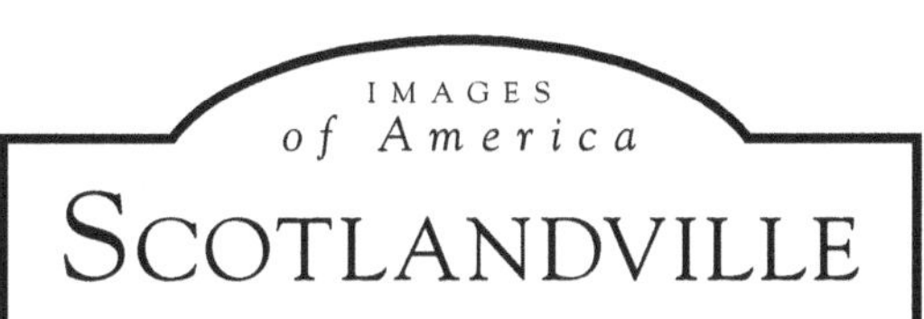
IMAGES
of America
SCOTLANDVILLE

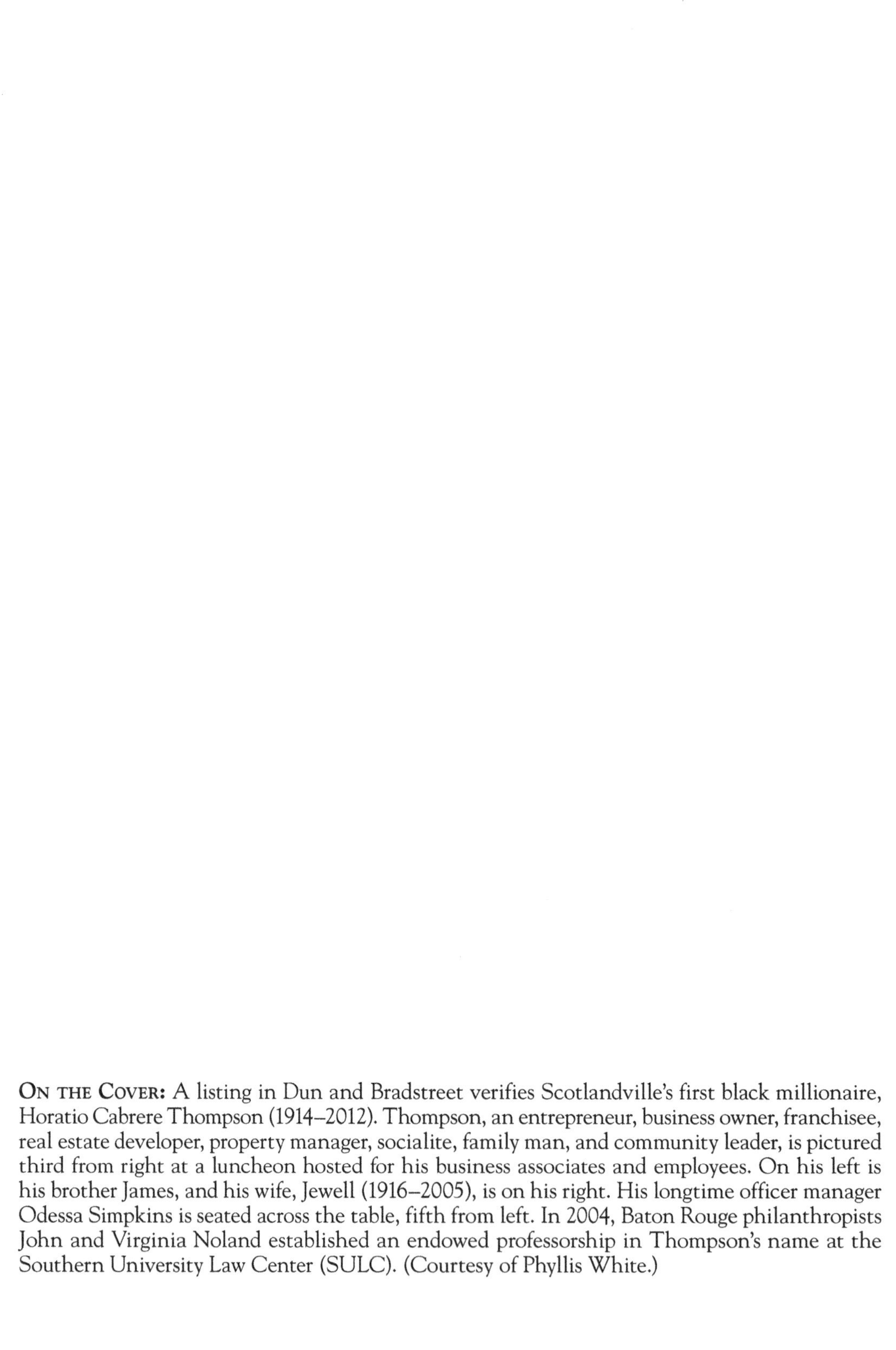

On the Cover: A listing in Dun and Bradstreet verifies Scotlandville's first black millionaire, Horatio Cabrere Thompson (1914–2012). Thompson, an entrepreneur, business owner, franchisee, real estate developer, property manager, socialite, family man, and community leader, is pictured third from right at a luncheon hosted for his business associates and employees. On his left is his brother James, and his wife, Jewell (1916–2005), is on his right. His longtime officer manager Odessa Simpkins is seated across the table, fifth from left. In 2004, Baton Rouge philanthropists John and Virginia Noland established an endowed professorship in Thompson's name at the Southern University Law Center (SULC). (Courtesy of Phyllis White.)

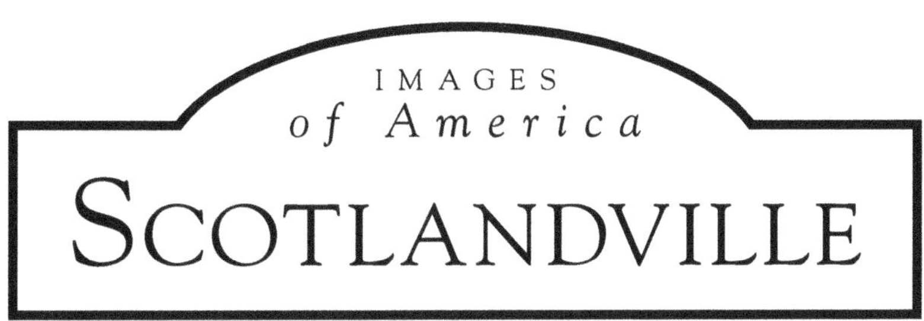

Rachel L. Emanuel, PhD, Ruby Jean Simms, EdD,
and Charles Vincent, PhD
Foreword by Mayor-President Melvin "Kip" Holden

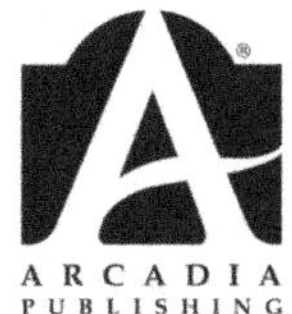

ISBN 978-1-4671-1314-4

Published by Arcadia Publishing
Charleston, South Carolina

Library of Congress Control Number: 2015937278

For all general information, please contact Arcadia Publishing:
Telephone 843-853-2070
Fax 843-853-0044
E-mail sales@arcadiapublishing.com
For customer service and orders:
Toll-Free 1-888-313-2665

Visit us on the Internet at www.arcadiapublishing.com

The authors dedicate this book to all the first families of Scotlandville who, along with community residents past and present, inspire us to share this valuable history of their lives and times.

Contents

Foreword

I can think of no better way to preserve the cultural, educational, business, religious, social, and political history of the self-determined, dedicated, and resilient people of Scotlandville than this pictorial history book. Readers are in for a treat because this publication has captured the flavor of this unique area in our state and nation. This historical account should delight the hearts and expand the minds of young and old. These words and images reveal our days gone by, and inspire and celebrate the victories of everyday folks overcoming challenges and making their way by faith and hard work.

As a lifelong resident of Scotlandville and an elected official blessed with the opportunity to represent and serve this community on the Metro Council, in the Louisiana legislature, and now as mayor-president, I have been shaped and motivated by the educators, entrepreneurs, clergy, community servants, and parental role models who have cared about their youth and fellow human beings. The richness of their lives and times are explored through these pages.

No doubt writing this book was a labor of love for authors who are longtime historians and documentarians of African American cultural, educational, and political experiences. With their work they can lift up our communities, inspire great achievements, and effect positive change.

For this pictorial history of my community presented by these committed authors through Arcadia Publishing's *Images of America* series, I express my appreciation for a valiant effort, one that most certainly will be continued in the work of Dr. Rachel L. Emanuel, Dr. Ruby Jean Simms, and Dr. Charles Vincent.

—Melvin "Kip" Holden, mayor-president
City of Baton Rouge and Parish of East Baton Rouge

Acknowledgments

This publication was made possible with the contributions of former and current Scotlandville residents. They were eager to share with us their photograph collections, as well as names and contact information of others who might have had photographs that we could use. (See names listed in credit lines of photograph captions.) Also, they enthusiastically revealed a story or two about their Scotlandville and "Dear Southern." Special thanks go to Mauretta Wailes Elbert, Carolyn Wilcox Fields, Marion Key, Sarah Starring, Brenda Sterling, and Aolar Wilson. We sincerely thank all for their valuable contributions.

Some images were taken from private/public organizational, church, governmental, and media archives. We appreciate help from the archivists we met and Southern employees, alumni, and other supporters who were eager to assist us if they could. Specifically, we thank Lena Armstead, Carla Ball of SULC, Carolyn Bennett of the Foundation for Historical Louisiana, Ann Boltin of the Catholic Diocese of Baton Rouge, Judy Bolton of Louisiana State University (LSU) Libraries Special Collections, Charlene Bonnette of the Louisiana Collection of the State Library of Louisiana, Bridgett Brister, Benjamin J. Dunbar Jr. of St. Paul Catholic Church of Baton Rouge, Richard Early, Elva Jewell "E.J." Carter of the Scotlandville Branch of the East Baton Rouge Parish Library, Melissa Eastin of the East Baton Rouge Parish Library Baton Rouge Room, Eldridge Etienne of the Southern Teachers and Parents Federal Credit Union, Nedina Flowers of the Southern University Laboratory School, Rosa L. Franklin, Harold Isadore of the Southern University Law Library, Kenneth and Regina Martin, Dr. Francesco Mellion-Williams, Mwalimu Institute for the Study of People of African Descent in the Western Hemisphere, Edward Pratt of Southern University and A&M College Media Relations, Angela Proctor of the Southern University Library Archives, Dianne J. Pullen of Greater Mount Carmel Baptist Church, Bertha R. Stewart, Joicelyn Southern, Peggy Wallace of Mount Pilgrim Baptist Church, and Lynn West of East Baton Rouge Parish School Board.

Other images are by professional photographers. We extend special thanks to N. John Oubre of Southern University Baton Rouge and longtime Baton Rouge photographer Steve Jarreau for their assistance.

Thank you to Chancellor Freddie Pitcher Jr. and Vice Chancellor John K. Pierre of the Southern University Law Center for their initial endorsement of this project. We spoke with many individuals who expressed excitement and appreciation for what we were doing and wished us well. And for that we are truly grateful.

Finally, we wish to thank our families and friends for their support. The Scotlandville story is not fully told in this one volume; however, we hope we have made a good start.

The names of organizations are abbreviated in the text and courtesy lines as follows: Order of Eastern Star–Prince Hall Affiliation (OES-PHA), Louisiana State School for the Deaf (LSSD), National Association for the Advancement of Colored People (NAACP), Southern Teachers and Parents Federal Credit Union (STPFCU), Southern University and Agricultural and Mechanical College (SU), and Southern University Law Center (SULC).

Introduction

The Scotlandville community, located in the northern part of East Baton Rouge Parish in Louisiana, has been in existence for more than 165 years. This book is the first pictorial history with text about the area, which is so intricately tied to the Southern University and Agricultural and Mechanical (A&M) College, the only historically black university system in the United States. Originally located in New Orleans from 1880 until 1913, Southern University and A&M College was relocated to Scott's Bluff on the western edge of Scotlandville in 1914.

With the mighty Mississippi River on one side and swamps on the other, the community of Scotlandville was initially described as "isolated" and "as nearly set aside as it is possible." The change in the university domicile from New Orleans withstood a lawsuit brought by residents of that city who were defeated on appeal to the Louisiana Supreme Court. Shortly after, the stipulations of Act No. 118 signed by Gov. Luther E. Hall on July 9, 1912, calling for the relocation of the institution to a rural area began. Despite the opposition of white residents to a school for "Negroes" in their village, the plantation, known as the Kernan Place and located on a high point, Scott's Bluff, along the Mississippi River in the rural area of Scotland (later Scotlandville) was chosen.

The same editorial that described the community as "isolated" also noted that two railroads, the Illinois Central Railroad (now Canadian National) and the Kansas City Southern Railroad, along with the riverfront, provided the area with the advantage of "quick and easy transportation." The State of Louisiana purchased the 531-acre site in Scotlandville, and the Mississippi River was used to transfer usable properties like chairs, desks, buggies and tally hoes, mules and horses, school records and reports, tools, printing equipment, pianos, dump carts, and band instruments from New Orleans to Scotlandville.

The story of Southern University and A&M College and Scotlandville, like that of many Jim Crow institutions and communities of the Deep South, is a tale of triumphs and struggles in the midst of racism, inequality, and oppression. Presented through the themes of firsts in business, churches, schools, residential developments, politics, social organizations, and community service, Images of America: *Scotlandville* will focus on the people who shaped the lives of the community in significant ways—economically, spiritually, educationally, politically, socially, and culturally.

This collection of photographs of the people, places, and events from 1914 to 2000 reveal the past of this rural village, once the entry point for the slave trade to cotton plantations, turned African American community. The families of the community are portrayed in photographs taken by both professionals and amateurs. Scotlandville residents provided many of the photographs. At one time only viewed by family and friends in private photo albums around their coffee tables, these images and the lives captured in them are now being shared with a larger audience.

We tried our best to reach residents in all of the neighborhoods of Scotlandville, through contact with churches, schools, neighborhoods, businesses, Greek organizations, and other social organizations currently in the vicinity. We sincerely apologize to anyone we missed who would have wanted to contribute. Some residents we contacted were not able to locate photographs, acknowledging that generations ago their families did not have the means to take them or that the ones that they once had were no longer available. Many were lost when family members moved or were destroyed by the elements when stored in attics or under beds.

The people and lives that are portrayed show that they have invested precious time and significant efforts working to establish and maintain a community. Commitment to spirituality, educational attainment, civil rights, environmental justice, equitable housing, artistic talents, and athletic prowess are hallmarks of the community. Through their share of hardships and struggles, they have enjoyed life, celebrating with each other during the joys of victories and consoling each other during storms, both natural and man-made. With great energy and enthusiasm, with innovation and skill, these individuals created a vibrant community.

Human fragilities, dysfunctions, and misfortunes took their tolls. Decades of resurgence in commitment, innovation, and skill have continued with purpose.

Southern University celebrated its 100th year on the bluff on March 9, 2014; in 2015, it celebrates 135 years as an institution. It is now a most opportune time to review this story of Scotlandville. Those who peruse these pages will discover an intriguing and inspiring record of the past.

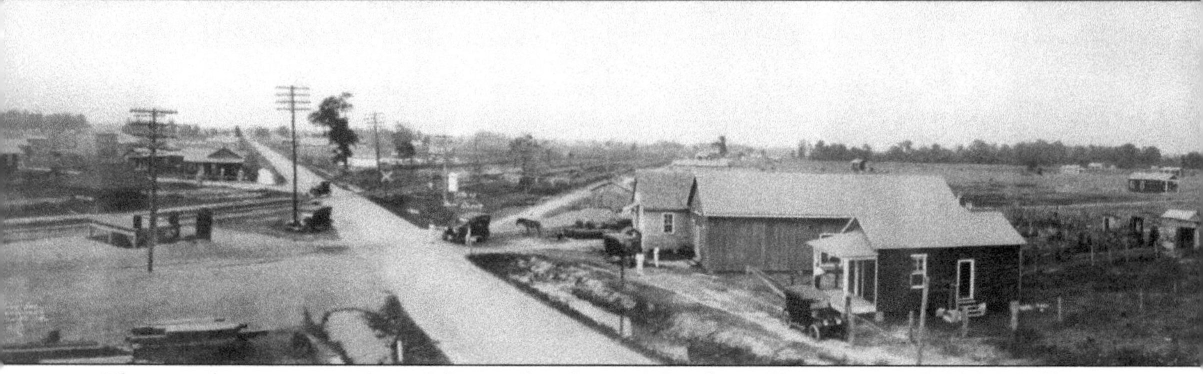

The initial coming together of the newly relocated Southern University and A&M College on Scott's Bluff with the neighboring Scotlandville community is captured in this photograph taken in 1915 at the intersection of Scenic Highway and Swan Street. Southern's president, Dr. Joseph Samuel Clark, at left, greets residents, including Arthur "Jack" Kelly sitting on a mule, a member of the first African American family to inhabit Scotlandville. (Courtesy of Earl Marcelle and Mildred Kelly Marcelle.)

One

First Families of Scotlandville

Building Community

In 1865, the beginning of Reconstruction, the population in the area that would become Scotlandville was a small number of mostly rural farmers, sharecroppers, laborers, and their families, scattered throughout the vast farmland and pastures.

Between 1878 (the year after Reconstruction ended) and 1912 (the year the area was being considered for the new location of Southern University), it is reported that approximately 34 families lived in the Scotlandville area. The few non–African American families included the families of Sam Drago, of Italian descent, and William Crumholdts, of German descent.

During the first Great Migration of African Americans out of the rural South to the Northeast, Midwest, and West from 1916 to 1920, a migration into Scotlandville took place. This "in-migration" was fueled by employment opportunities at the newly chartered Standard Oil Refinery just south of Scotlandville in 1909 and Southern University's relocation to Scott's Bluff in 1914. Joseph Samuel Clark, the first president of Southern, recruited students, faculty, and staff to the university from far and near. The Mengel Lumber Company and Ethyl Chemical Plant, Solvay, Dupont Chemical, the Munition Works, and the Kansas City Southern and Illinois Central Railways provided employment for Scotlandville residents.

With the Great Depression of the 1930s and the coming of World War II in the 1940s, Scotlandville experienced another wave of growth with employment opportunities in the Works Progress Administration (WPA) programs and the opening of Harding Air Field, Baton Rouge's first and only Army air base.

The names of some of the first African American families of Scotlandville are Ball, Banks, Bradford, Brown, Coleman, Cook, Cooper, Cox, Crockett, Davis, Diggs, Douglas, Dunn, Eames, Early, Flanders, Foster, Finney, Franklin, Goings, Hammond, Hansberry, Hardesty, Hayes, Haynes, Jackson, Johnson, Jones, Jordan, Kelly, Kirk, Knox, Lewis, Lipscomb, London, Maybuce, McGee, Morrison, Netters, Patty, Pidgeon, Reed, Reese, Sewell, Simms, Spruel, Talbert, Theus, Thomas, Veal, Watkins, Williams, Wilcox, and Wilson.

Employment and educational opportunities spawned the establishment of locally owned businesses, more churches, housing, and a vibrant social and civic life through dedicated leadership and commitment to a vision of building community in Scotlandville.

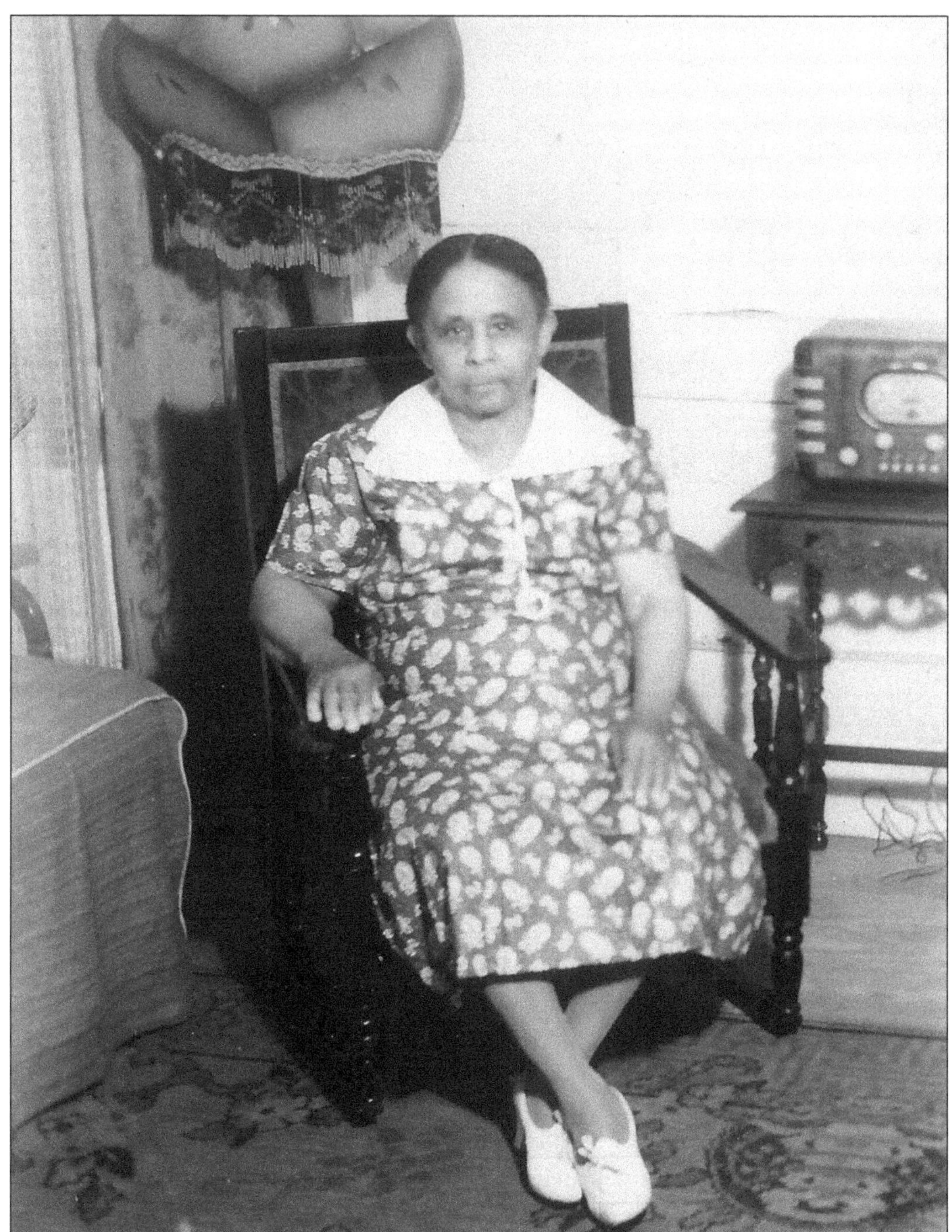

The only black family living in Scotlandville prior to the opening of Southern in 1914 was the Kelly family. The patriarch of the family was William "Dreher" Kelly (1866–1954), the son of Saul Kelly, a native of Kansas. William began using the name "Dreher" when he moved to Scotlandville as a young man. He married Priscilla Barnes (pictured), a native of Alsen, a community north of Scotlandville. The couple had 10 children. Nolan Kelly, a biologist, said that 33.3 acres of land located on Rosenwald Road was given to his grandfather Dreher for laying out the roads of Scotlandville. (Courtesy of Russell L. Kelly Sr., Arthur and Mildred Donaldson Kelly Collection.)

The Kelly children were longtime residents of Scotlandville. Alma, pictured at right, was a beautician. Her sisters were SU graduate Sadie, the wife of SU industrial arts professor Dr. Nicholas Harrison Sr.; Althea "Alta," the wife of Fred Davis, a Standard Oil Company/Esso employee; SU graduate Etha, who taught in public schools in the St. Francisville, Louisiana, area; and SU graduate Ora, the wife of SU biology professor Dr. James Warren Lee. Arteal, pictured below, was the youngest of the five sons. His brothers were Timothy, a World War I veteran; Major, a Standard Oil Company employee; and Irvin and Arthur James "Jack." (Both, courtesy of Russell L. Kelly Sr., Arthur and Mildred Donaldson Kelly Collection.)

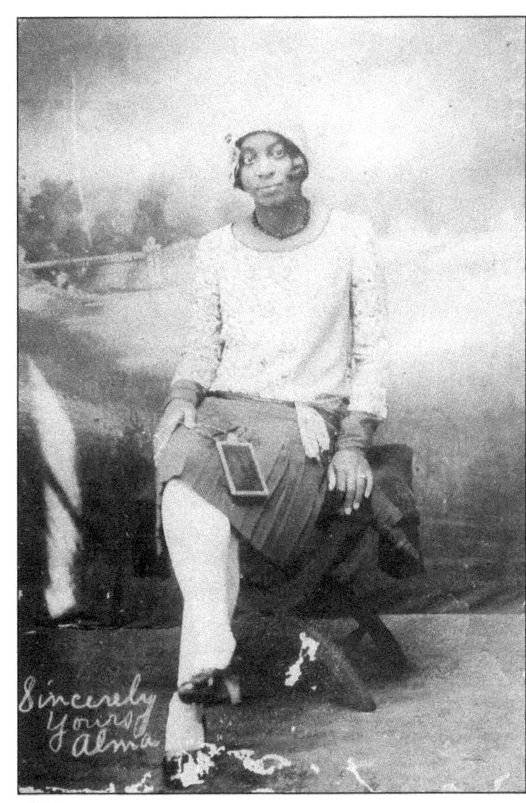

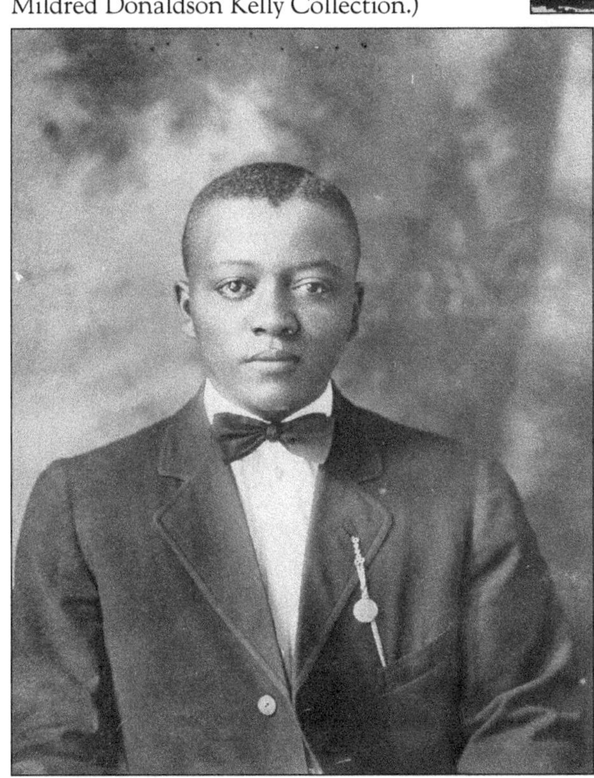

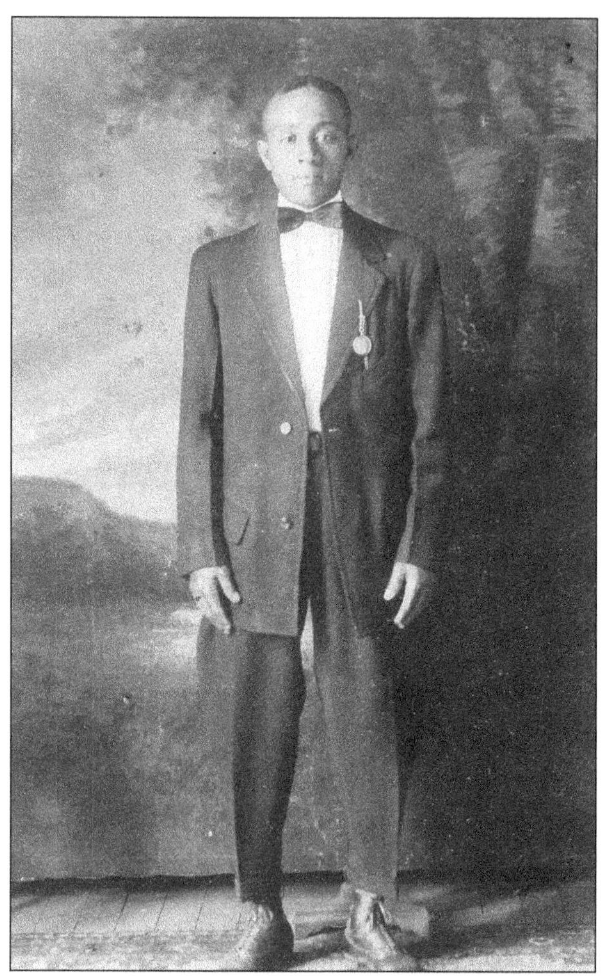

Pictured at left, Irvin Kelly, one of Dreher and Priscilla Kelly's five sons, was the owner and operator of a barbershop and nightclub at the junction of Highway 19 and Scenic Highway. His brother Jack was a longtime employee of the Esso Refinery. Jack and Felton G. Clark, the son of Southern's first president, J.S. Clark, were friends and classmates at Southern Demonstration School (now Southern Laboratory School or Southern Lab) and fellow members of the school's football team. Clark was five years older than Jack. Pictured below are, from left to right, Elizabeth Smith Donaldson, Richard Donaldson Jr. (rear), Jack, and Beatrice Donaldson Brown. (Both, courtesy of Russell L. Kelly Sr., Arthur and Mildred Donaldson Kelly Collection.)

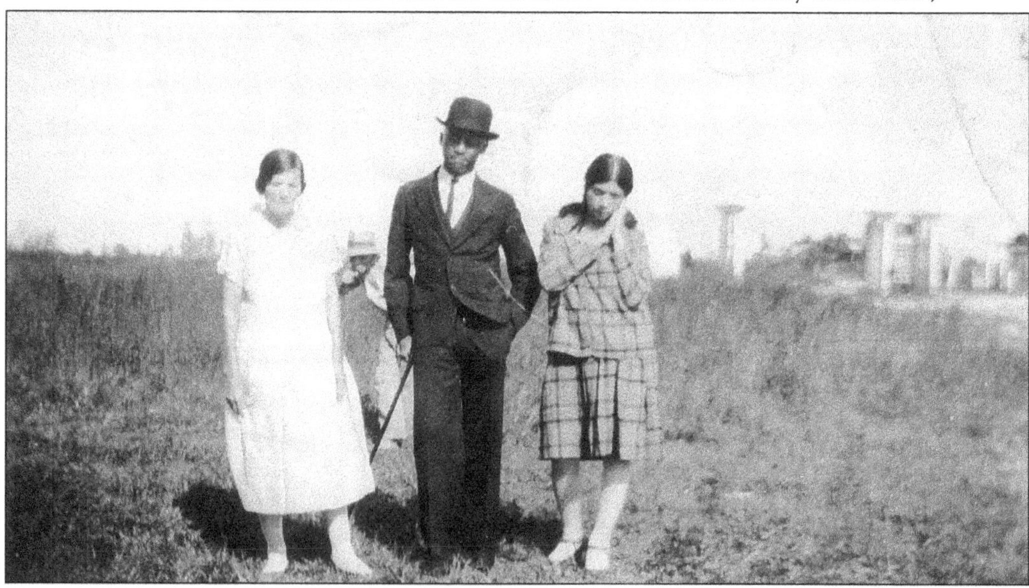

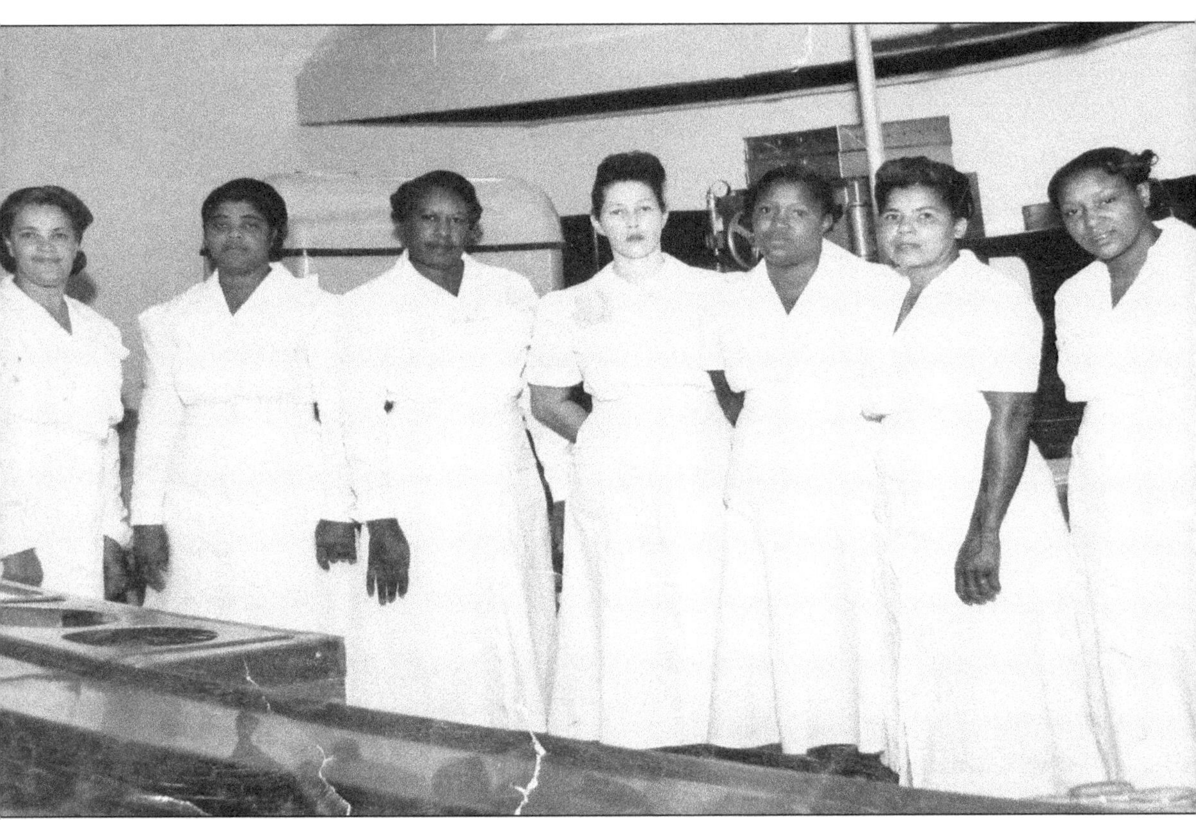

The Kelly family was upset about the marriage of their son to his 16-year-old bride Mildred Donaldson because it thwarted plans for Jack to become the family's first medical doctor. Mildred, at center, is shown with fellow cooking staff at North Scotlandville Elementary School. Jack and Mildred's children were Southern graduates Gloria Dean; Delores, Miss Southern 1951; Mildred, wife of SU graduate Earl Marcelle; Jacqueline, an educator and businesswoman; Nolan "Bergeron," retired Scotlandville High biology teacher and car salesman; and Exxon/Mobil retiree Frank "Ruzi," a Southern Lab graduate who attended Southern. (Courtesy of Nolan Kelly.)

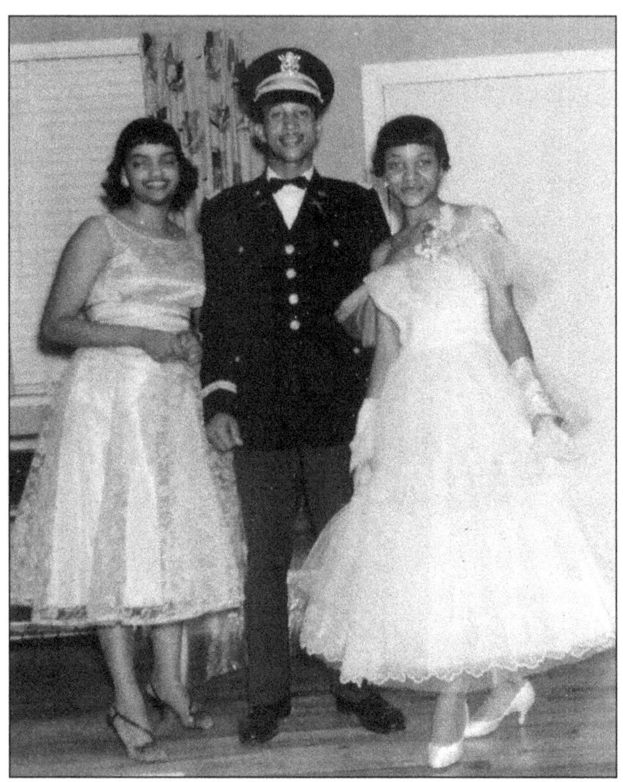

Nolan Ferdinand Kelly, one of two sons of Jack and Mildred Kelly, married Jewel Amelia Smith. He is pictured with his wife, Jewel (left), and sister Mildred before departing for military duty in Korea in 1957. The photograph was taken in his grandmother Elizabeth Smith Donaldson's home on Avenue A in Scotlandville. (Courtesy of Russell L. Kelly Sr., Arthur and Mildred Donaldson Kelly Collection.)

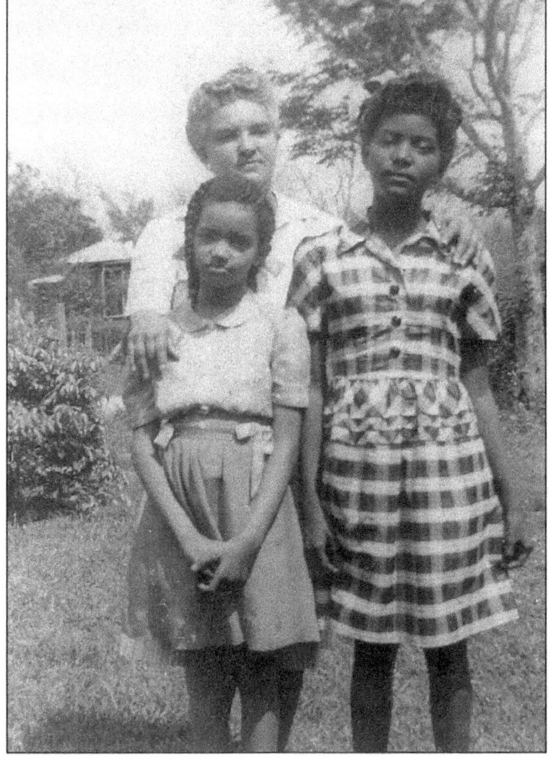

Angie Corrine "Synetta" Tacneau-Smith (1907–1954) and her husband, Theodore Roosevelt "Prexy" Smith Sr. (1901–1975), were the maternal grandparents of Nolan and Jewel Kelly's children. Angie Tacneau-Smith is pictured with her daughters Jewel and Constance "Connie." Jewel attended Southern Lab and, in 1953, was voted Miss Southern Lab. (Courtesy of Russell L. Kelly Sr., Arthur and Mildred Donaldson Kelly Collection.)

William L. "Bill" Kelly (right) was the son of Ernest and Teatsey Hayes Kelly. Ernest, a cousin of Dreher Kelly, owned the only lumberyard in Scotlandville until the 1950s. Using a team of horses to carry lumber from his yard, Ernest helped to build the foundation for a number of buildings on Southern's campus. He earned a degree in masonry at Tuskegee Institute, now Tuskegee College, in Alabama and later constructed a family home for himself and his wife, Hattie. He also built his family's business and the homes of Amanda Kelly and Ruffin Paul Sr., a fellow Tuskegee graduate and owner of the first and only electrical company in Scotlandville. Hattie (below) and Bill were the parents of five children, Shirley, Lois, Yvonne, Lloyd, and Donald, all of whom attended Southern Lab and Southern University. (Both, courtesy of Shirley Kelly Hammond.)

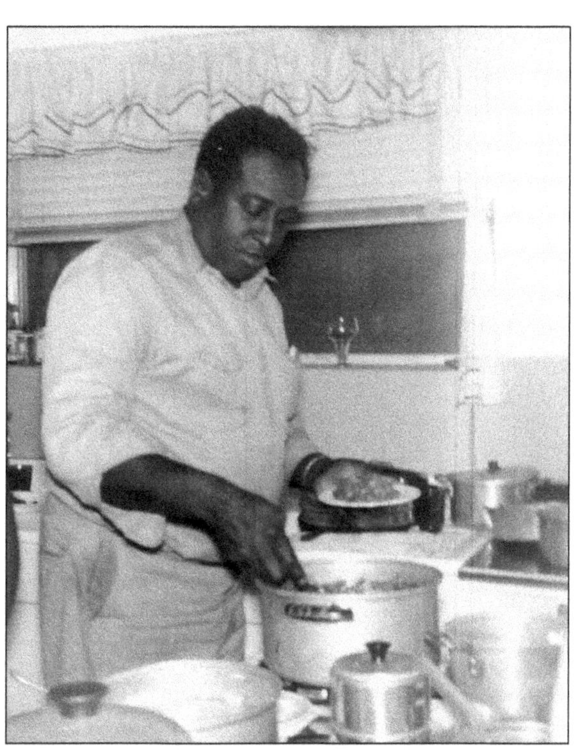

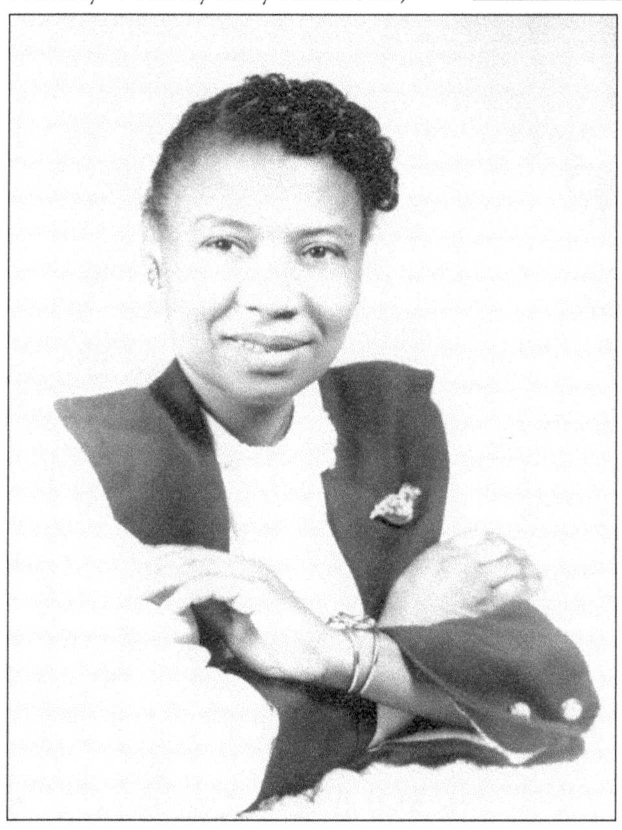

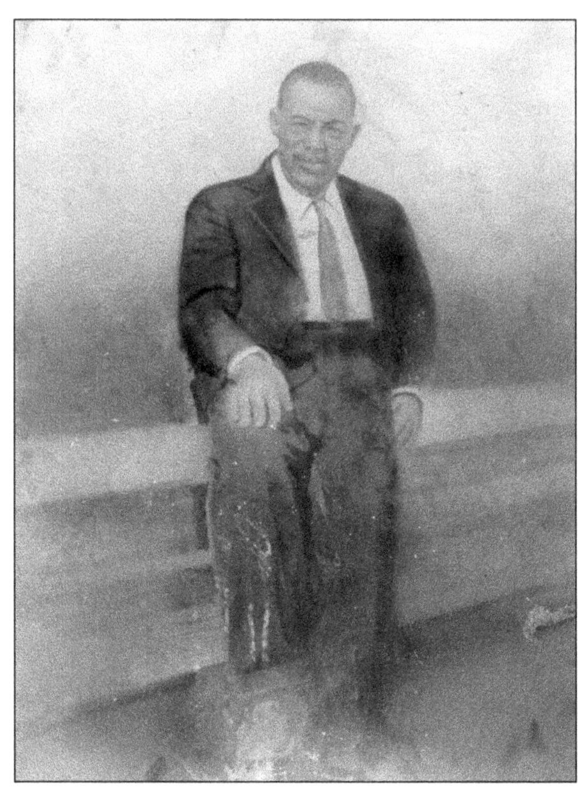

Although he was not a US Postal Service employee, Joseph Lewis (left), pastor of a small church in Scotlandville, was considered the first black mail carrier of the town. Frank Reiger Sr., owner of Reiger's Pharmacy, hired Lewis to retrieve a mail sack placed on a pole near the railroad tracks by a passing train and bring it to the pharmacy. The pole was in front of the area designated for black passengers at the segregated train depot. Lewis would take the mail for processing to the contracted post office inside the pharmacy. Joseph and his wife, Emma Barnes Lewis, had one son, Simon. Emma is pictured below with one of the couple's granddaughters, Bernice. (Both, courtesy of Ruth Lewis Crawford and Rhonda Crawford Stewart.)

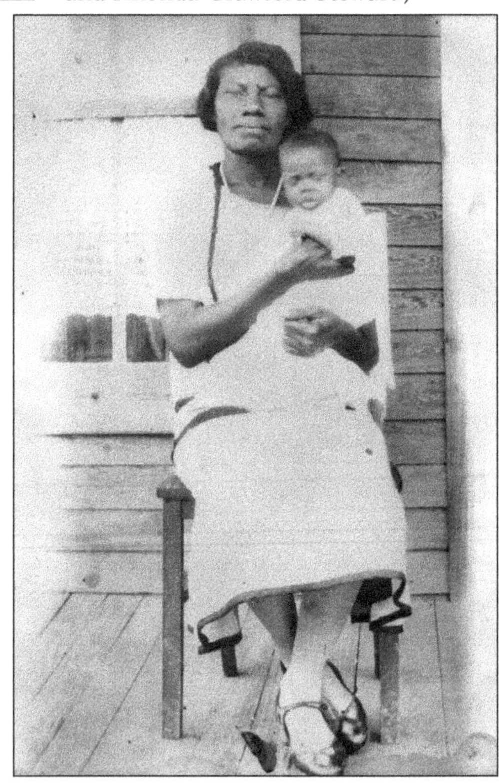

Simon Lewis met Pearl Morton Lewis (1910–1987) of South Carolina when the two were enrolled at Stillman College in Tuscaloosa, Alabama. The couple was married in the 1920s, made their home on Robin Street in Scotlandville, and became the parents of two daughters, Bernice and Ruth. Simon was an employee at Standard Oil, and Pearl was employed first by Cox Cleaners on Swan Avenue, and later as a dormitory counselor at the Louisiana State School for the Deaf. Theirs was a talented singing family, all becoming members of the senior choir at Camphor Memorial United Methodist Church. (Courtesy of Rhonda Crawford Stewart.)

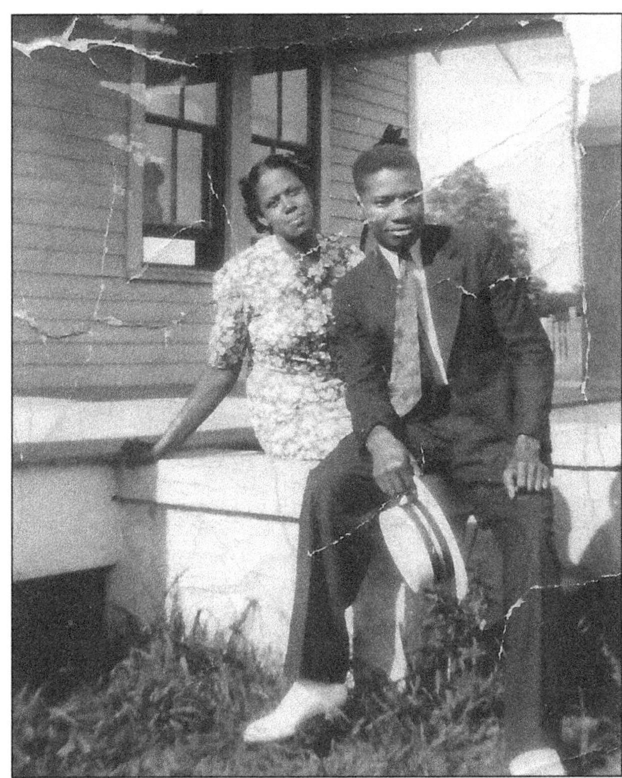

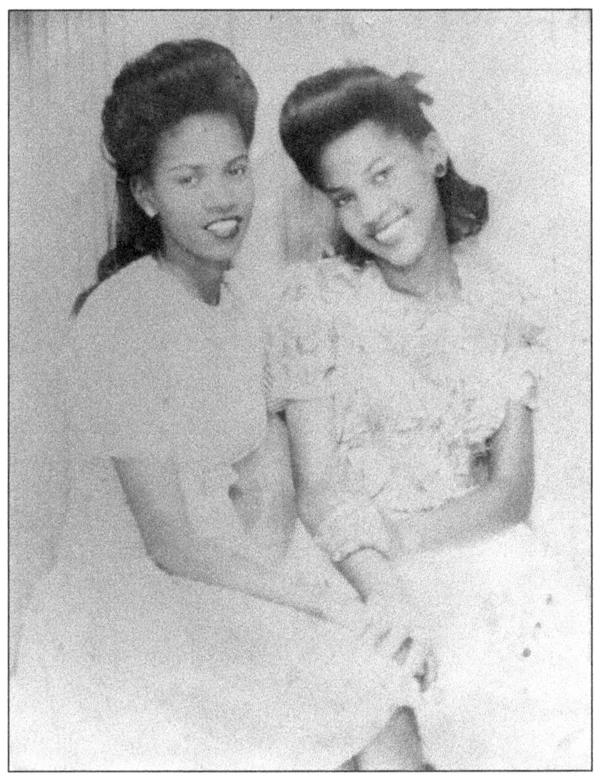

Educators Bernice and Ruth Lewis, third-generation Scotlandville residents, were graduates of Southern Lab and Southern University. Bernice taught at Harding Elementary and Claiborne Elementary schools. She was also a pilot reading teacher at Bakersfield and Progress Elementary schools. Ruth taught at North Scotlandville Elementary. She was helping teacher and supervisor for East Baton Rouge Parish Schools, and retired as administrative assistant to Dr. Edward Elloie, dean of the SU College of Education. Both sisters became members of Baton Rouge Sigma Alumnae Chapter of Delta Sigma Theta Sorority. Ruth pledged Delta Tau at Southern. (Courtesy of Rhonda Crawford Stewart.)

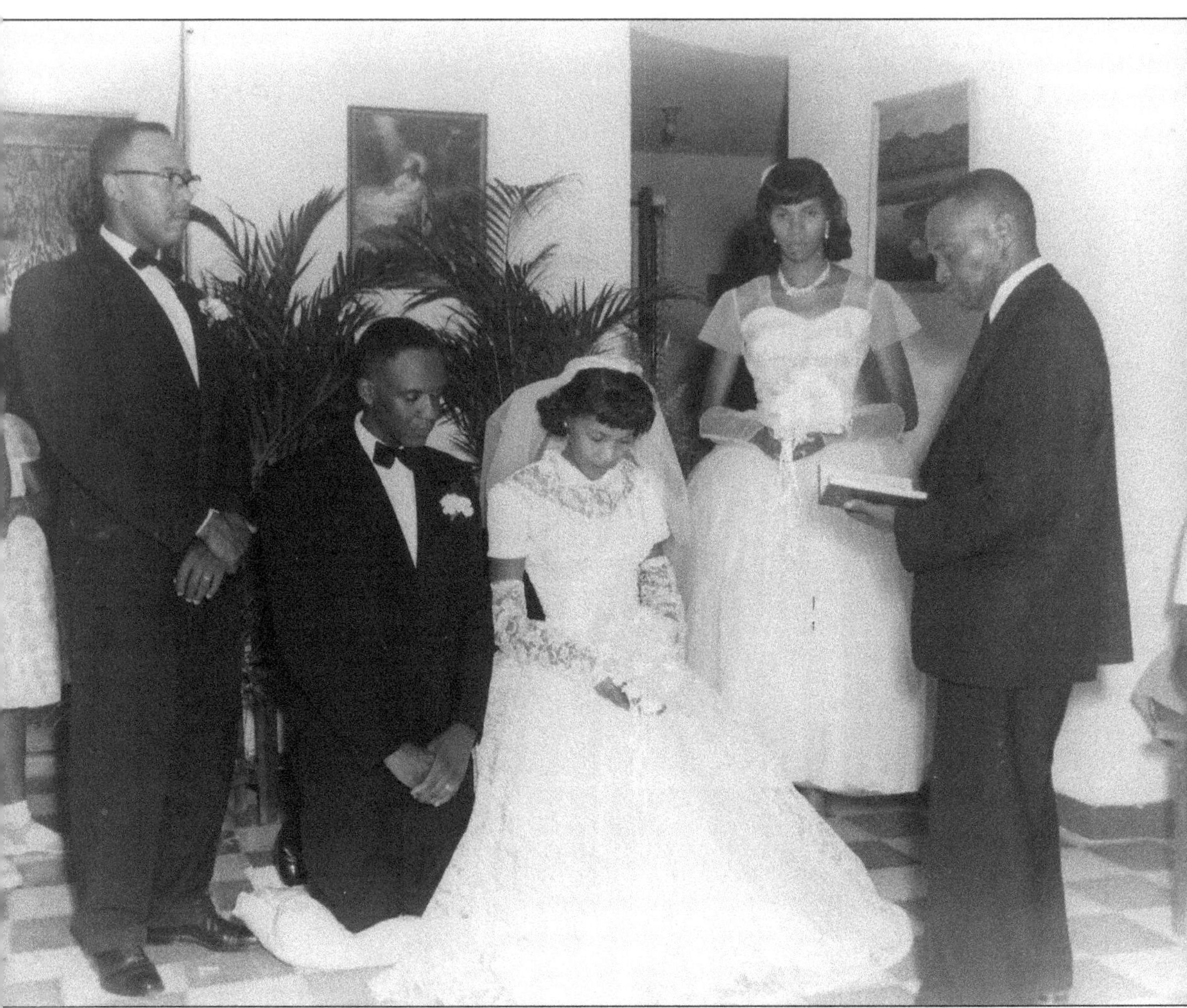

Ruth Lewis and Matthew Crawford exchange their wedding vows on August 30, 1953. Pictured are, from left to right, best man Wesley Crawford, standing; groom Matthew, bride Ruth; maid of honor Bernice Lewis Lemons; and Pastor Leslie H.P. Norris. The couple's two daughters are Rhonda and Karlene. Crawford, a math professor, was a charter member of the SU chapter of the National Association of Mathematicians, Louisiana Beta, established in October 1960. Other charter members are Percy Milligan, Dr. Lovenia DeConge-Watson, Dr. Roger Newman, and Dr. Dolores Spikes, who later served as the first female president of the Southern University System. World War II veteran Alvin Lemons Sr. (1925–2014) was Bernice's husband and was the son of Walter and Daisy Bolden Lemons. The couple had three children, Kathy, Tonya, and Alvin Jr. (Courtesy of Ruth Lewis Crawford.)

William Haynes (right), a bricklayer and carpenter, and his wife, Mary Hayes Haynes (below), a graduate of Straight University (now Dillard University) in New Orleans, were members of first-generation families of Scotlandville and among the 12 founders of Camphor Memorial United Methodist Church. Haynes built the store that he and his wife owned and operated, Haynes Grocery, opened in 1922. The store was located on the corner of Scotland Avenue and Stilt Street. The couple's seven-room home, which William also built, was attached to the store. The couple reared two sons, Paul Haynes, a graduate of Tuskegee University in Alabama with a degree in masonry, and Victor Earl "Vic" Haynes, who earned a degree in pharmacy at Xavier University in New Orleans. (Right, courtesy of Geraldine A. Simms; below, courtesy of Louise Smith)

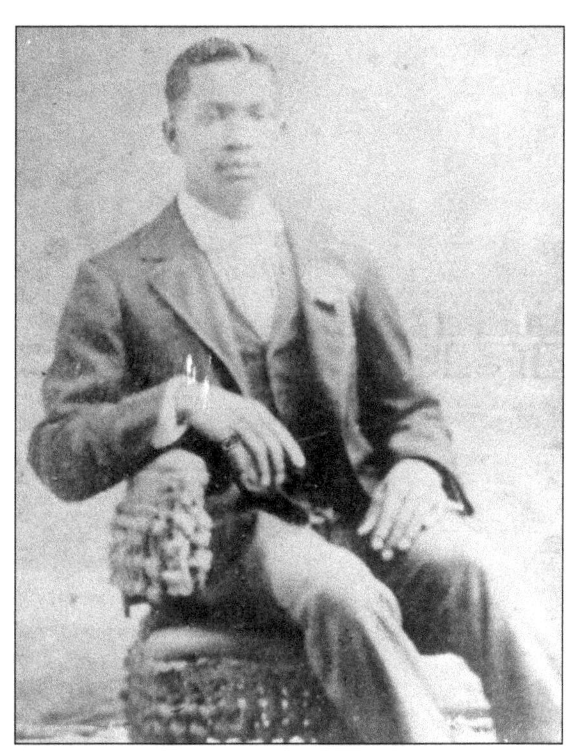

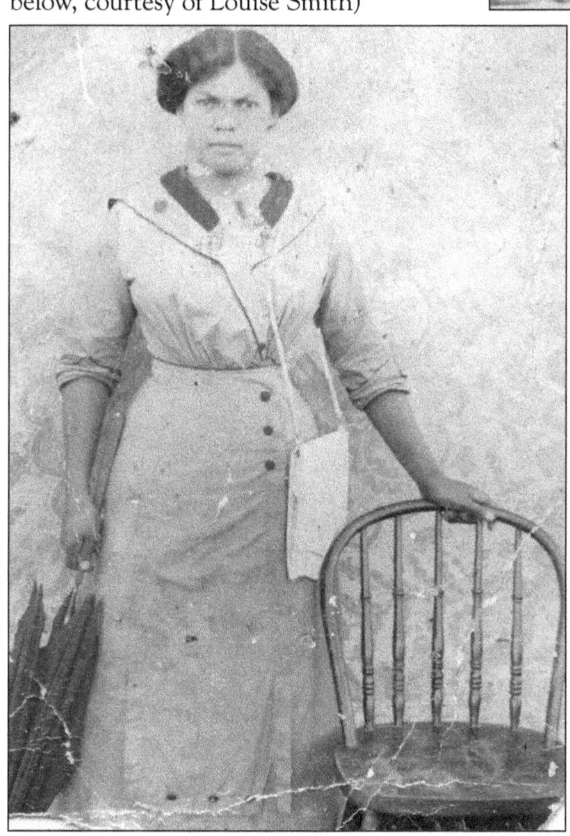

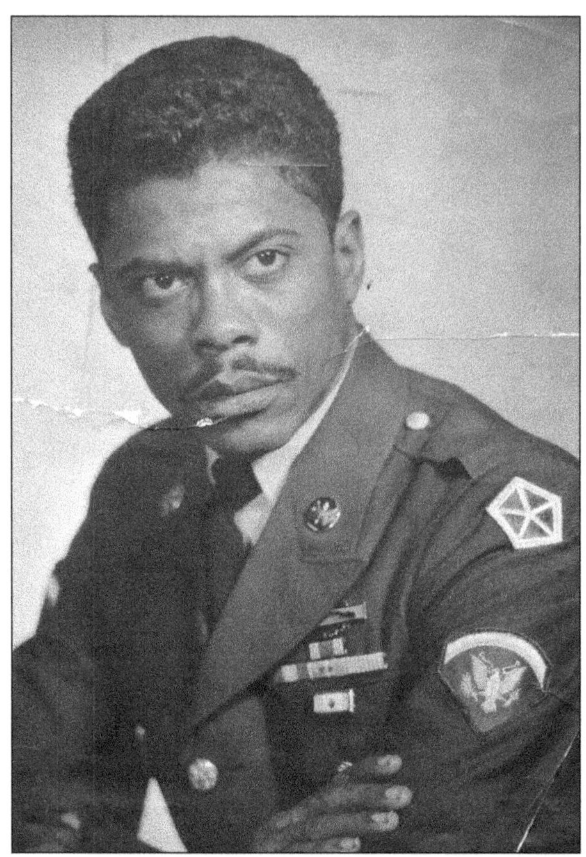

Among the many military men of Scotlandville were World War II veterans Luttrell Cox and Folden Thomas. Cox, pictured at left, moved with his parents and siblings to Scotlandville in 1920 when his father secured a job at Standard Oil. In the early 1980s, Luttrell and his wife, the former Bernice Wheellock, opened the second funeral home in the community. A master in facial restorations, Cox was called upon by other morticians to perform this service for their clients. Returning from active duty in 1945, Folden Thomas secured employment at Standard Oil and advanced his career by completing a welding certification program. He and his wife, the former Aline Davis, had two children. As a member of the Bonnette-Harrison Post No. 504 of Scotlandville, Thomas continued his family's legacy of helping others, reflected in the origins of the Thomas Benevolent Society. Thomas is pictured below, second from left, with his military cohorts. (Both, courtesy of Jacqueline Thomas.)

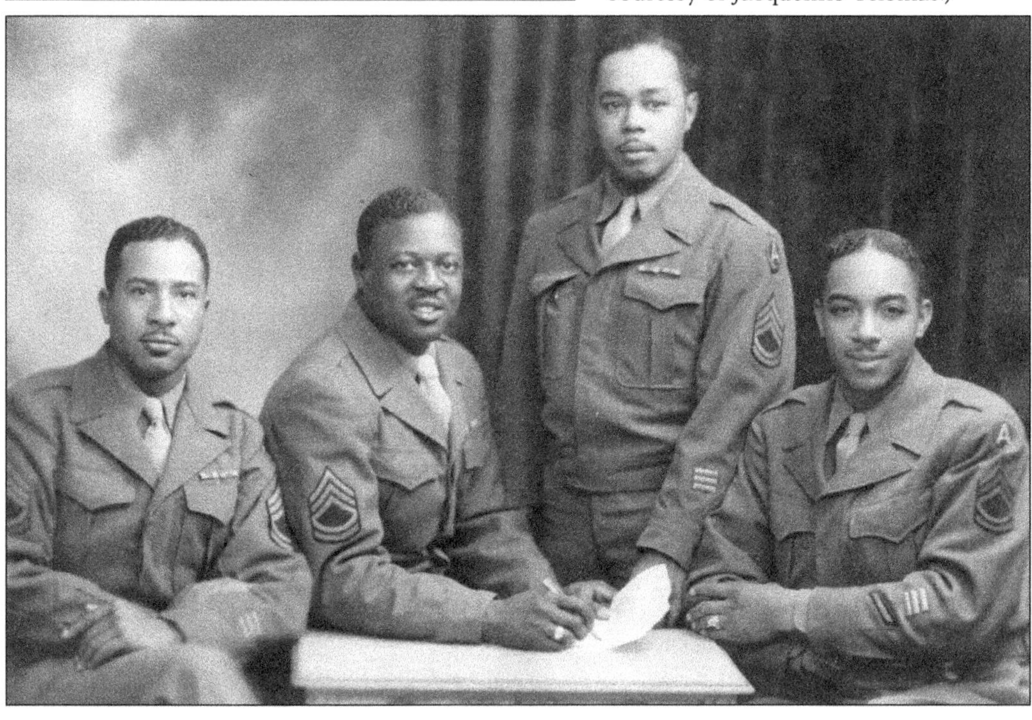

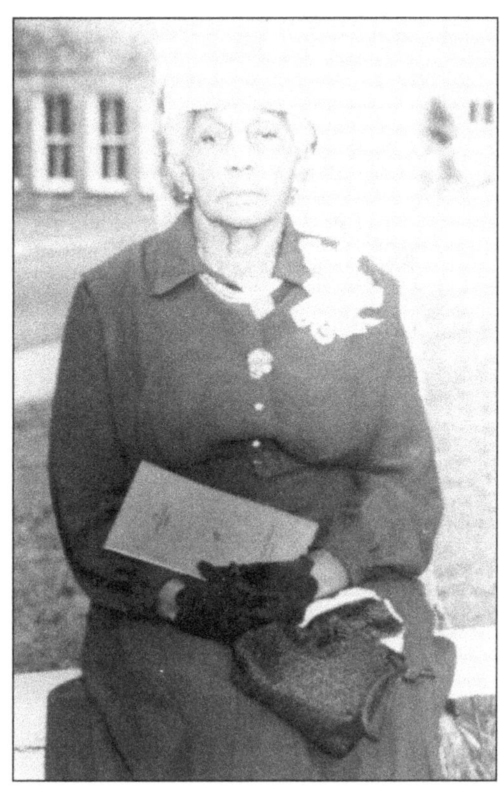

Ada Hansberry was born in Scotlandville in 1872. She was the mother of three children, Ernest, Robert, and Ruth, and is believed to be a relative of noted playwright Lorraine Hansberry, author of *A Raisin in the Sun* and the first African American woman to produce a drama on Broadway. Ada, a founding member of Camphor Memorial United Methodist Church, owned a dairy farm on Scenic Highway and Rosenwald Road. (Courtesy of Geraldine A. Simms and Louise Smith.)

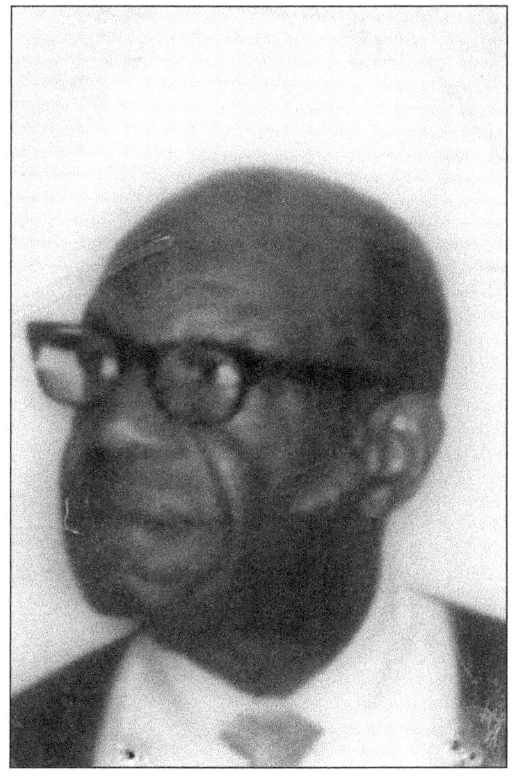

Vanderbilt Sewell Sr. was one of Scotlandville's entrepreneurs in the grocery, real estate, and housing businesses. Sewell was born on April 11, 1905, to parents Dane and Ada Sewell of Tunica, Louisiana. He received his formal education from the public schools of Tunica. He and his parents moved to Scotlandville in the early 1920s. Vanderbilt was a graduate of Southern Laboratory School, and later completed courses in law and business at Southern University. (Courtesy of Douglas and Ethel Sewell.)

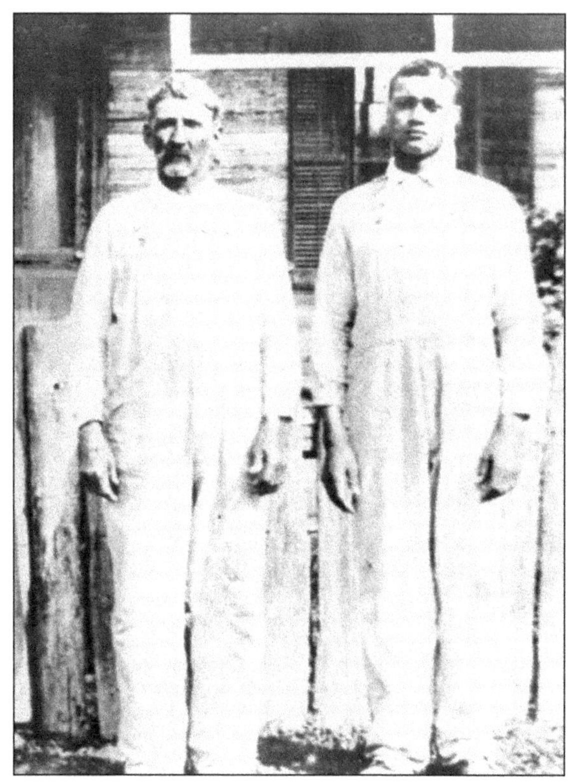

Samuel Devall Sr. (1857–1934) and son William Sigure "Sig" Devall Sr. stand in front of the Samuel and Celeste Hollins Devall homestead between Scenic Highway and Highway 19 and the railroad track west of Blount Road. Celeste, who was born a slave, and Samuel, a plantation owner, had 10 children. Two of their offspring, Mary Jane and Sig Devall Sr., founded the Devall Construction Company, located on Kingfisher Street in Scotlandville. Sig trained generations of Devalls and Morrisons, including his son Theodore, who are skilled in these trades today. (Courtesy of Marjorie Green.)

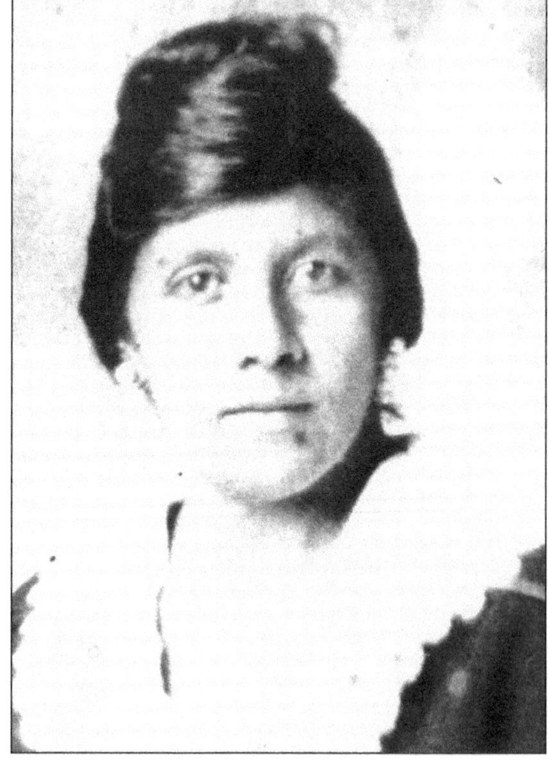

Mary Jane Devall, the sixth daughter born in 1889, grew up with her siblings on the original Devall family homestead, located on what is now the Blount Road area from Scenic Highway to the railroad tracks on Scotland Avenue. The property line extended to the present Park Vista subdivision on the south. She married Abraham Sanders Morrison Jr. and the couple had 12 children. (Courtesy of Marjorie Green.)

Maria Molex is believed to be the daughter of a white plantation owner. Not to reveal her mother's out-of-wedlock pregnancy, Maria was reared as a mulatto, the product of a slave mother. She married a Native American with the last name Molex, and they lived in Morganza, Louisiana. The two had 10 children, who she encouraged to move to Scotlandville and attend Southern. (Courtesy of Ruby Jean Simms.)

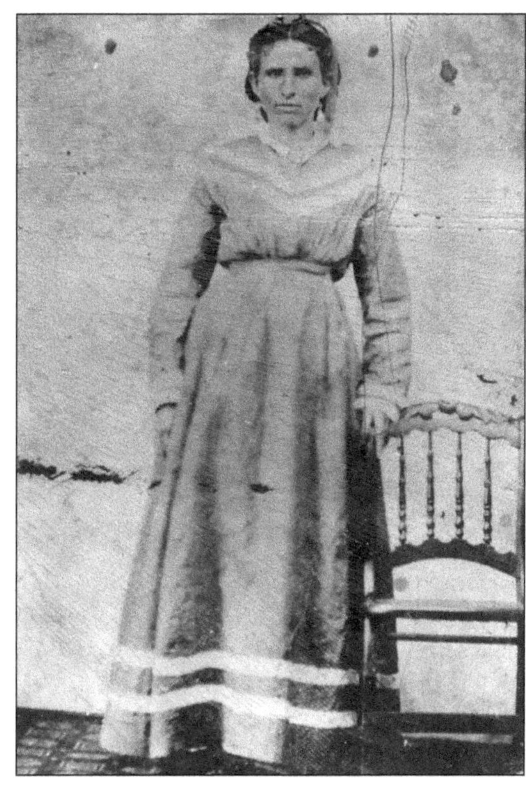

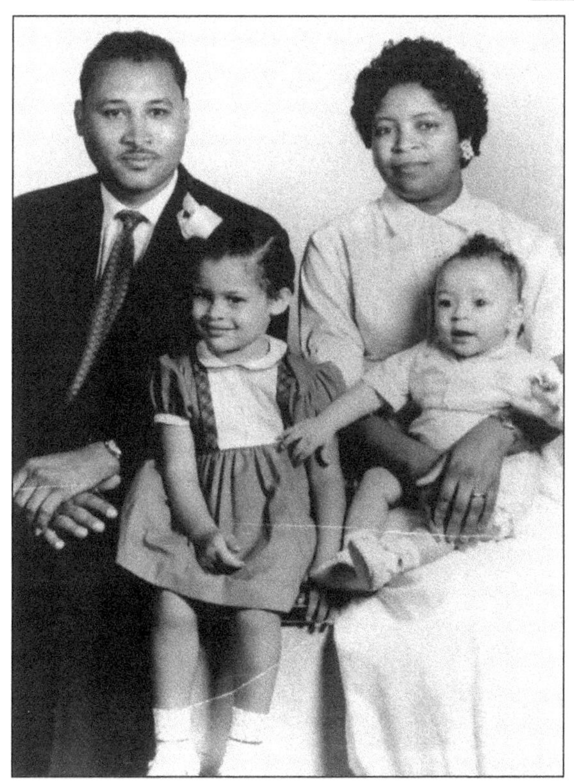

John E. "Pool" Simms, a businessman, and his wife, Evelyn Handy Simms, were longtime residents of Scotlandville. The couple and their children were fourth and fifth generations of the Molex, Veal, and Simms families. (Courtesy of Geraldine A. Simms, Vallory Simms Hills, and Ruby Jean Simms.)

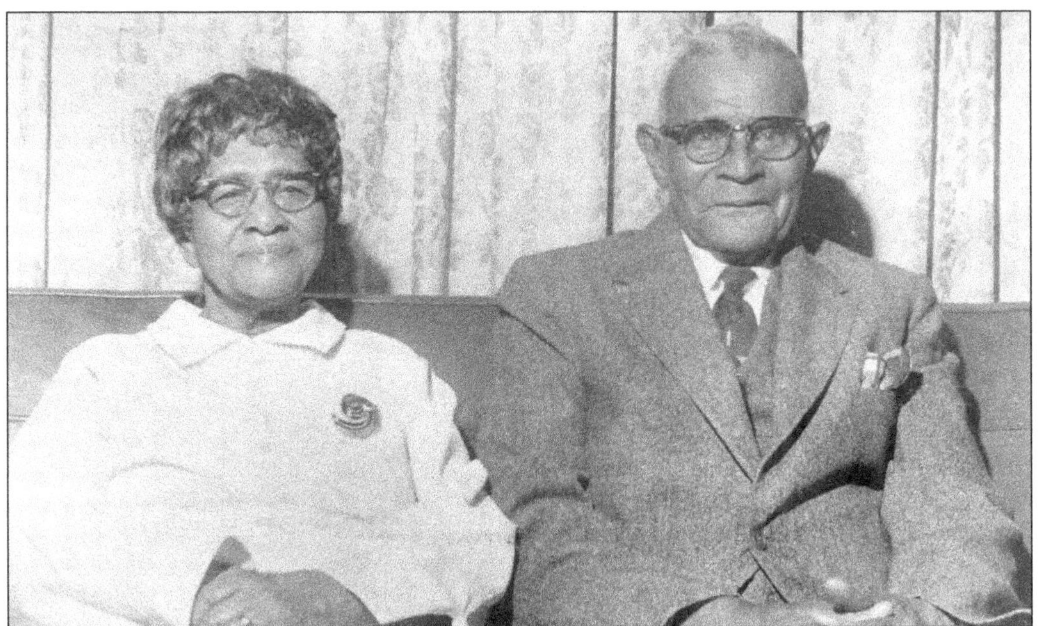

James Bradford and his wife, Mary, were the parents of two sons, Wallace and Lawrence. The Bradfords were founders of Camphor Memorial United Methodist Church in Scotlandville. In 1917, the 12 founders met in the Bradfords' home on Marsh Street. James and Mary are the grandparents of Lawrence Bradford Jr., first black page in the US Senate, who was appointed by Jacob Javits of New York in 1965. (Courtesy of Julia Bradford Moore.)

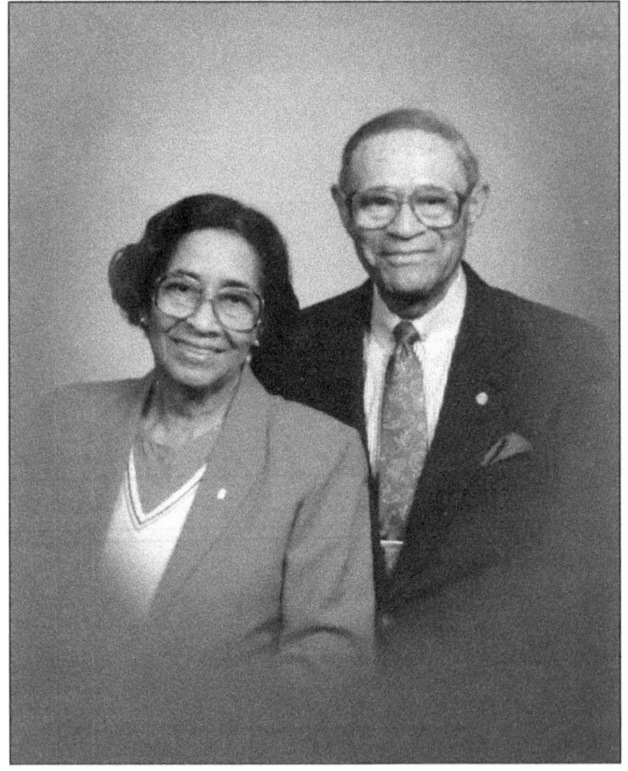

Wallace Lee Bradford, one of two sons of James and Mary Bradford, attended Tuskegee Institute and later became the second principal of the Louisiana State School for the Deaf (LSSD) for Negroes at Southern University. Established in October 1938, LSSD was open to deaf African American children of the state between the ages of 6 and 21 whose hearing impairment could not be addressed in traditional public schools. Academic offerings included extensive training in trade and vocational areas. Wallace married the former Earlene LaMotte. Wallace Lee Bradford Hall, a men's dormitory on the Southern campus, is named for him. (Courtesy of Dr. Marilyn Ray-Jones.)

Scotlandville native Earlene LaMotte Bradford (right) was crowned Miss Southern in 1933. During the school's early operation, she served as school matron for LSSD; her coworkers included beautician Helena Arthur, physician Dr. Raymond M. Baranco, residential school nurse Mary Ellen Brown, and secretary Nellie Wilder Hamms. Wallace and Earlene Bradford's daughter Dr. Marilyn Ray-Jones (below) is a retired administrator of Southern University in New Orleans. She served more than 36 years as a professor of education and was interim dean of the College of Education in 1997–1998. (Both, courtesy of Dr. Marilyn Ray-Jones.)

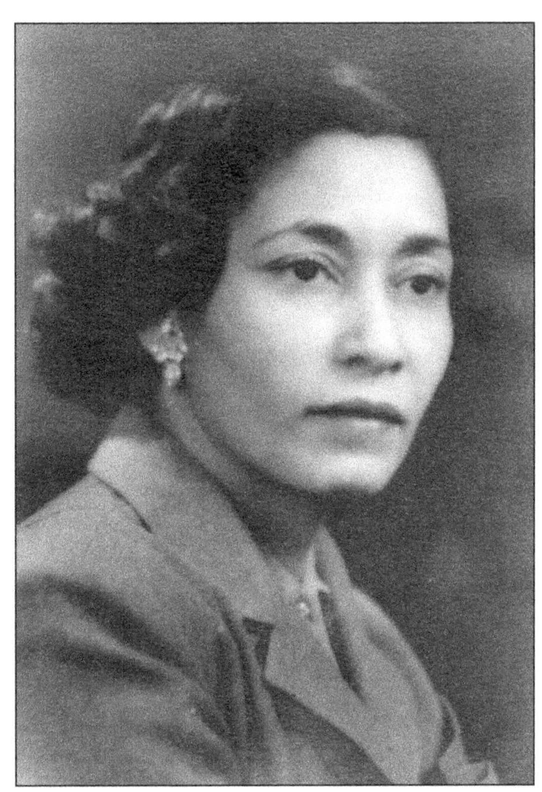

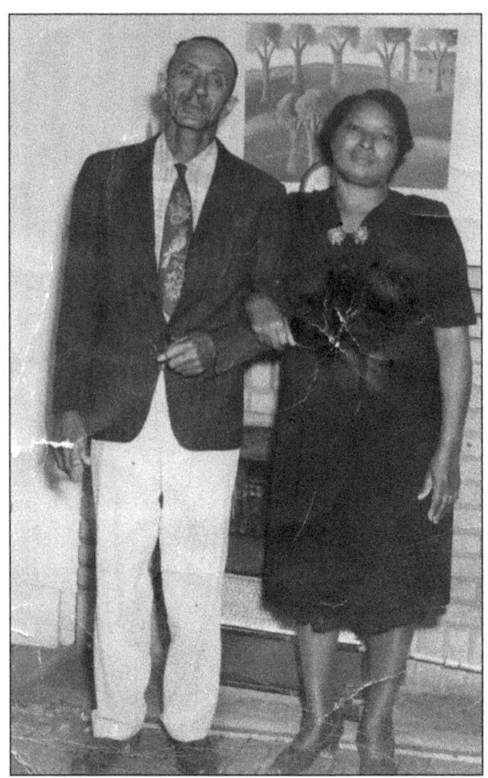

Hartzel and Beatrice Bradford were married on March 13, 1918. The couple was among the first members to join Camphor Memorial United Methodist Church. Hartzel was the brother of James Bradford and the father of longtime Scotlandville community activist Julia Bradford Moore. (Courtesy of Julia Bradford Moore.)

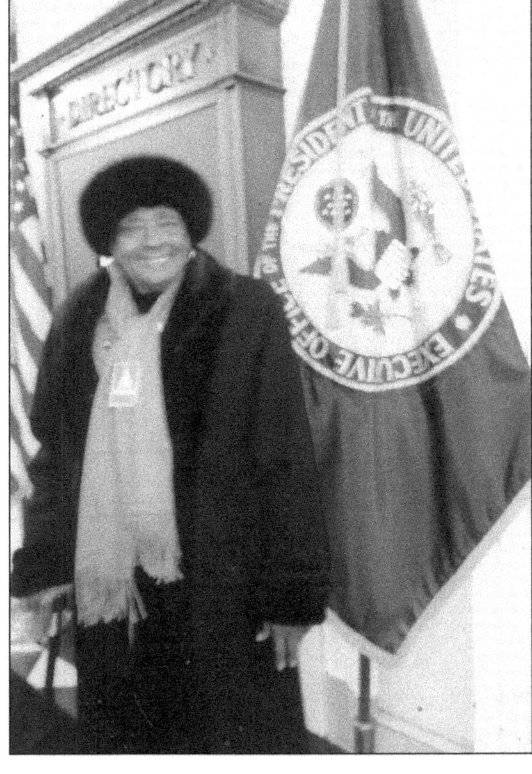

Julia Bradford Moore, a retired teacher from the East Baton Rouge Parish School System, organized the national award-winning group Sisters Supporting Sisters and the Louisiana Coalition of African American Breast Cancer Survivors. Both support groups have had a positive impact. Through genetic testing, Moore learned that she is a carrier of the cancer gene. This information has helped her family members live a healthier lifestyle. (Courtesy of Julia Bradford Moore.)

Bertrand L. Cook owned a poultry yard and icehouse in Scotlandville. He and his wife, Pearl Lees Cook, had nine children, Howard, Ruth, Eugenia, Joseph, Emma, Silas, Ora Mae, Margaret, and Handy. The Cook children all attended the Southern University Demonstration School. Bertrand Cook was one of the founders of Camphor Memorial United Methodist Church. He is also pictured in chapter five. (Courtesy of Geraldine A. Simms, Dr. Marilyn Ray-Jones, and Louise Smith.)

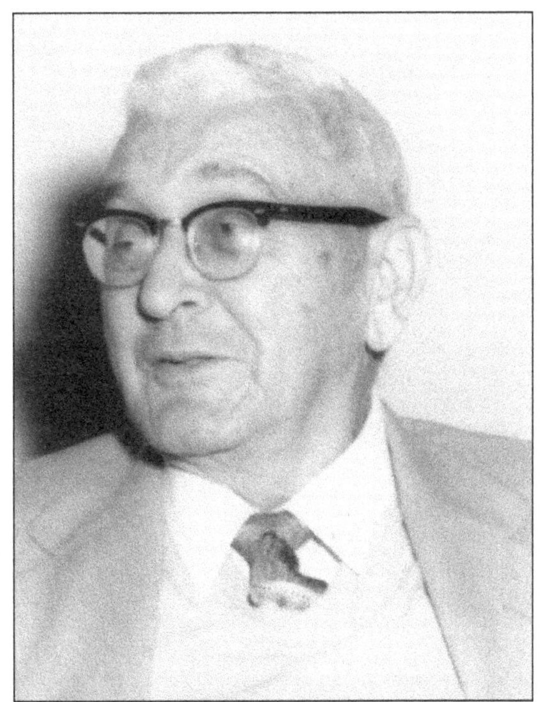

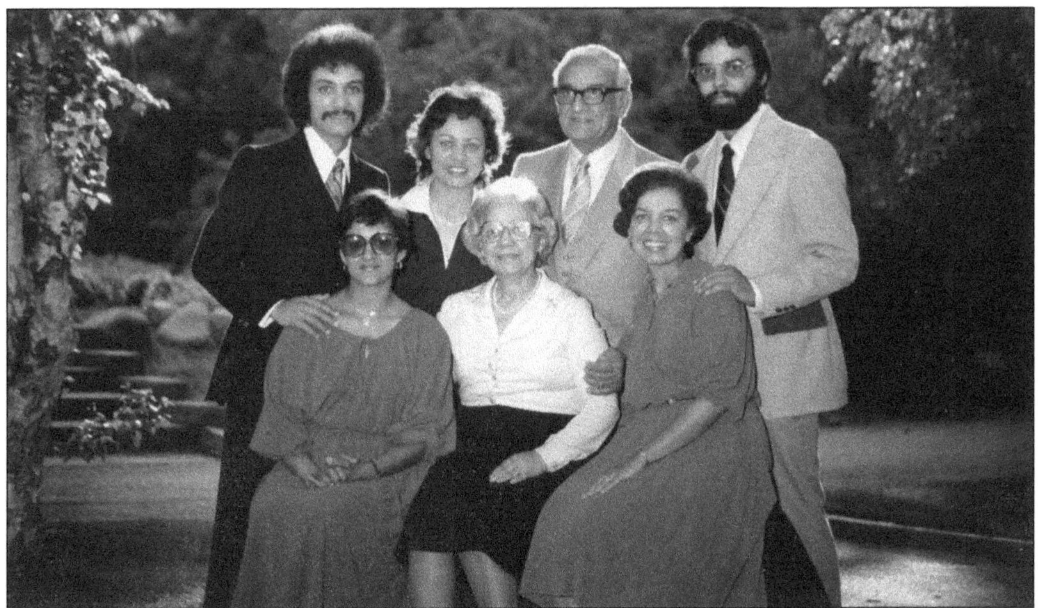

James Carl Cook Sr. moved with his parents, James Alexander and Ora Hunter Cook, and siblings from Jackson, Louisiana, to Scotlandville in 1917. The senior Cook owned a blacksmith shop in Scotlandville. James Sr. enrolled as a first grader at Southern Lab School. His teacher Myrtle D. McLeod was also the first-grade teacher for all five of his children. Cook earned a bachelor's degree in mathematics from Southern University in 1936. In 1938, he married the former Ruby J. Darensbourg of South Baton Rouge, also a Southern graduate. Pictured are, from left to right, (sitting) Ora Anita, Ruby, and Linda; (standing) James Jr., Marvel Ann, James Sr., and Harold. (Courtesy of Dr. James Carl Cook Jr.)

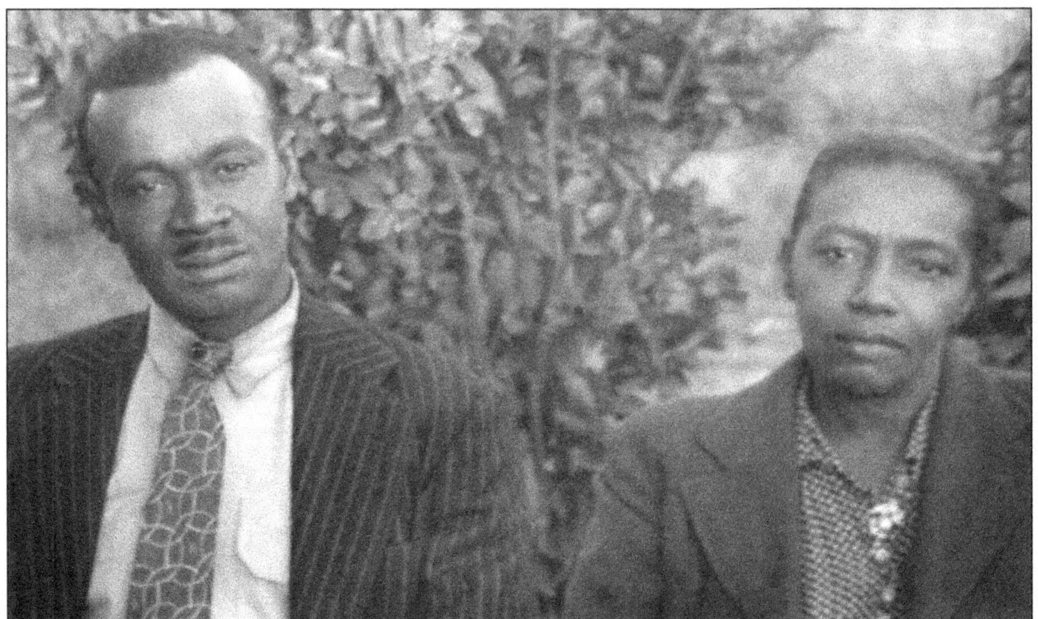

Foster Reese Sr. and his wife, the former Corinne Wheelock, made their home on Fairchild Street, across from Immaculate Conception Catholic Church of Scotlandville. Foster was a boilermaker/welder for Illinois Central Railroad for 15 years. The couple had 10 children; all of them graduated from Southern Lab, attended Southern University, and were members of Mount Carmel Baptist Church. (Courtesy of Rodney Reese.)

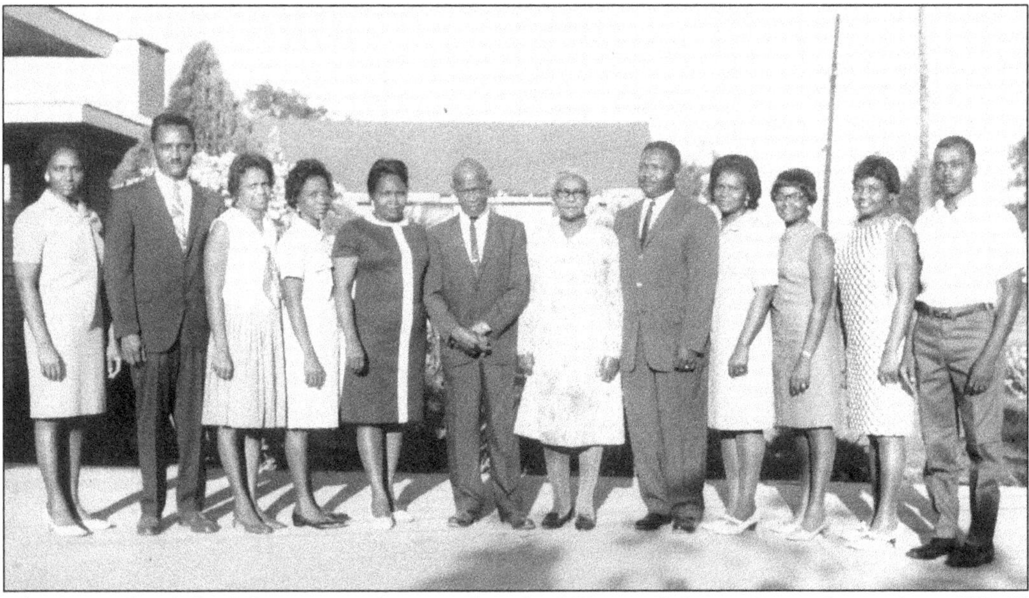

The Reese family had three sons who served in the US armed forces, Foster Jr., an Army World War II Buffalo Soldier; Willie, a Marine in the South Pacific in World War II; and Norman, an Airman. There were also five daughters involved with education, Irene, Dolores, Armedia, Johnnie, and Gloria, who were teachers employed in East Baton Rouge Parish Schools and in Biloxi, Mississippi. Two daughters were homemakers, Ruth, now deceased, and Ogarita. (Courtesy of Rodney Reese.)

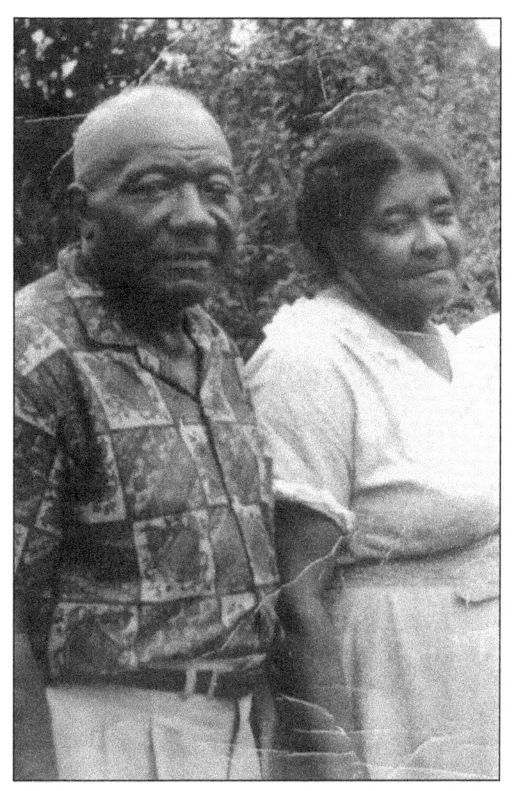

Farmer Jessie and homemaker Clara Thomas Early moved to Scotlandville in the early 1920s seeking a place to work and rear children. They lived Franz Kafka's adage, "Better to have, and not need, than to need and not have." Jessie retired after more than 40 years as a laborer at Standard Oil. The couple's 10 children were Gladys Brown and Almeanda Knowles, 1946 SU graduates; Florida Smith, 1950; Dorothy Davis, 1952; Georgia Daniels, 1953; Geraldine Jackson, 1963; Zeniola, a beautician; Richard, an auto mechanic; Jessie Wash; and Earline Tyrone. Three worked at Southern. (Courtesy of Dorothy E. Davis.)

Harold H. Handy Sr., who was married to Gloria Murray Handy, was one of a number of Scotlandville first families to serve in World War II. The Handy family represents several generations of Scotlandville residents. Pictured are, from left to right, Wayman Bryant, Harold H. Jr., Gerald Wayne, mother Gloria Murray Handy, Gregory Reynaud, and father Harold H. Handy Sr. (Courtesy of Chaz Handy and Vallory Simms Hills.)

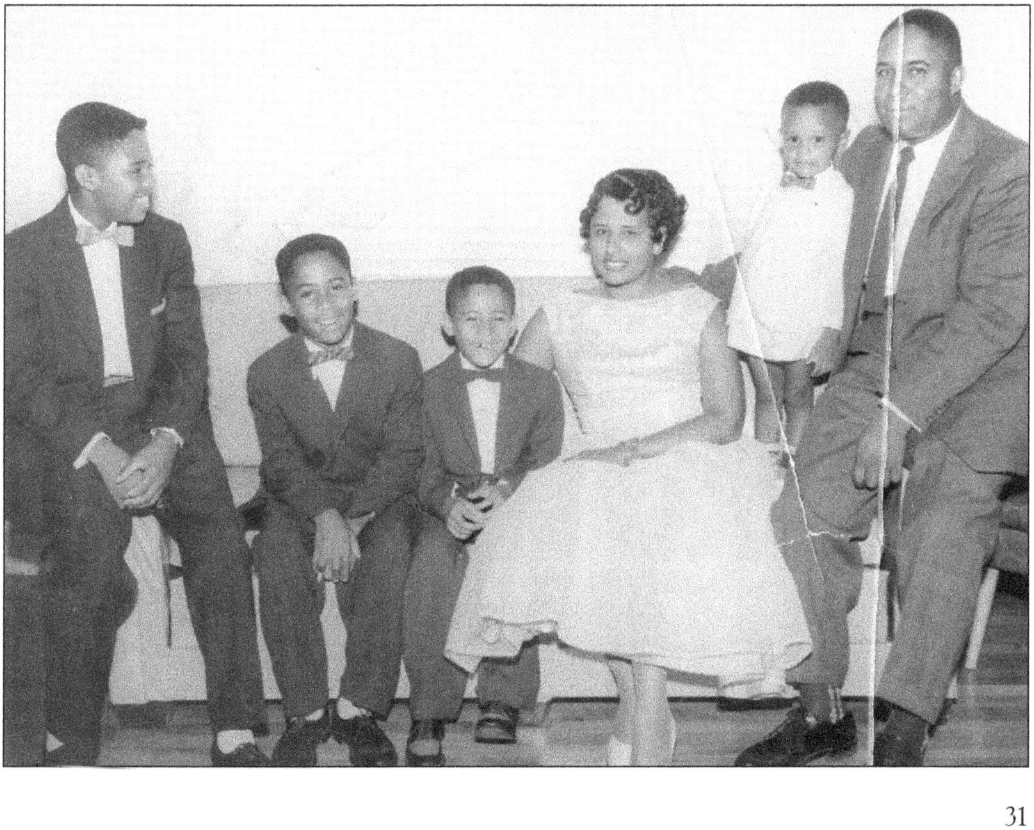

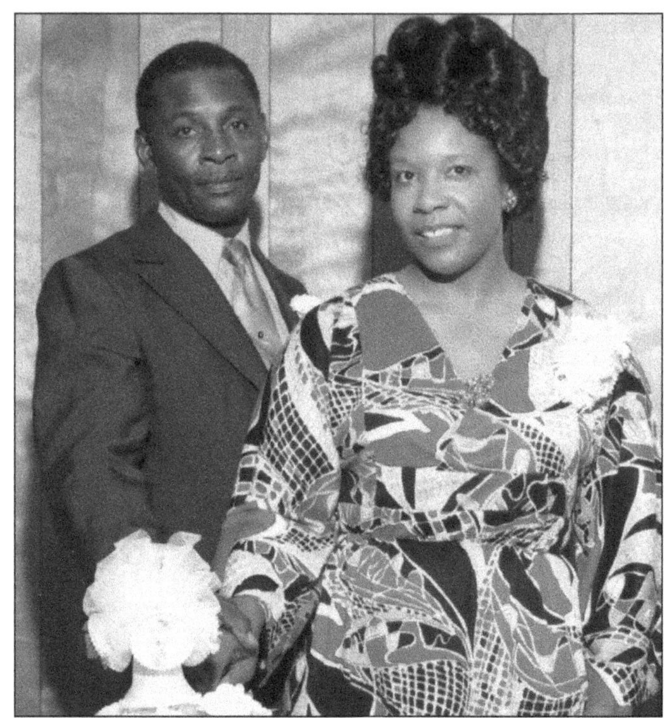

Percy and Lillian Jackson moved to Scotlandville in the 1920s from Zachary, Louisiana. Percy, the son of Howard and Alice Jackson, was a longtime employee of Standard Oil Company/Esso. After he retired from Standard Oil, he served in several positions as a state and city employee, from which he is now also retired. His wife, Lillian, is the daughter of the Reverend Pompey Ellis and Dafiney Wallace Square, who were among the first families of Scotlandville. A Southern University graduate, Lillian is a former public school teacher in East Baton Rouge Parish. The couple's current home is on Harding Boulevard. They have two daughters, Joyce and Paula, both graduates of Southern Lab. (Courtesy of Lillian S. Jackson.)

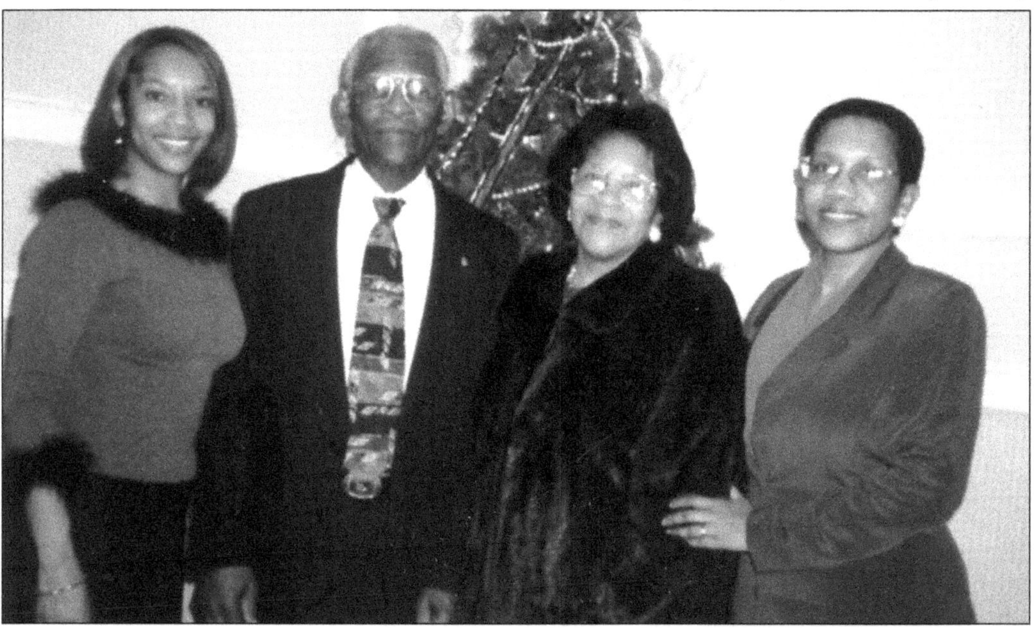

Joyce M. Jackson earned bachelor's and master's degrees in music from Louisiana State University in Baton Rouge and a doctorate from Indiana University in Bloomington. She is an associate professor of geography and anthropology and director of African and African American studies at LSU. Paula L. Jackson has an MBA and is an assistant athletic director for Compliance & Student Services/Senior Woman Administrator (SWA) at Hampton University Department of Athletics. Pictured are, from left to right, Paula L. Jackson, Percy L. Jackson, Lillian S. Jackson, and Joyce M. Jackson. (Courtesy of Lillian S. Jackson.)

The wedding day portrait at right of Charlie and Estella Square Banks, who were married on February 17, 1960, was taken in the cafeteria of Progress Elementary School. Charlie, the oldest of three children, was a graduate of Southern Lab. Estella, the oldest of 12, was in the first graduating class of Scotlandville High School, where her father, Willie T. Square, served as the first PTA president. Both graduates of Southern University, Charlie and Estella Banks pursued careers in secondary education, counseling, and administration. They always lived in Scotlandville and reared their four children in the community. Their daughter Chauna, who was educated at Progress Elementary, Southern Lab, and Southern University, is pictured below in her paternal grandparents' home on Cardinal Street. In 2012, Chauna was elected as the first female to serve District 2, encompassing Scotlandville, on the East Baton Rouge Metro Council. The photograph below was taken by Daisy Jones, Scotlandville's first female photographer. (Both, courtesy of Chauna Banks-Daniel.)

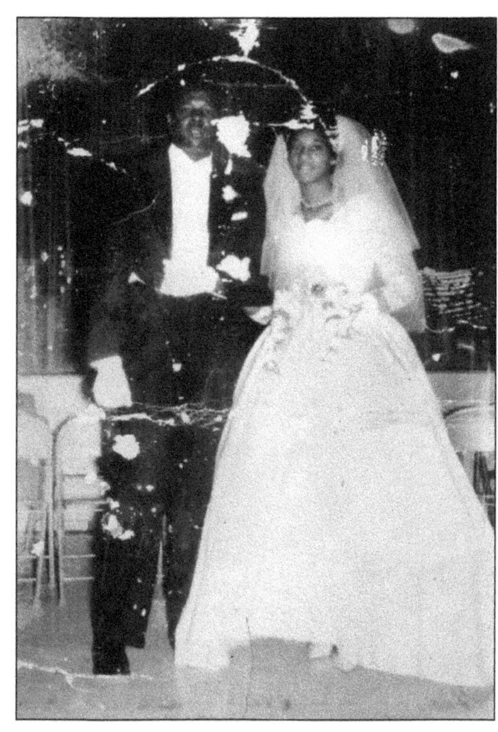

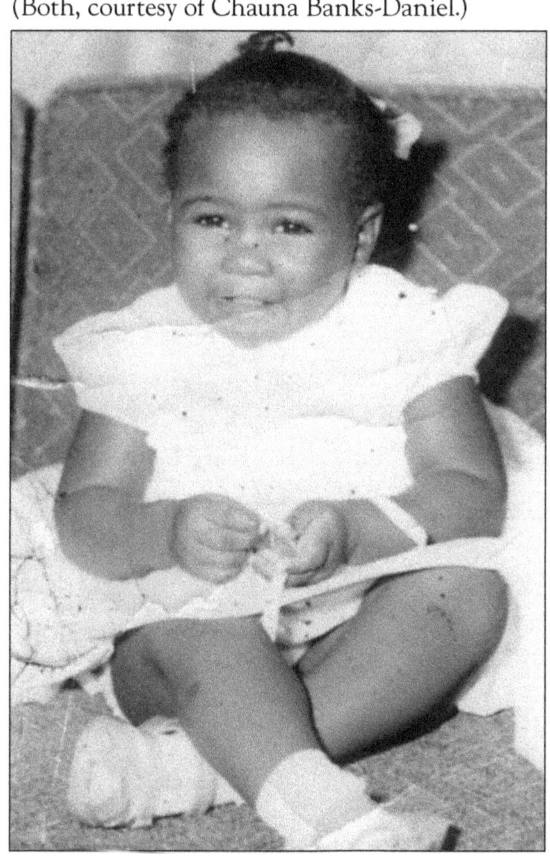

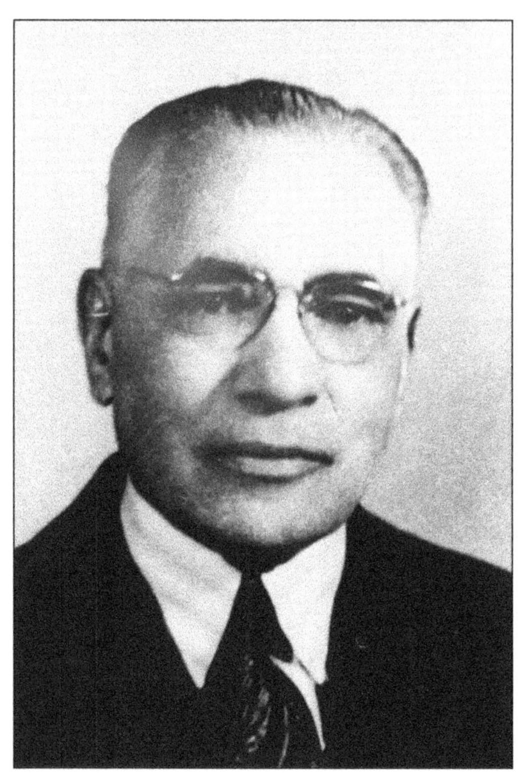

With the building of community in Scotlandville came the building of a university on the site of Scott's Bluff. On June 7, 1871, on Bill Poland Plantation located on the rural western side of Black Lake Bayou in Shephardtown, Bienville Parish, a baby boy was given the name Josiah Clark, meaning "Jehovah support." In 1890, his Christian name was changed to Joseph Samuel Clark. J.S. Clark (left) became one of the most powerful black education leaders in the state of Louisiana from the late 1880s until his death in 1944. He came to Scotlandville in 1914 to serve as first president of the "new" Southern University, bringing with him his wife, Octavia Head Clark (below), and their son, Felton Grandison Clark. Octavia served as Southern's first registrar and director of music and was the university's first lady until her death in 1959. (Both, courtesy of the Archives Department/John B. Cade Library/ Southern University and A&M College.)

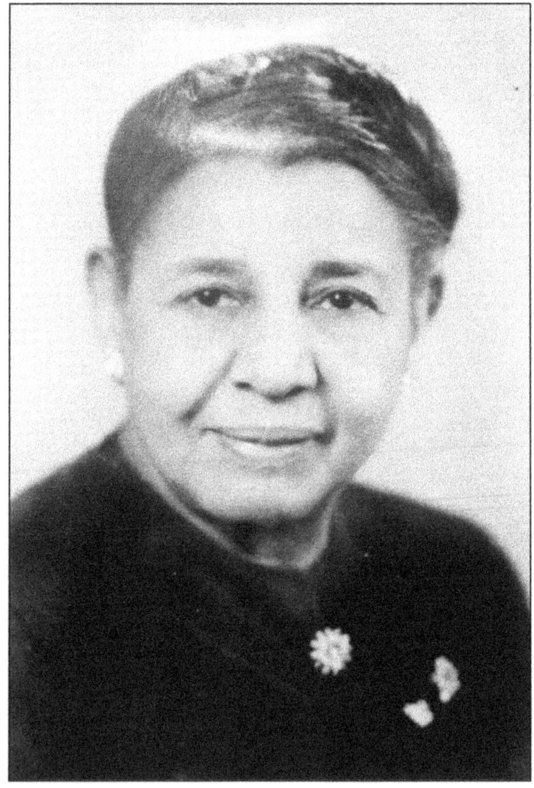

Two

Central Business District

Once the Heart of the Scotlandville Community

The heart of the Scotlandville community was its business district, located around the intersection of Scenic Highway and Scotland Avenue, which is Highway 19. Many businesses were found along this main thoroughfare and on Scenic Highway, across from the Scotland Station of the Kansas City Southern Railroad, once a passenger railroad line.

The first black families of Scotlandville included individuals who became leaders in the business community. They, along with white business owners, exercised their entrepreneurial skills in family-owned enterprises. Operating their own businesses built pride, dignity, and worth for these residents. A more self-sustaining existence proved beneficial in combating the indignities of Jim Crow society, where discrimination and inequality based on race were rampant.

Initially, these enterprises were primarily in the service and entertainment industries, such as grocers, transportation, realty services, barbers and beauticians, auto and shoe repair shops, clothing stores, funeral homes, printing shops, pharmacies, bakeries, restaurants, movie theaters, dance halls, liquor stores, and automotive sales. There were also musicians, artists, builders, photographers, reporters and editors, and contractors.

Scotlandville's first professional offices and financial institutions opened with the assistance of Southern University. University administrators were concerned about health care, legal, and financial services for not only faculty, staff, and students, but also to the neighborhood at large. From the opening of Southern in 1914, individuals with credentials and expertise in these areas were employed by or were trained at the university. Many of them opened offices in the neighborhood.

A third generation native notes that Scotlandville residents had practically everything needed to survive and to pursue happiness within the neighborhood. This self-sufficiency empowered many. It limited the need for them to venture outside the community's borders, shielding them from the oppression and degradation of second-class citizenship. The neighborhood's youth found role models in the local business leaders as well as educators, clergy, parents, and civic leaders. Having these role models within their neighborhood inspired many to develop the skills, abilities, and motivation to become engaged citizens.

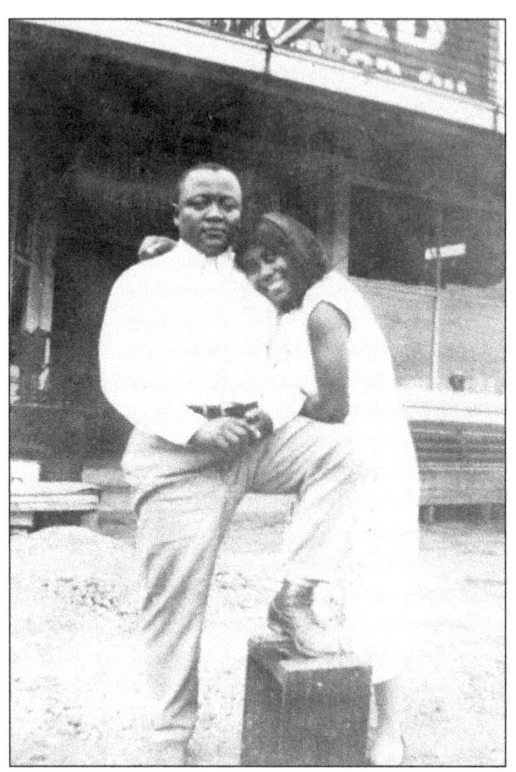

Located on the corner of Scenic Highway and Swan Street, Drago's Grocery was the first grocery store owned by a non–African American family living in Scotlandville prior to 1912. In 1919, Arteal Kelly and his wife, Amanda (both pictured at left), opened the first black-owned grocery in Scotlandville, serving the community for 25 years. The Kellys' store formed the centerpiece of a larger complex that included a gas station and post office. The Kellys cemented the link to the Standard Oil Company/Esso that not only employed Scotlandville residents but also initiated a product supply chain with the community's small-business owners. (Courtesy of Beverly A. Vincent.)

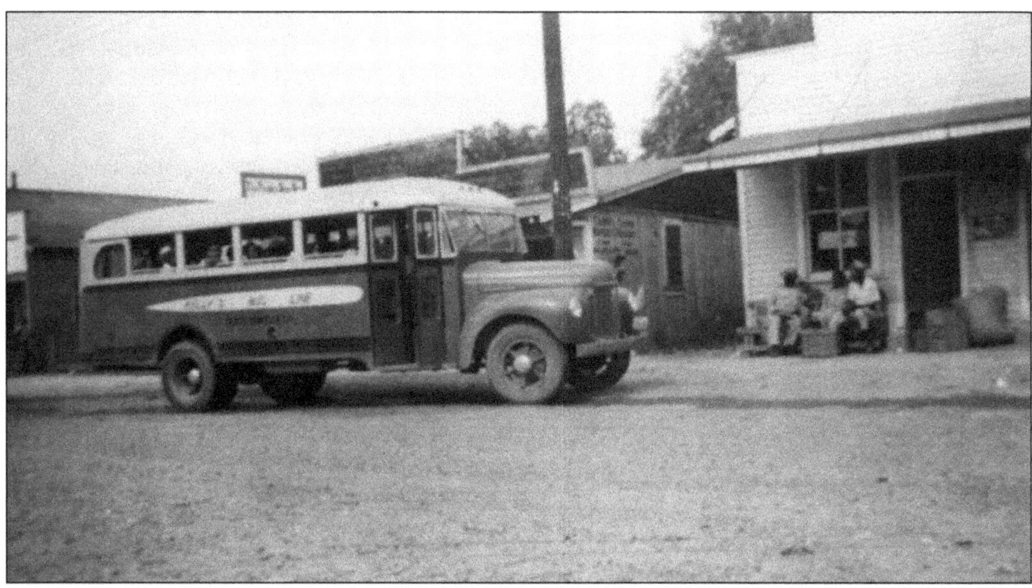

Once called a trading center, Scotlandville was a place travelers passed through en route to other towns. After Southern University's move to the area, people stopped passing through and began to venture into the area to live. To serve the needs of residents who needed to travel throughout and outside the community, newlyweds Arteal and Amanda Kelly founded Kelly's Blue Line, Scotlandville's first bus company, in 1919. An advertisement in Southern University's Yearbook, *The Cat*, in 1928 described the services available to their customers, including transfers and additional amenities. (Courtesy of Beverly A. Vincent.)

Franklin brothers Henry (below) and Arthur (right), Hayes brothers Clarence and Oliver "Scoobie," and the London family (next page) also operated Scotlandville bus transportation enterprises. Shortly after the end of World War II, the limited public transportation available for black residents was segregated. These black business owners provided a local service and also daily transportation to work at plants and industries along the Mississippi and various points in downtown Baton Rouge and area businesses and neighborhoods. For more than 30 years, the Franklins' central transit locale was in the area of Swan Street, near their residences. Arthur also operated the community's leading auto repair shop, which he established in the 1940s. All 11 children of these two Franklin families attended Southern University. (Both, courtesy of Gracie Franklin Perkins and Rosa Franklin.)

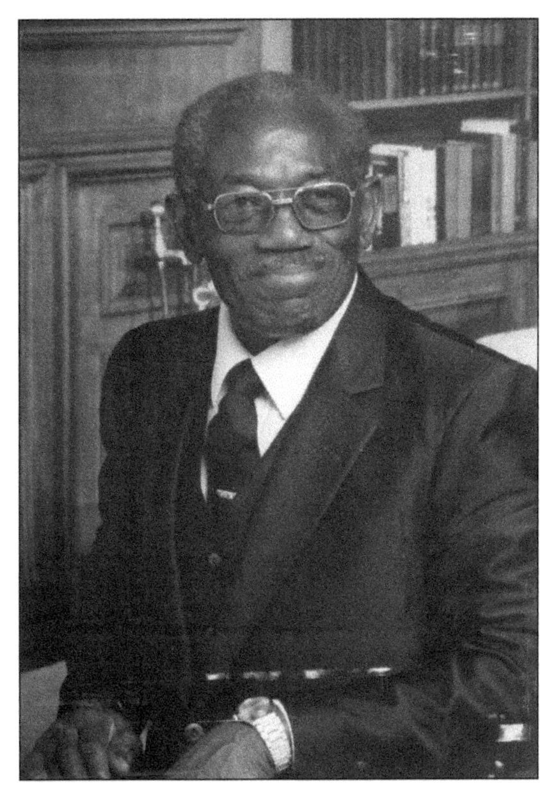

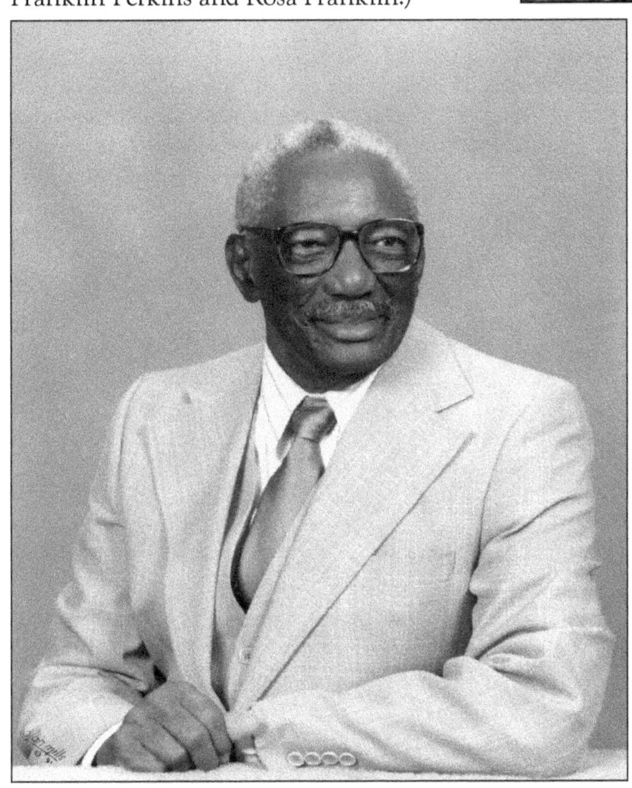

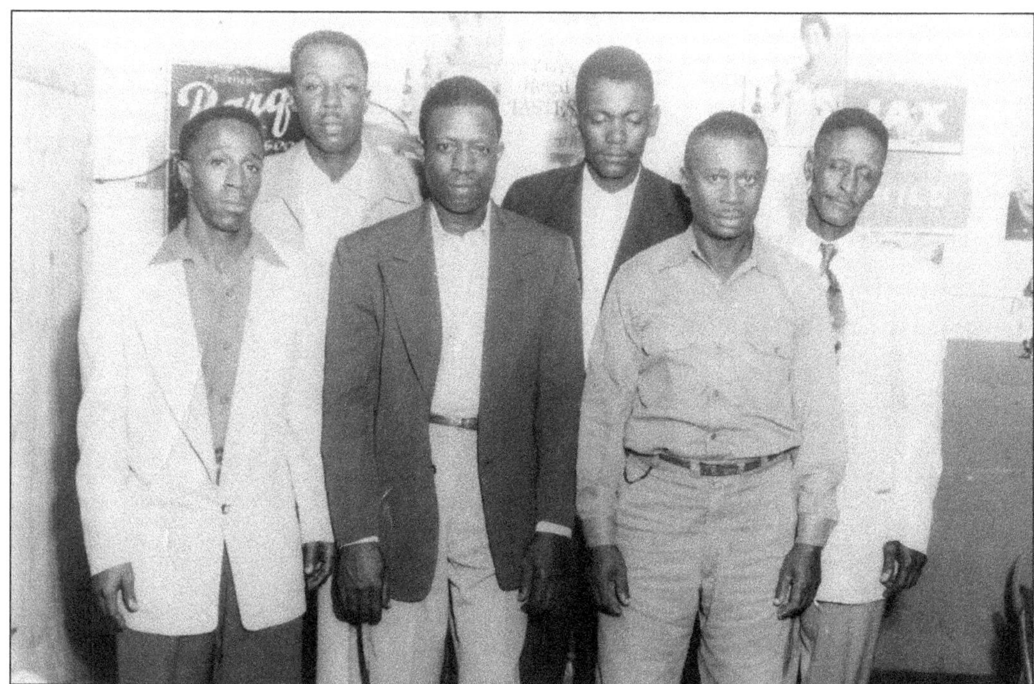

The Hayes brothers principally served students traveling to and from Southern University. Going door-to-door rather than corner-to-corner, the bus service was more like a taxi, though charging only 25¢. Clarence died in 1933. Scoobie still lives in his home in Southern Heights subdivision. Members of the Henry London Sr. family were also successful businesspersons in the bus transportation sector for more than 40 years until the early 1980s. Pictured above are drivers for London's bus service. Harold and his wife, Carrie, and their sons, Harold Jr., Henry, and Harding, along with daughters Ethel and Wilhelmenia, assisted in serving the transportation needs of Scotlandville residents. Pictured below are, from left to right, (sitting) Harold Sr., Carrie, and Harding; (standing) Ethel, Wilhelmenia, and Henry Jr. (Both, courtesy of Mary Wheelock Emerson.)

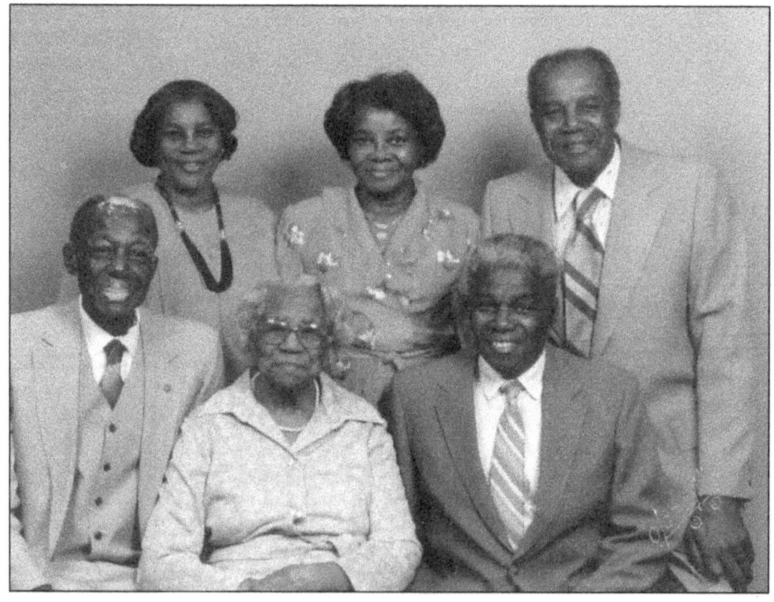

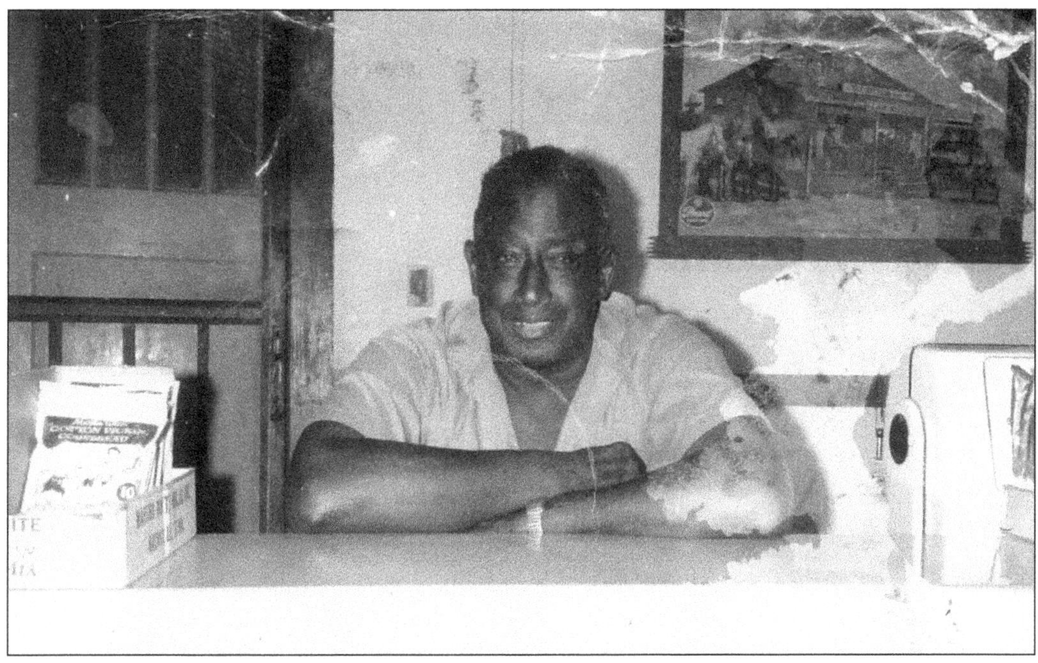

William "Bill" Kelly sits behind a counter in his store, Kelly and Sons Grocery Story, in the photograph above, taken in 1940. The store was located at 9515 Scenic Highway in the northwestern section of the community. Kelly and his wife, Hattie, were the parents of five children who they enrolled at Southern Lab. All attended Southern University. Shirley became an instructor in the University's English department, Lois earned degrees in English and library science, Lloyd graduated in masonry, Yvonne was a speech therapist who was employed in several local schools, and Donald studied visual arts. Below, Shirley and Hattie Kelly are pictured in the family store in 1950. (Both, courtesy of Shirley Kelly Hammond.)

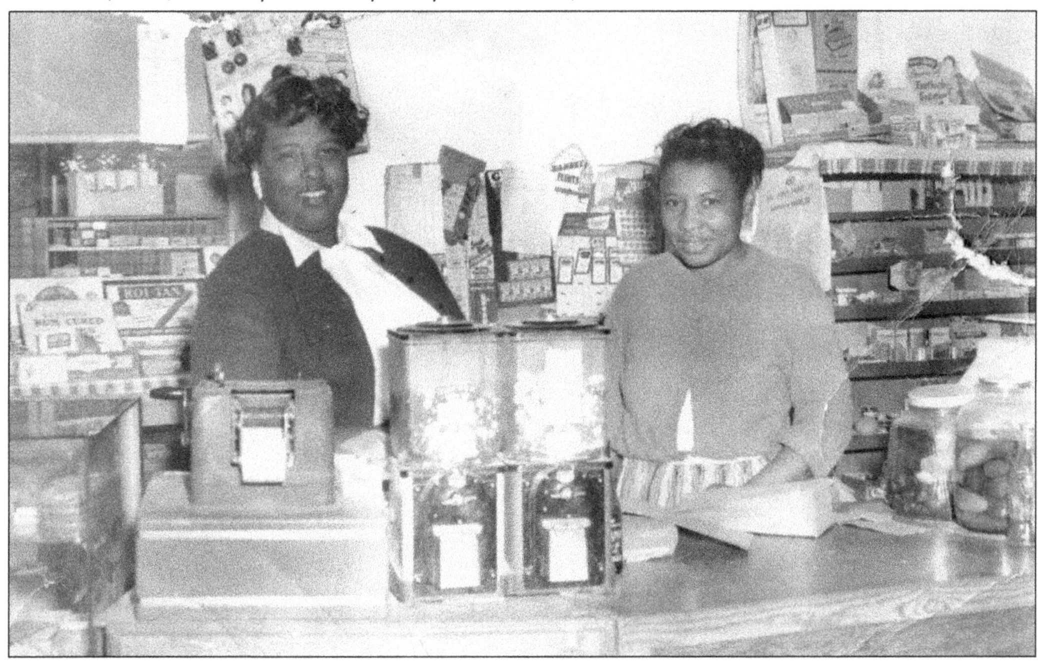

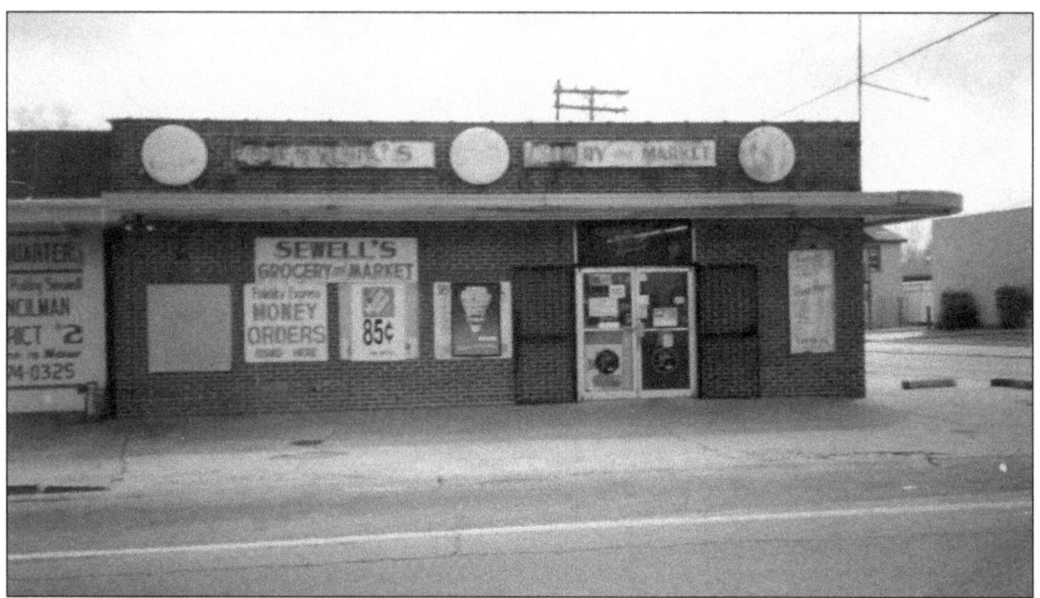

Sewell's Grocery and Market, owned and operated by Vanderbilt Sewell and his wife, Ellen, was a family business in every sense of the term. Four sons, Vanderbilt Jr., Kerry, David, and Douglas; and two daughters, Fairy Lee and Ada Mae, assisted in all operations of the store. The original location on the corner of Scotland and Swan Avenues was modernized and expanded in the 1950s, as shown here. (Courtesy of Douglas and Ethel Sewell.)

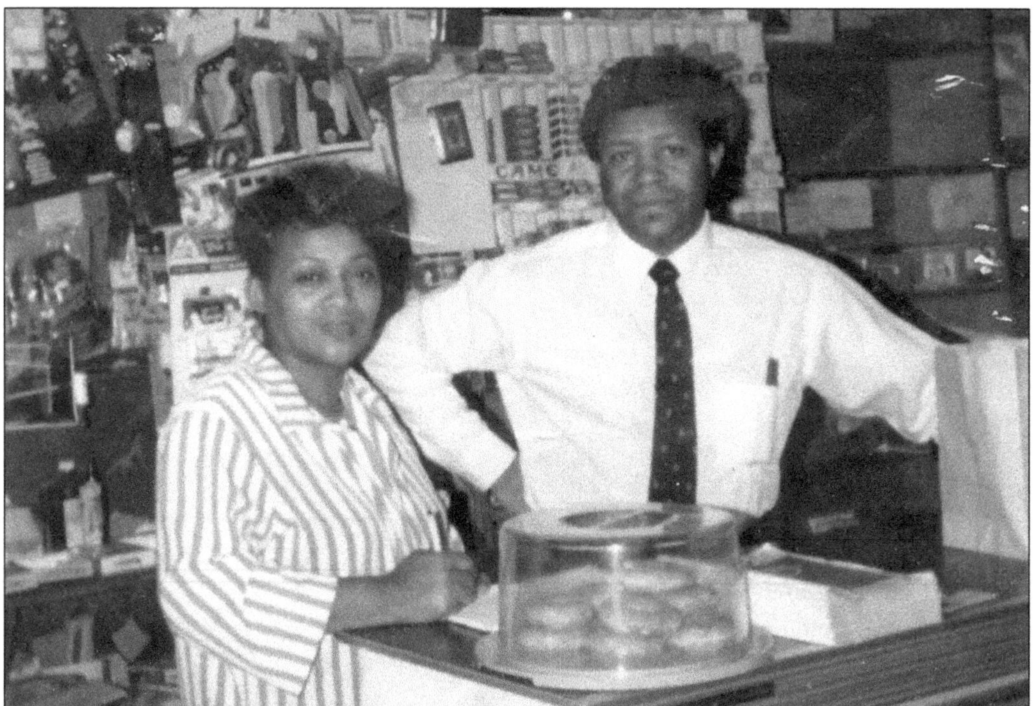

In the 1960s, approximately 20 years after the establishment of the original store, Sewell's had four separate locations in Scotlandville, each owned by Vanderbilt's four sons. Douglas Sewell Sr. and his wife, Ethel, are shown in one of the stores in 1970. (Courtesy of Douglas and Ethel Sewell.)

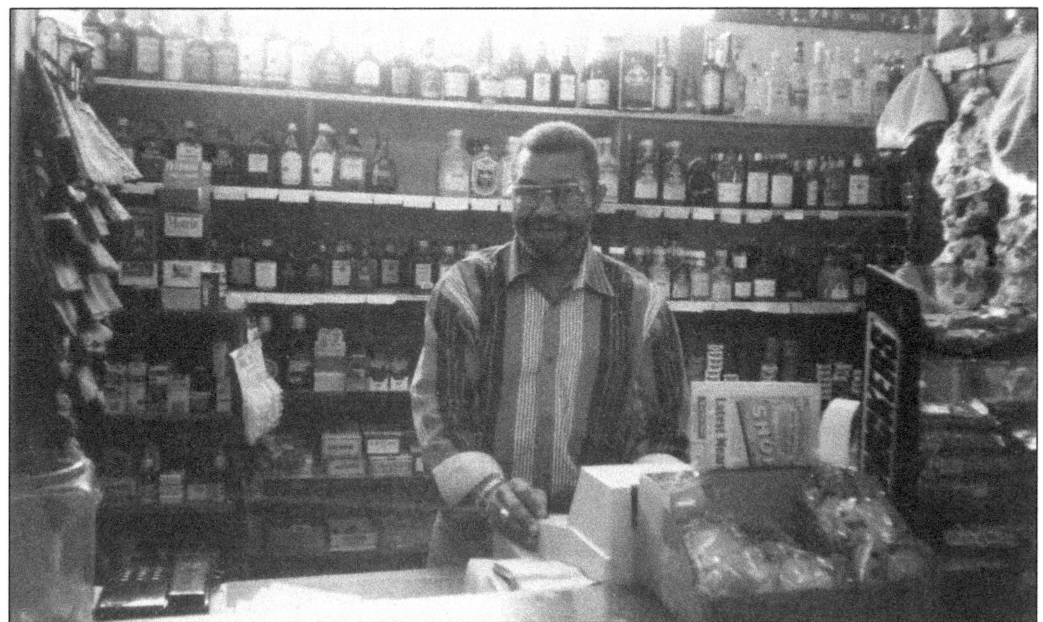

Vanderbilt and Ellen Sewell provided jobs and granted credit for the townspeople and Southern University students and employees in their stores. After his parents' deaths, Douglas Jr. was the last family member to operate the original store. A gunshot wound to his leg during an armed robbery at the store in July 2011 prompted Douglas to close the business after more than 40 years. (Courtesy of Douglas and Ethel Sewell.)

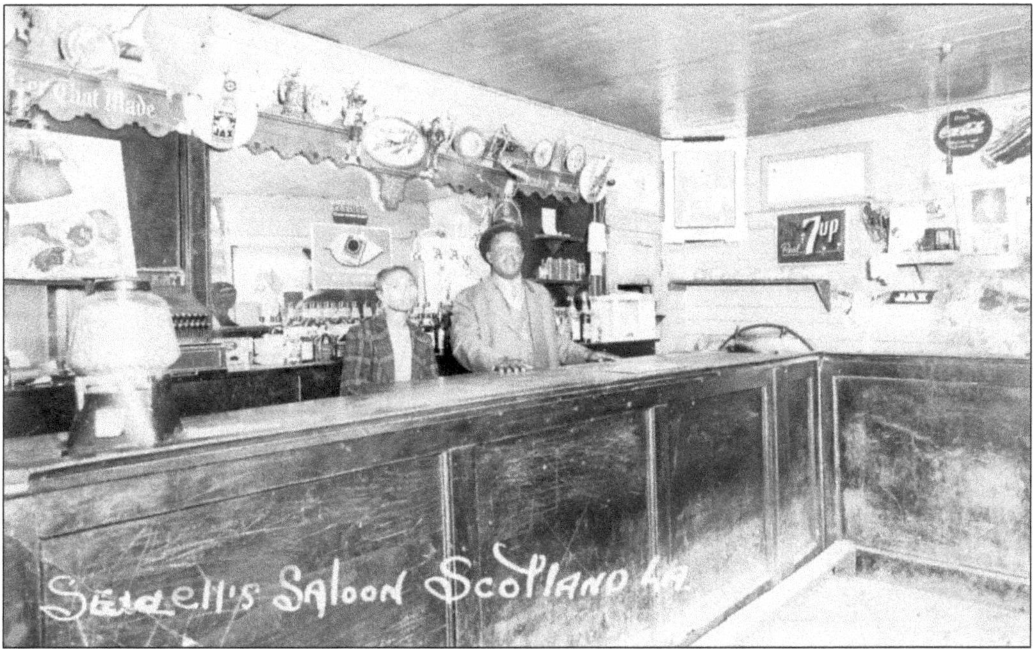

Scotlandville by the 1940s offered residents access to groceries, sundries, fuel, housing, entertainment, and much more because of entrepreneurs like the Sewells. Employees are pictured in Sewell's Saloon, a forerunner to bars; many with eateries, such as Moreco's, opened on Harding Boulevard. (See page 48.) (Courtesy of Douglas and Ethel Sewell.)

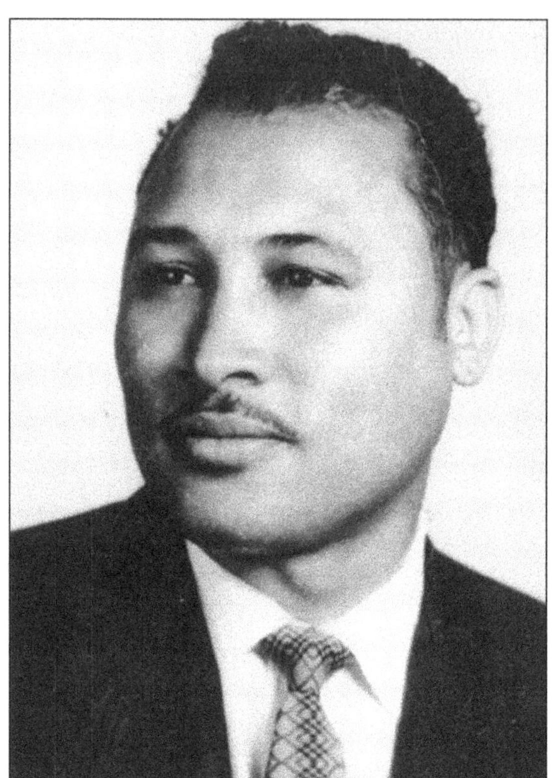

At the age of nine, John E. "Pool" Simms held two jobs, one working for Sam McCoy's ice truck business and the other in Rieger's Pharmacy in Scotlandville. Lewis Rieger, president and general manager, operated 12 stores in Louisiana, Mississippi, and Florida. Using the skills acquired while working in Rieger's Pharmacy, Pool later became an employee, owner/manager, and partner at Pool's, University, and Simms Discount pharmacies, totaling more than 60 years. As a business manager, Pool contributed generously to community service projects and church initiatives. A little league baseball team was sponsored by his business for many years. Pool was a lifetime member of the NAACP. He died at the age of 80 in 2010. (Courtesy of Geraldine A. Simms and Ruby Jean Simms.)

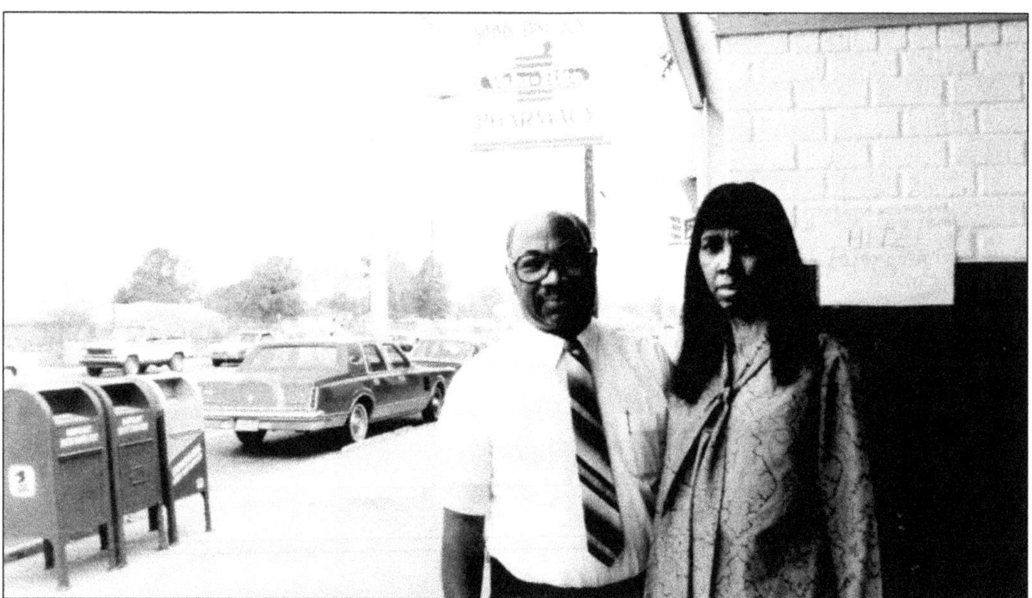

When Simms' Discount Pharmacy was opened in 1985 by Pool's sisters, Geraldine A. "Gerry" and Ruby Jean Simms, it became Scotlandville's first female business associated with a chain, the Value-Rite Chain. When the pharmacy section was closed, the store became affiliated with T. G and Y, McCrory's, and Newberry's. The two secured contracts with the US Postal Service, Entergy, and South Central Bell (Bell South/AT&T) until 1996, when the store was closed. Co-owner Ruby Jean is pictured in front of the store with Councilman Thomas Woods. (Courtesy of Ola J. Woods.)

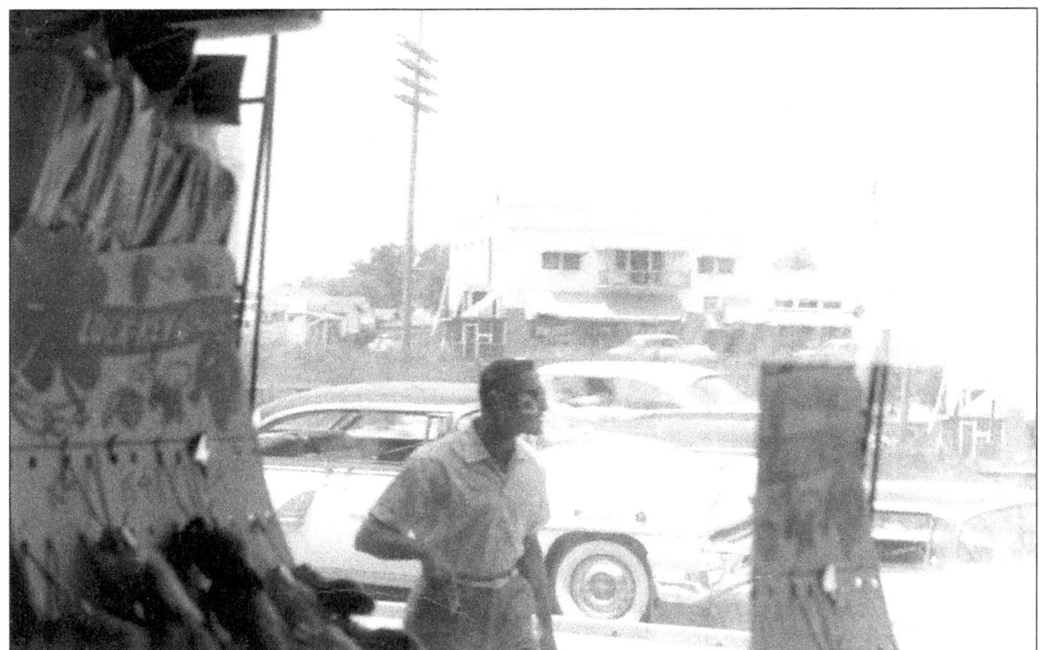

Paul Haynes taught at a New Orleans college on weekdays, and in the evenings and on weekends managed his family's building on Highway 19. Until the 1990s, space on the first floor was leased for apartments, a restaurant, and a liquor store. On the second floor was a nightclub. The Haynes building is visible in this photograph taken from a shop window across the street. (Courtesy of Ruby Jean Simms and Vallory Simms Hills.)

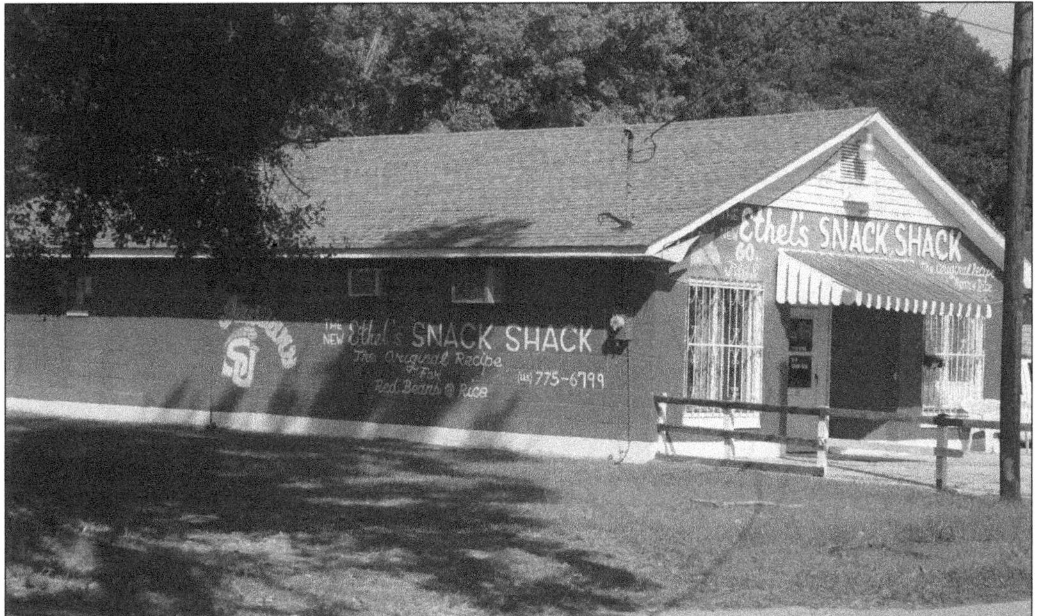

Ethel's Snack Shack, 1553 Fairchild Street, achieved the long-running title of "No. 1 Soul Food" restaurant in the area shortly after opening its doors in the 1930s. Ethel's was not only a place to get a bite to eat, but also a noon meeting place for SU administrators, faculty, staff, and students. For home football games, "all roads led to Ethel's." (Courtesy of Steve Jarreau Photography.)

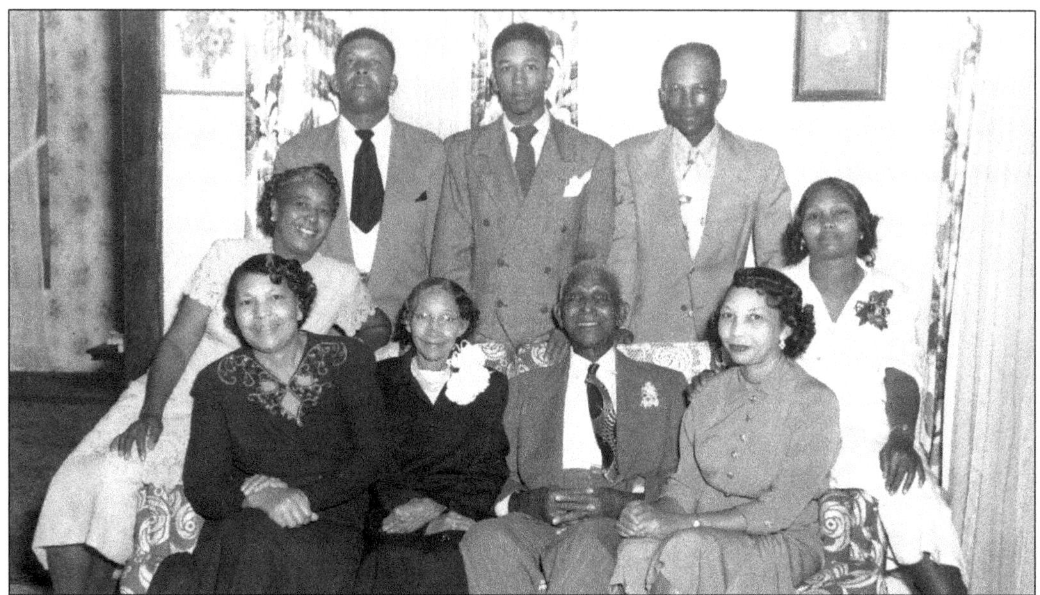

When greeting visitors from Scotlandville, alumni across the nation always inquired about Ethel's delicious home cooking. However, Ethel did not cook; she employed the best cooks in the community. Ethel was married to Melvin Kaufman, a Standard Oil Company/Esso employee. The couple had no children of their own. Pictured from left to right are (sitting) Bernice Ricks, Ida Green Lewis, Robie Green, Charles Green, Ethel Green Kaufman, and Bessie Green Rheames; (standing) Charles Green, Theodore Green, and Allen Green. (Courtesy of Juanita Lewis Franklin.)

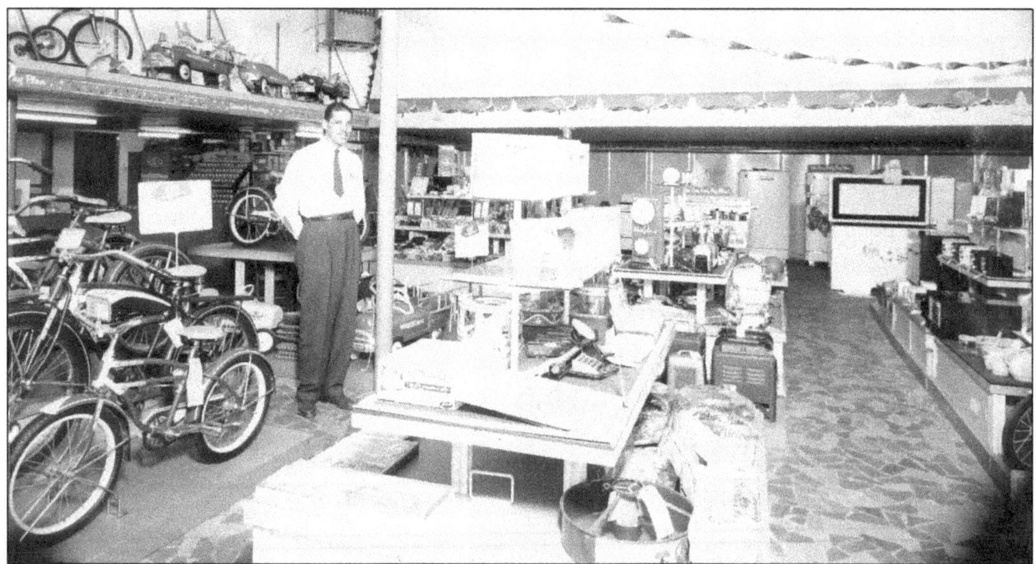

Son of James and Eleanor Cabrere Thompson Sr. of New Orleans, Horatio Cabrere Thompson opened his first Esso service station shortly after he earned his degree from Southern in 1937. Within 10 years, Thompson expanded his business to two other locations and 35 employees. He and his wife, the former Jewell Tatum, a public school teacher and principal, had two daughters, Phyllis and Paula. One of the first African Americans in Louisiana granted a General Electric and Esso Service Station franchise and Goodyear distributorship, Thompson is shown in one of his stores in this c. 1940 photograph. (Courtesy of Phyllis White.)

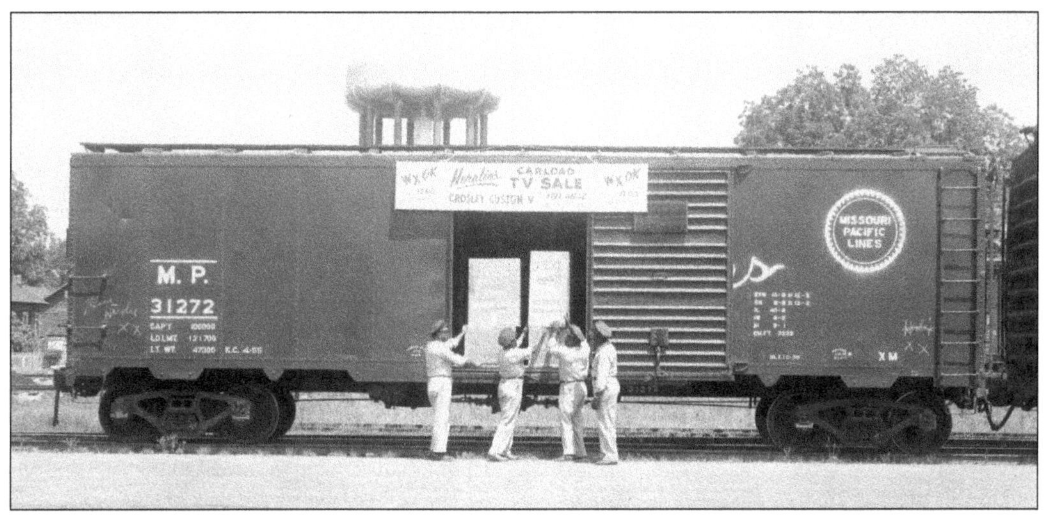

In addition to the usual items for purchase at a service station, Horatio's offered Goodyear car tires and GE home merchandise including sporting goods, housewares, small appliances, accessories, bicycles, toys, and games. Patrons could purchase these items on installment plans through the company's own finance department. Pictured are employees preparing for Thompson's railroad carload television sale, which was broadcast via WXOK radio at his appliance store. Below, Horatio Thompson is pictured at his station with manager "Smitty." The building displayed the trademark Esso slogan, "Happy Motoring!" In the 1950s, Thompson helped to develop the Southern Heights subdivision where he lived, built apartment complexes, and owned a fleet of taxis and buses. (Both, courtesy of Phyllis White.)

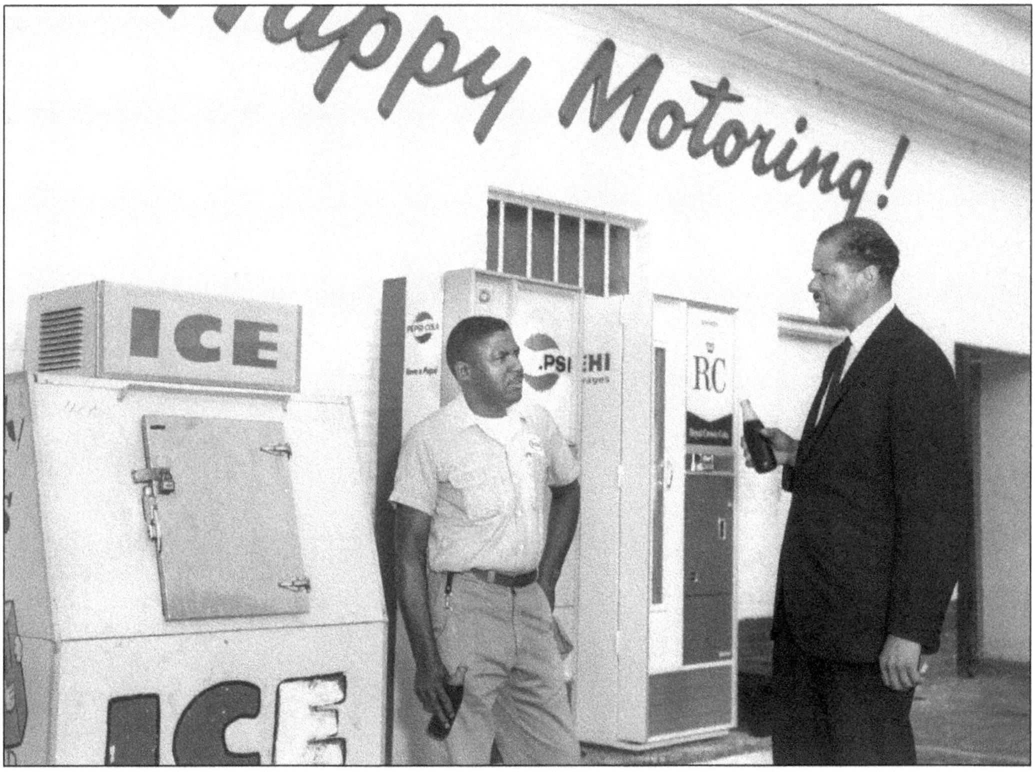

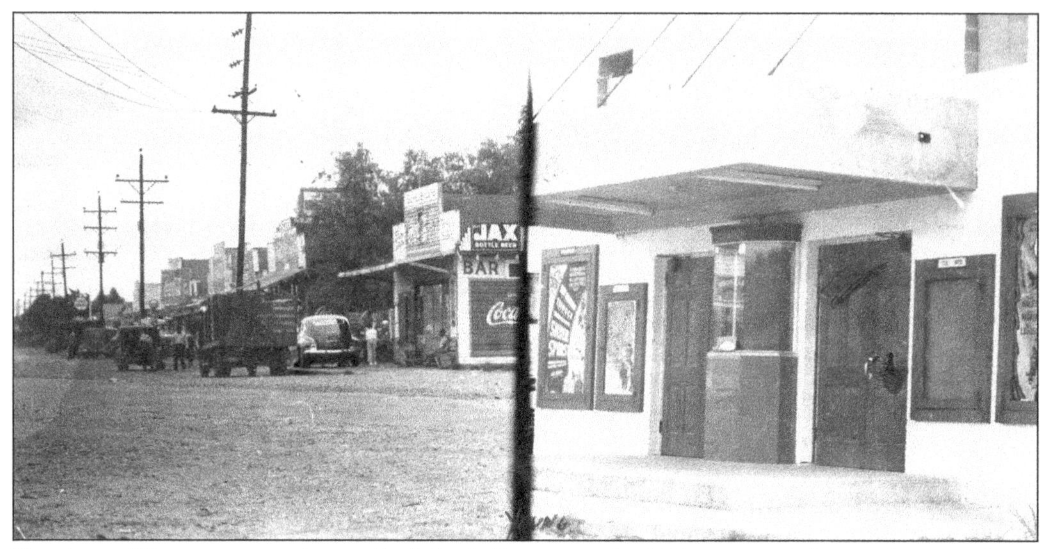

For almost 30 years, owner James Carl Cook Sr. operated a 300-seat movie house for second-run films and classics, especially the popular cowboy movies. Tickets were 14¢ for children, 36¢ for adults, and $1 for a family of four. The theater was known by grateful parents for providing after school and weekend entertainment for the children of Scotlandville. Cook, a longtime employee at Standard Oil, would rise at 5:00 a.m., have breakfast with his wife, and take the Kelly Bus to the refinery for his 7:00 a.m. to 3:30 p.m. shift. He would return home on the bus and have dinner before opening the theater at 6:00 p.m. The theater closed when the last show ended shortly before midnight. On weekends, the theater opened at 2:00 p.m. Pictured below from left to right are unidentified, businessman Horatio Thompson, and James "Jimmy" C. Cook Sr. (Above, courtesy of Dr. James Carl Cook Jr.; below, courtesy of Phyllis White.)

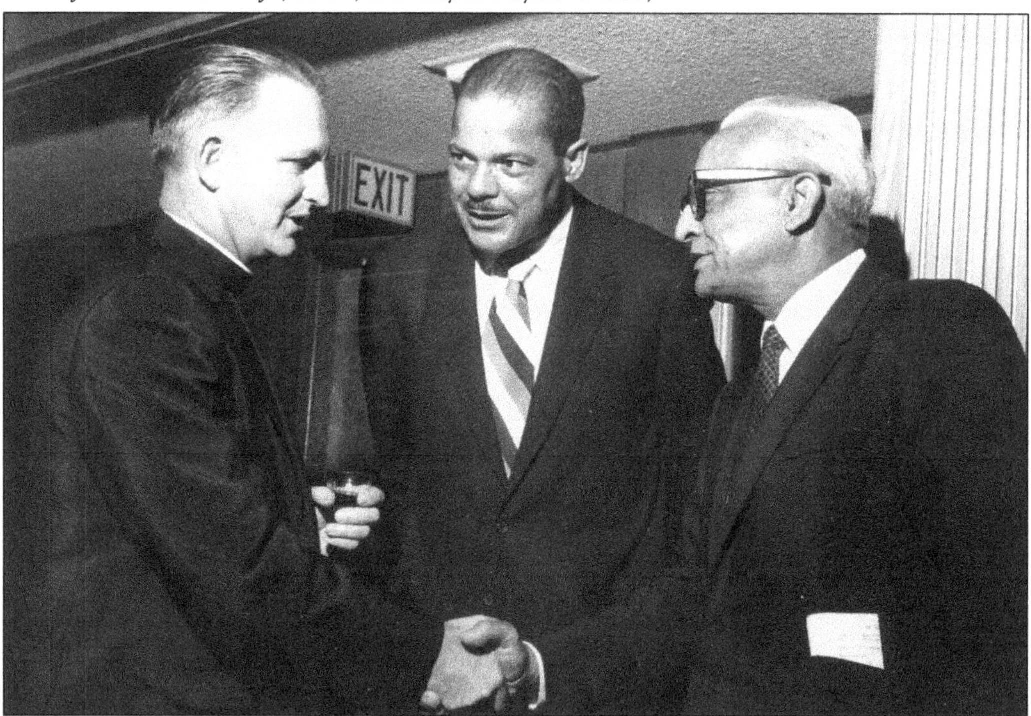

The original theater, a wood-frame building, burned in 1944. *Motion Picture Daily* reported the reopening of Cook's Theatre on April 1, 1945, the same day Cook's daughter, Linda, was born. Cook Sr. and friends, assisted by a $300 loan from Louisiana National Bank, rebuilt the new cinder block structure. In addition to movies, cartoons, and *Newsreel of the Week*, the theater patrons were treated to traveling magic and puppet shows performed on stage before the Saturday afternoon and evening features. Olympic gold medalist Jesse Owens was a guest speaker at the theater. Below, Sarah Starring, ticket manager for more than 30 years, recalled a visit by Roy Rogers, Gabby Hayes, and Rogers's horse, Trigger, in 1946. One of the Cook daughters is pictured at right helping out at the concessions. (Both, courtesy of Dr. James Carl Cook Jr.)

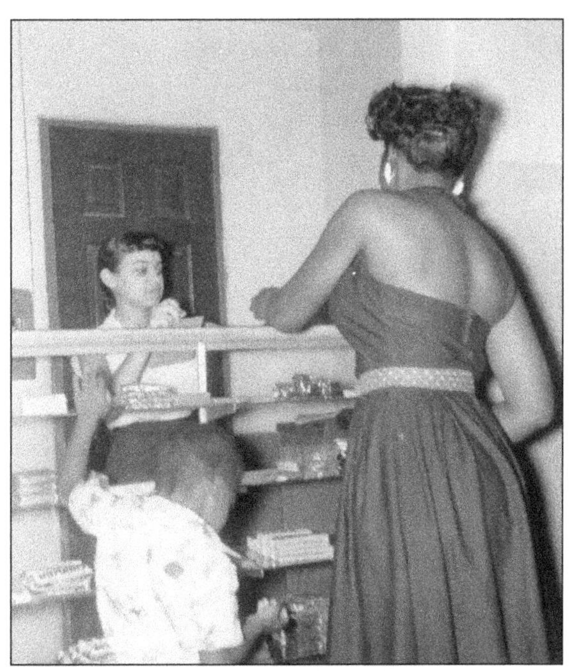

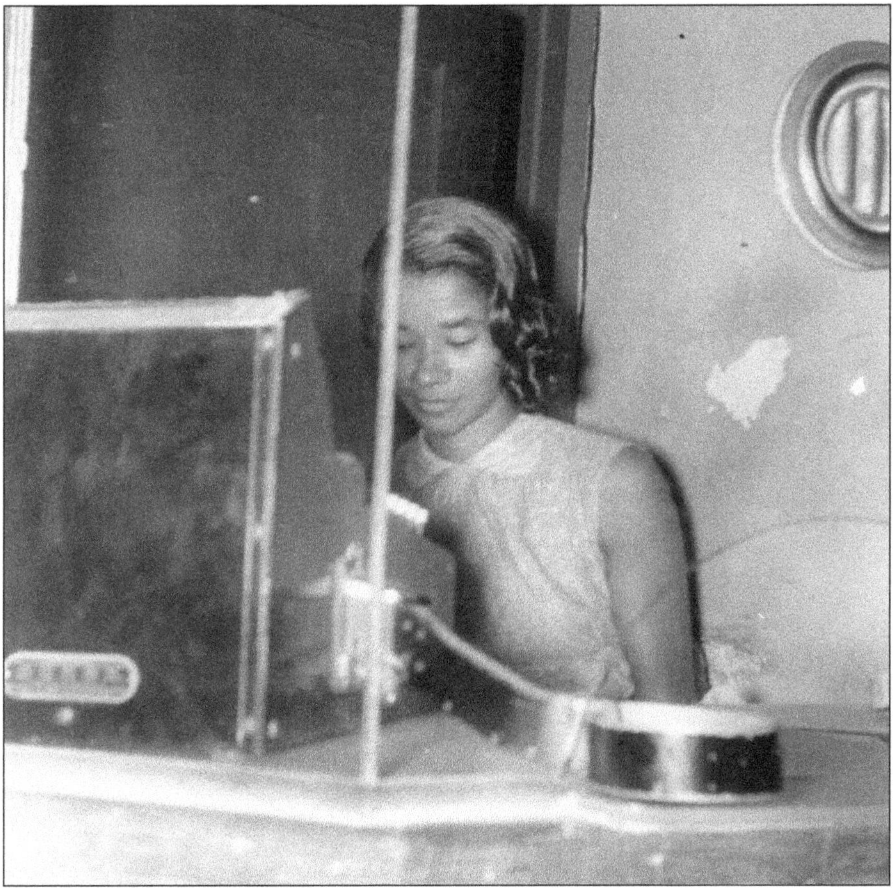

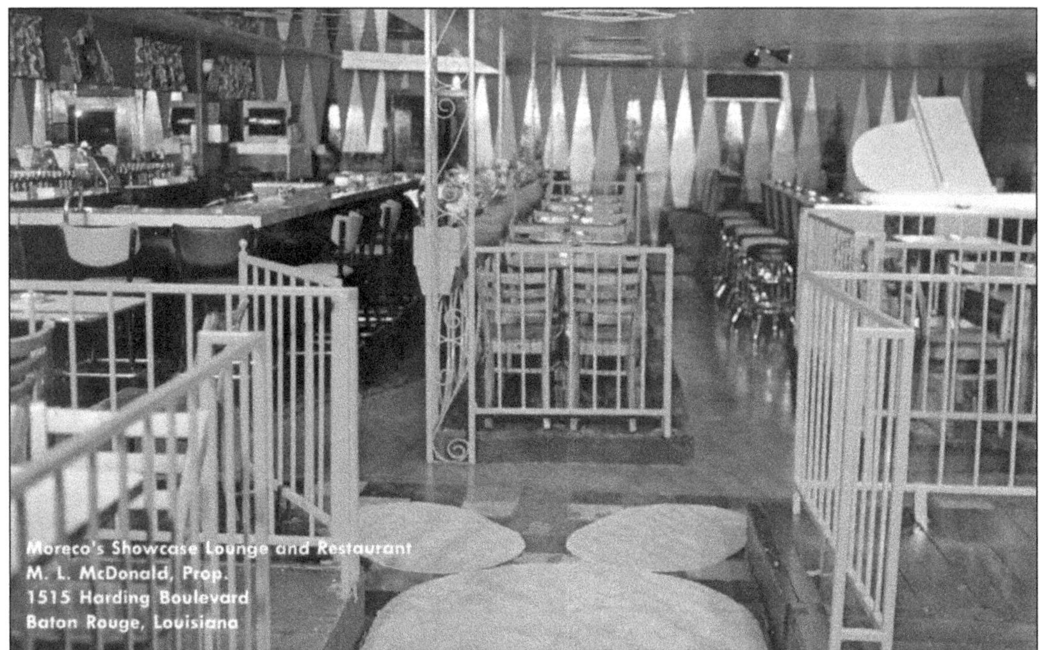

Moreco's Showcase Lounge and Soul Restaurant, which opened at 1515 Harding Boulevard in January 1960, was owned, operated, and managed by Moses L. McDonald. Patrons could enjoy fine dining and elegant décor. Entertainment at this popular nightspot included nationally known performers Nancy Wilson and the Chilites, along with musicians James Rivers, Red Tyler, Katie Webster, Bobby Powell, and Donnie Williams. It closed in 1981. (Courtesy of Mada McDonald.)

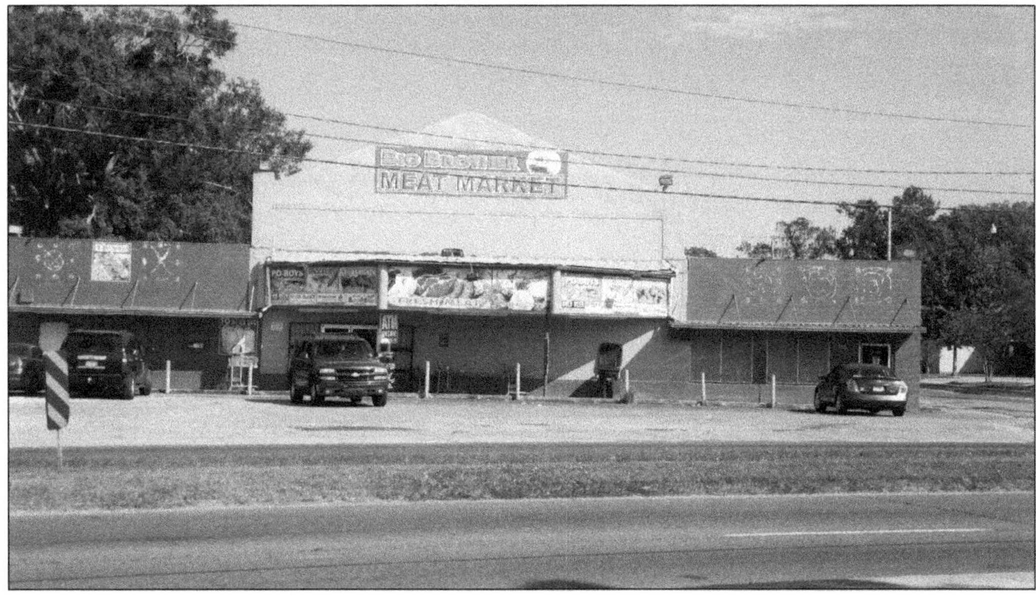

Opening on February 26, 1953, the Ann Theater, 6704 Scenic Highway, was owned and operated by Fred and Ida Freeman Williams off and on until its final closure in the 1980s. American Blaxploitation films, such as *Shaft*; *Super Fly*; *Cornbread, Earl, & Me*; and *Cooley High* were shown here. Hollywood celebrities Gail Fisher and Rudy Rae Moore made personal appearances. The former theater building currently houses a meat market, as seen here. (Courtesy of Steve Jarreau Photography.)

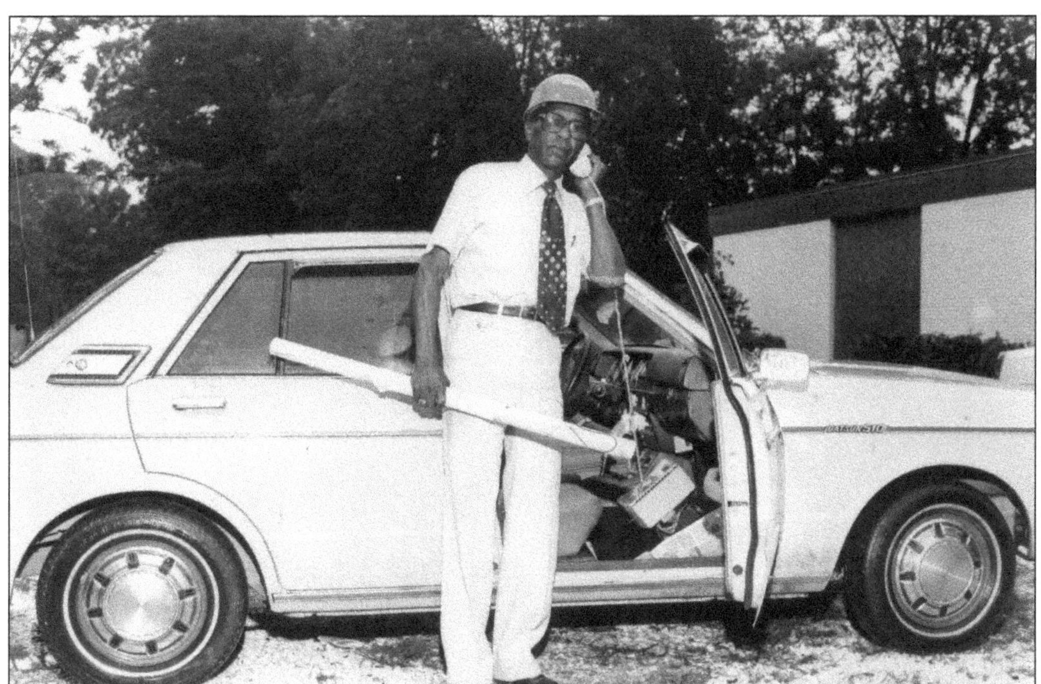

Son of Joseph "Papa" Newman and the former Florence Knox, Jewel Joseph Newman (1921–2014) was a 1941 graduate of McKinley Senior High School and attended Southern University, where he was a member of the Reserve Corps program. Shortly after enrolling at Southern, Newman was called to active duty in the US Army and was discharged in 1945 at the rank of sergeant 4th class. For 15 years, he owned and operated an Esso service station in Scotlandville. A neighbor for more than 20 years, Katie Fluker, a Southern graduate and current employee, recalled Newman coming to her rescue and giving her car a jumpstart. Newman was married to the former Sallie Gillespie in 1963. He was the father of six children. Even before he entered politics (see chapter seven), he was involved in helping to bring Little League baseball to Scotlandville. (Both, courtesy of Judge Trudy M. White.)

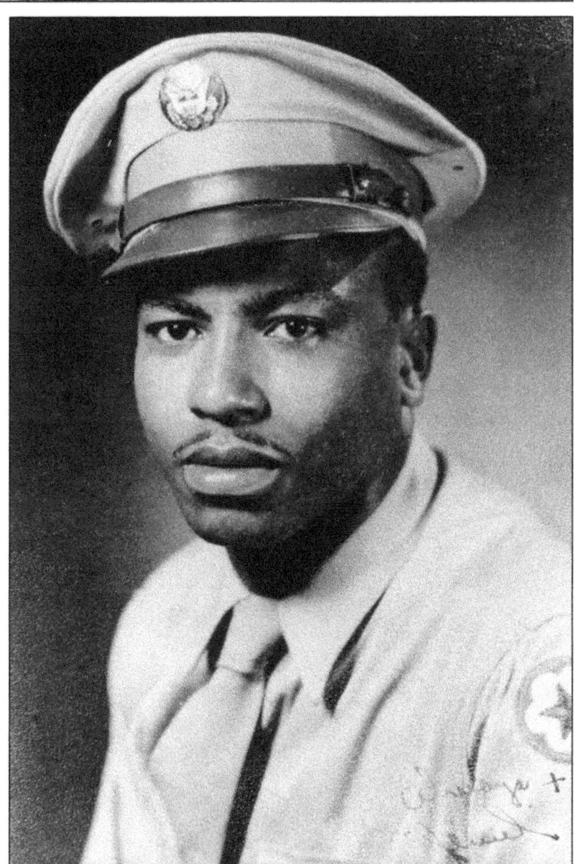

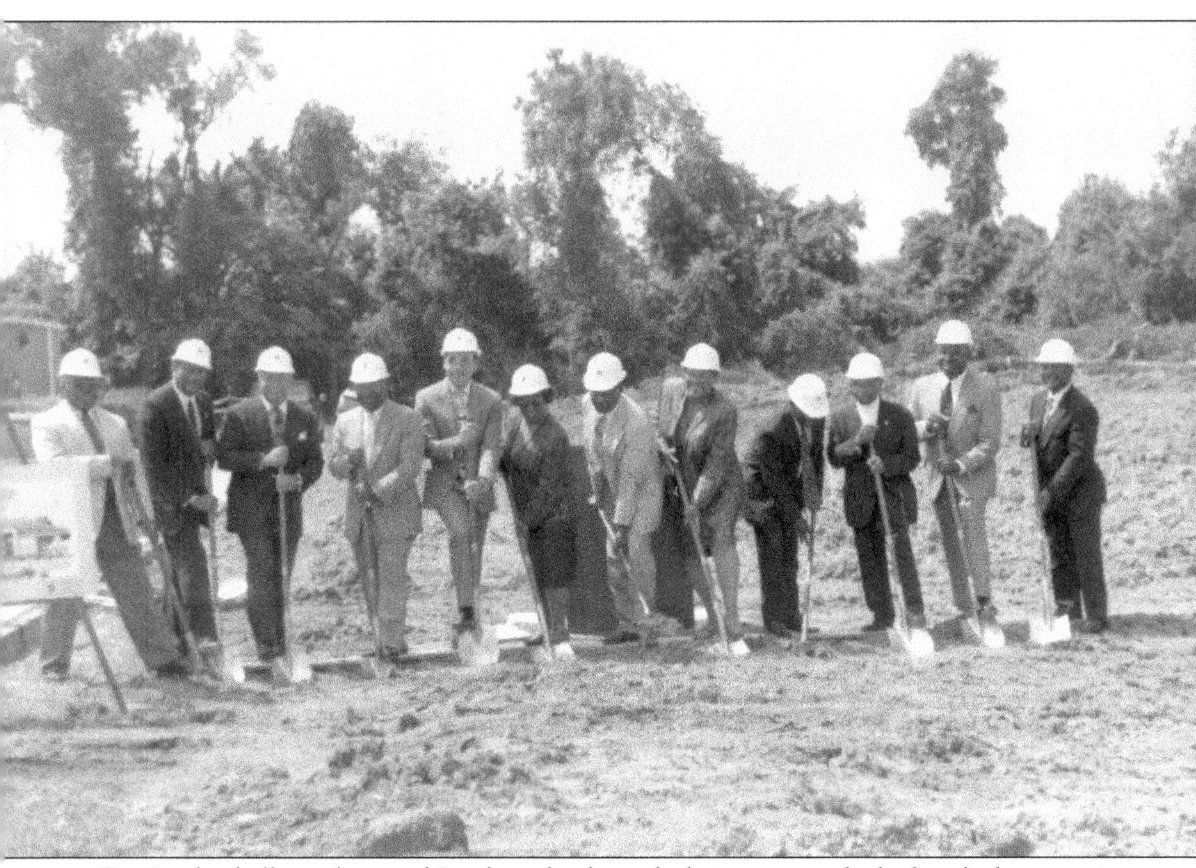

Ten Scotlandville residents and Southern faculty and administrators who had applied to organize and operate a federal credit union on January 9, 1937, were granted a charter three months later for the Southern Teachers and Parents Federal Credit Union (STPFCU). One of the founders, James B. Moore, an instructor in the university's industrial arts program, was the first STPFCU treasurer and manager. Moore operated the credit union business out of his home before the first office space was donated by Southern. Southern graduate Richard Turnley took over the financial institution on January 1, 1959. In 1997, fifty years after its founding, a ground breaking for the present facility was held. From left to right are Southern University administrators and Scotlandville residents Dewitt Jones, Marvin Yates, Leon Tarver, Thomas Woods, Flandus McClinton, Marilyn Ray-Jones, James Fortenberry, Doris Alfred, Jesse Perkins, B.A. Little, Kirkland Alfred, and Richard Turnley. (Courtesy of STPFCU.)

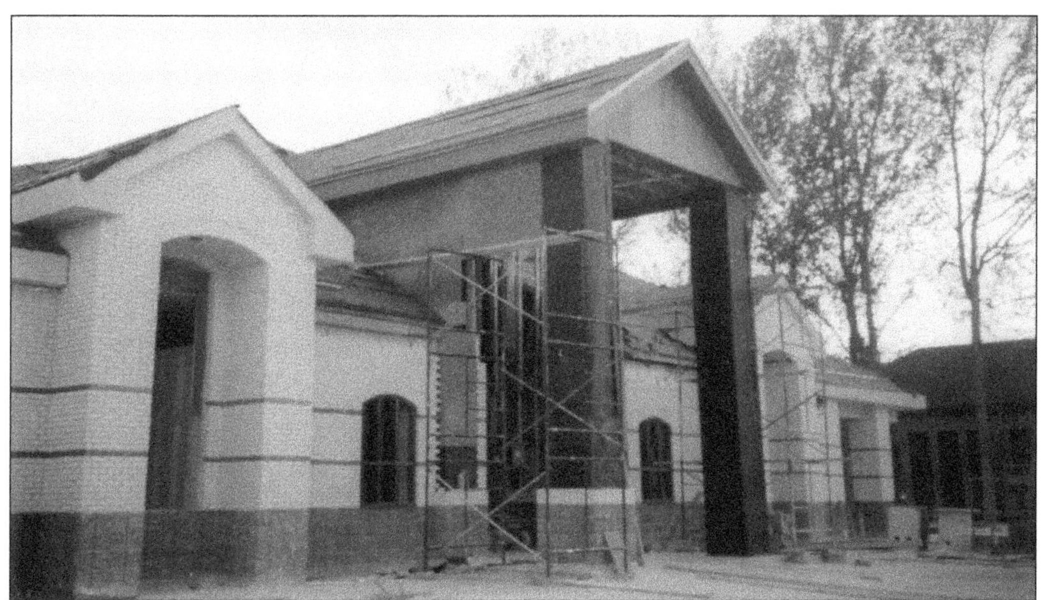

The new STPFCU building, pictured above under construction, represented the fulfillment of a dream for a financial institution where members were able to take out small loans and were taught to save their money. The initial STPFCU annual membership grew from 7 to 17 in one year. More than 4,000 were members by the mid-1980s, with total assets just under $1 million. Services offered included Visa cards with cash advances, ATM cards, automated response system, IRAs, traveler's checks, payroll deduction and direct deposits, and competitive rates on CDs. It was not until 1956 that the first bank, First Federal Savings and Loan Association, was established by black residents in Scotlandville. STPFCU staff below are, from left to right, (standing) Shirley Williams-Combs and Richard Turnley; (sitting) Venita Perkins, Carrie Germany, and Rosie Williams. (Both, courtesy of STPFCU.)

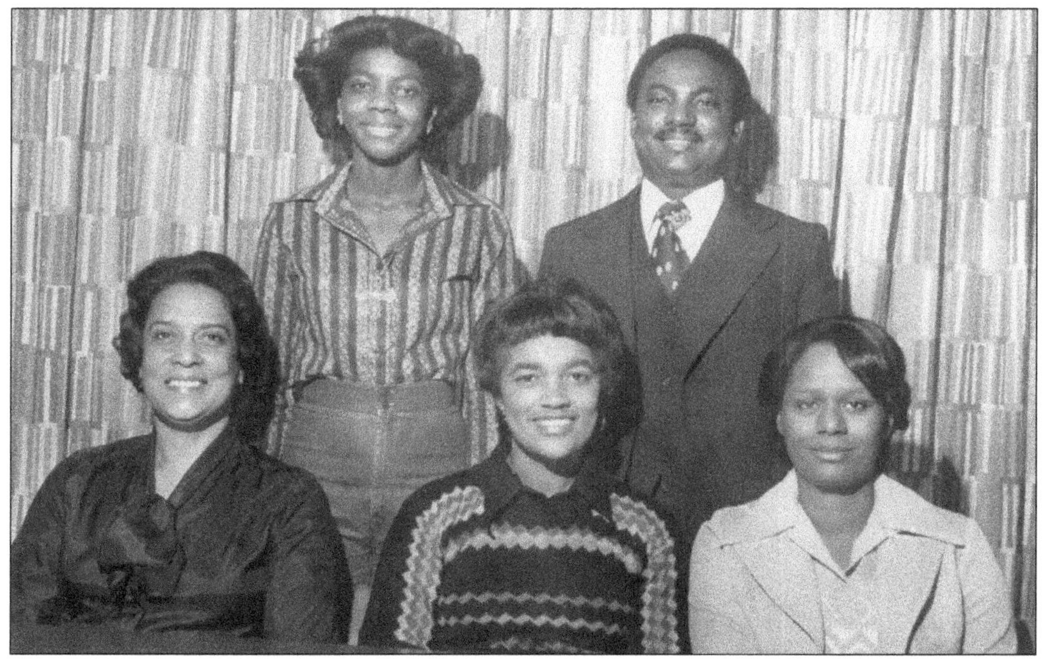

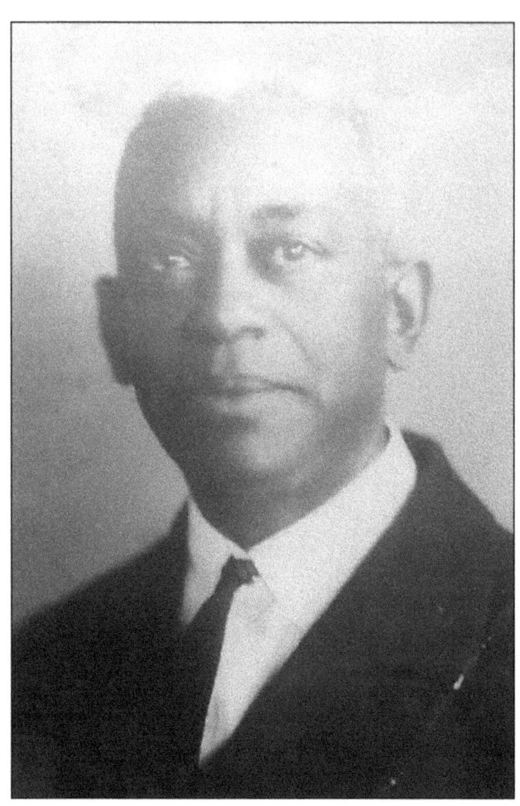

Health care for students was a primary concern of Dr. J.S. Clark and other university administrators. Initially, campus residents had no electricity and no running water. Water from the Mississippi River was first boiled on a flat-belly woodstove to be safe for drinking and cooking. President Clark solicited the assistance of the few local black physicians, who also provided services to the town of Scotlandville. These black doctors and dentists were graduates of Meharry and Howard universities' medical and dental schools, historically black institutions in the South. From 1914 to the 1960s, Dr. Beverly V. Baranco Sr. (left), his son Dr. Raymond M. Baranco, Dr. William H. Wethers I, and other physicians conducted a physical examination for entering students and shared their knowledge and skills in keeping them healthy and fit. The university has never been without a "physician in residence." The infirmary, completed in the 1990s, has staff doctors and nurses and a pharmacy. Dr. Beverly V. Baranco Jr., pictured below, was a campus dentist. (Both, courtesy of Dr. Patricia Baranco.)

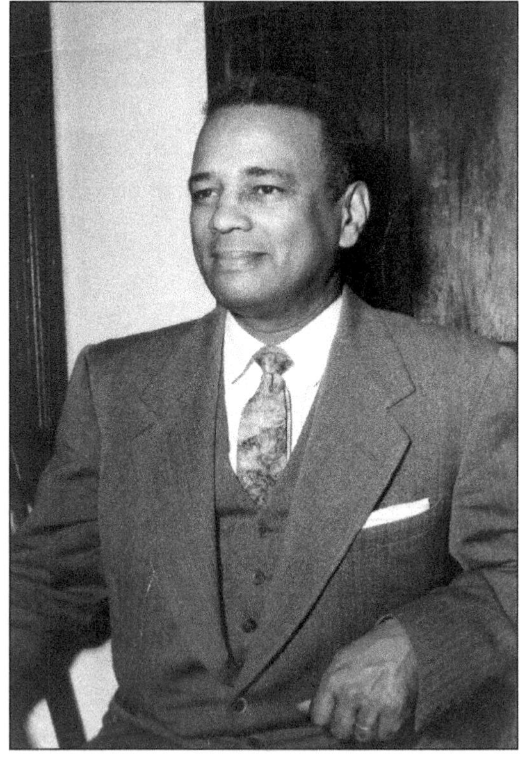

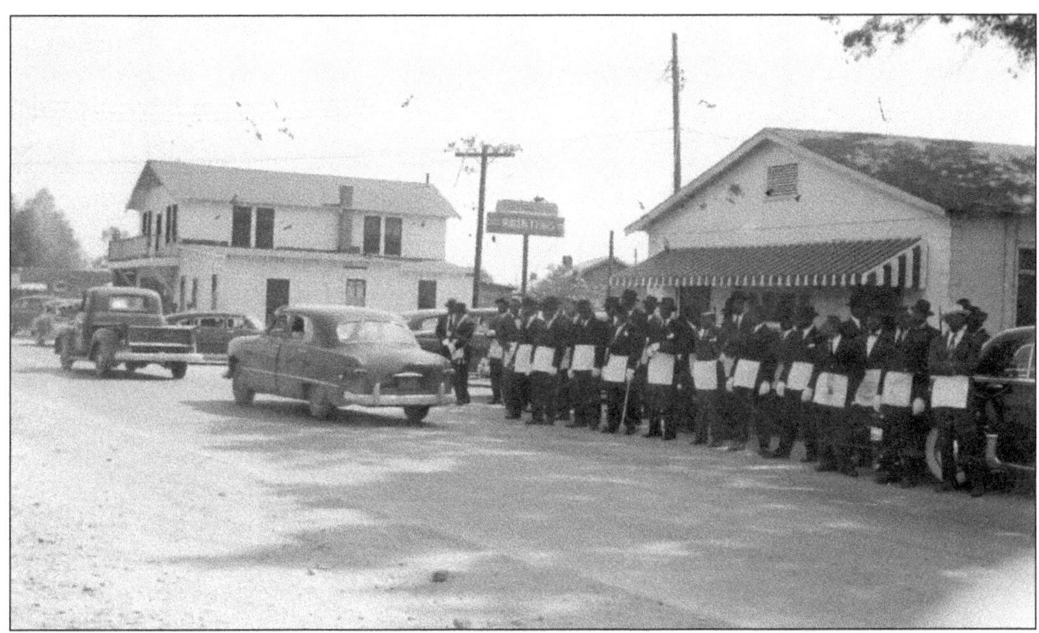

Owned and operated by Samuel Jenkins, Fraternal Press was the first and only printing business in Scotlandville for more than 40 years. Located across the highway from Scott's Bluff Morticians on Scenic Highway and next door to John Sebastian Jones, one of the first administrators of Southern employed in 1914, the press offered services for business and individual customers. Among the employees at the press were Charles Gray and Palmer Ray Dent. (Courtesy of Vallory Simms Hills and Kevin M. Simms.)

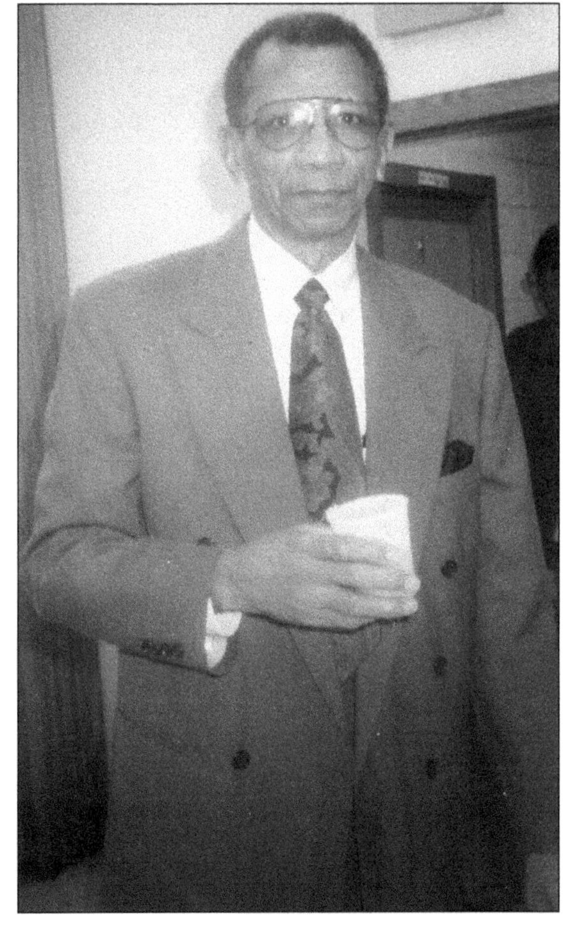

Mitchell Albert of Monroe was co-owner with Lawrence Wallace of Albert and Dixie Printing, before going solo as Albert Printing in the 1960s. Mitchell, his wife, Malvia Catherine Garner of Manny, and three children were members of Mount Pilgrim Baptist Church. He handled the printing business for Mount Pilgrim and other local churches. (Courtesy of Peggy M. Wallace.)

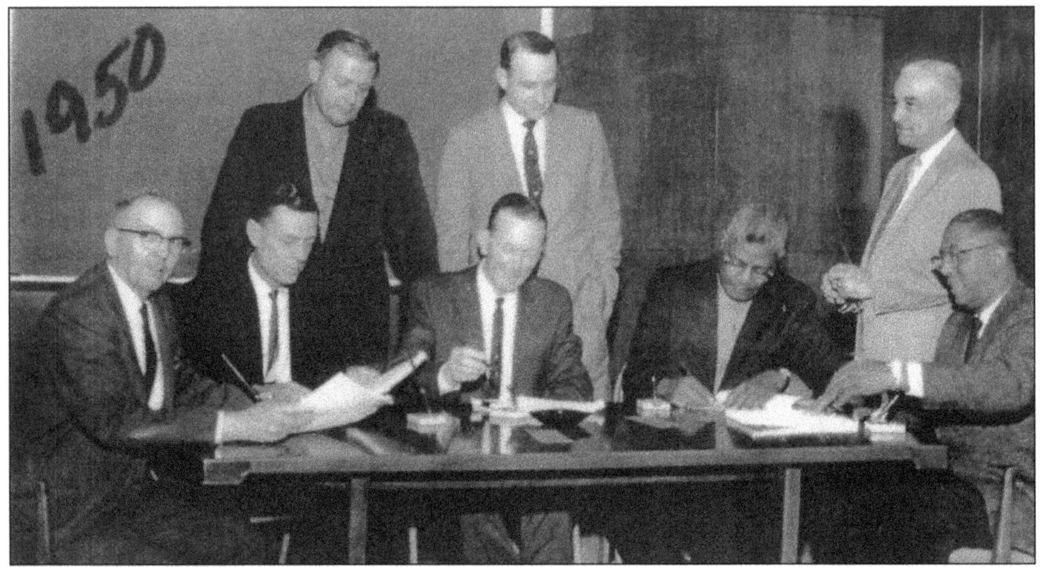

Union officers and management of the Baton Rouge Refinery signed Exxon Union employee contracts in 1950. Pictured are, from left to right, (sitting) Henry Voorhees, president/manager of the refinery; two unidentified union officers of the white section; T. Roosevelt, union president of the black section; and Thomas Davis, union secretary of the black section; (standing) two unidentified union officers of the white section, and James C. Cook Sr., union vice president of the black section. Cook, a laborer, said it was "the best paying job I could get, at $29.40 every two weeks." (Courtesy of Dr. James C. Cook Jr.)

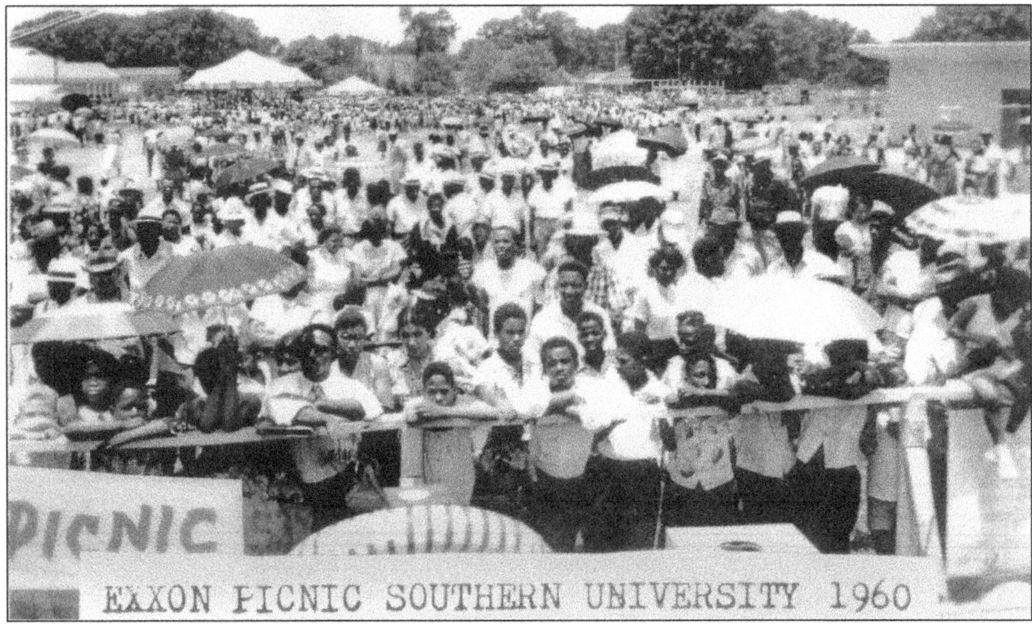

African American men were employed at Standard Oil Company/Exxon from the time of its charter in 1909. Several thousand black employees and their families and friends attended a 1960 Exxon picnic at Southern University. Attendees enjoyed a day of fun, food, rides, games, and prizes. The Exxon president addressed the crowd, and university president Felton G. Clark welcomed them. (Courtesy of Dr. James C. Cook Jr.; photograph by Fred C. Matthews Jr.)

The Weekly Press, located in the heart of the Scotlandville community, is the oldest continuously published weekly newspaper in the Baton Rouge area. Since 1974, Ivory Payne has published this "Peoples' Publication," with the philosophy: "We believe in the value of people and their community." Bishop Ivory J. Payne is pictured in an interview at radio station Q106.5. (Courtesy of Ivory Payne.)

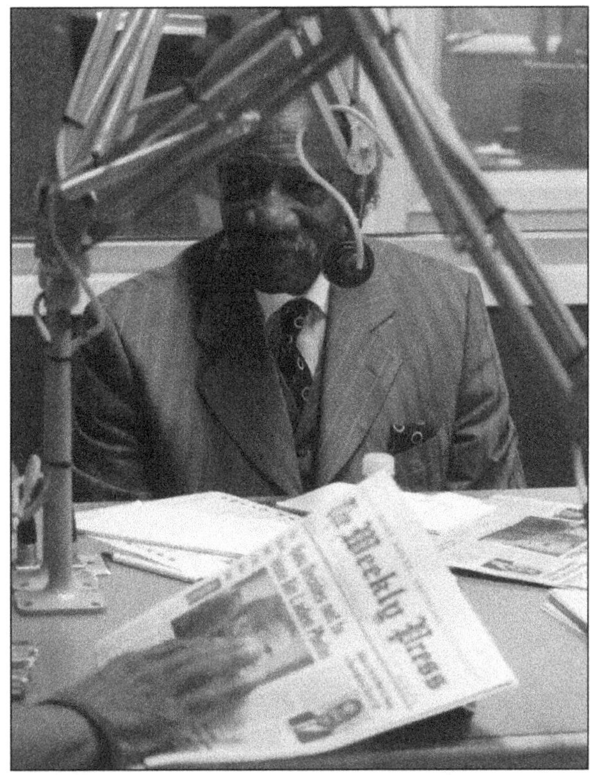

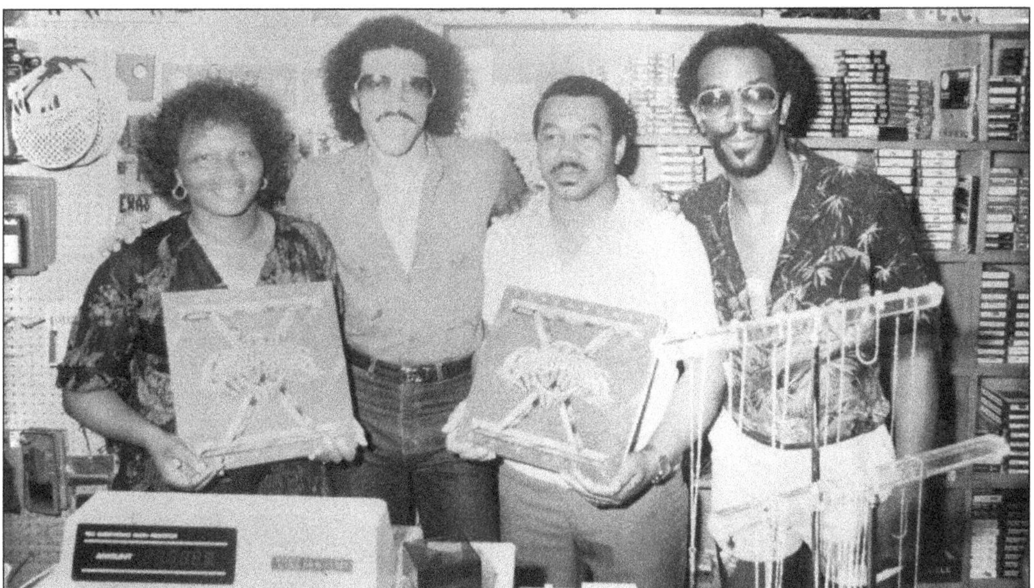

Herman "Poochie" Bowie (1943–2012), a 1961 Scotlandville High School graduate, was owner of Bowie's Record Shop, the first black-owned music store in the Baton Rouge area. The shop has brought numerous recording artists to the Scotlandville community, including members of The Commodores. Pictured here from left to right are Bowie's wife, Lucille Jackson; Lionel Richie; Bowie; and Thomas McClary. The couple's children are Kenneth, Karl, Kerry, and Kellee. (Courtesy of Kellee Bowie.)

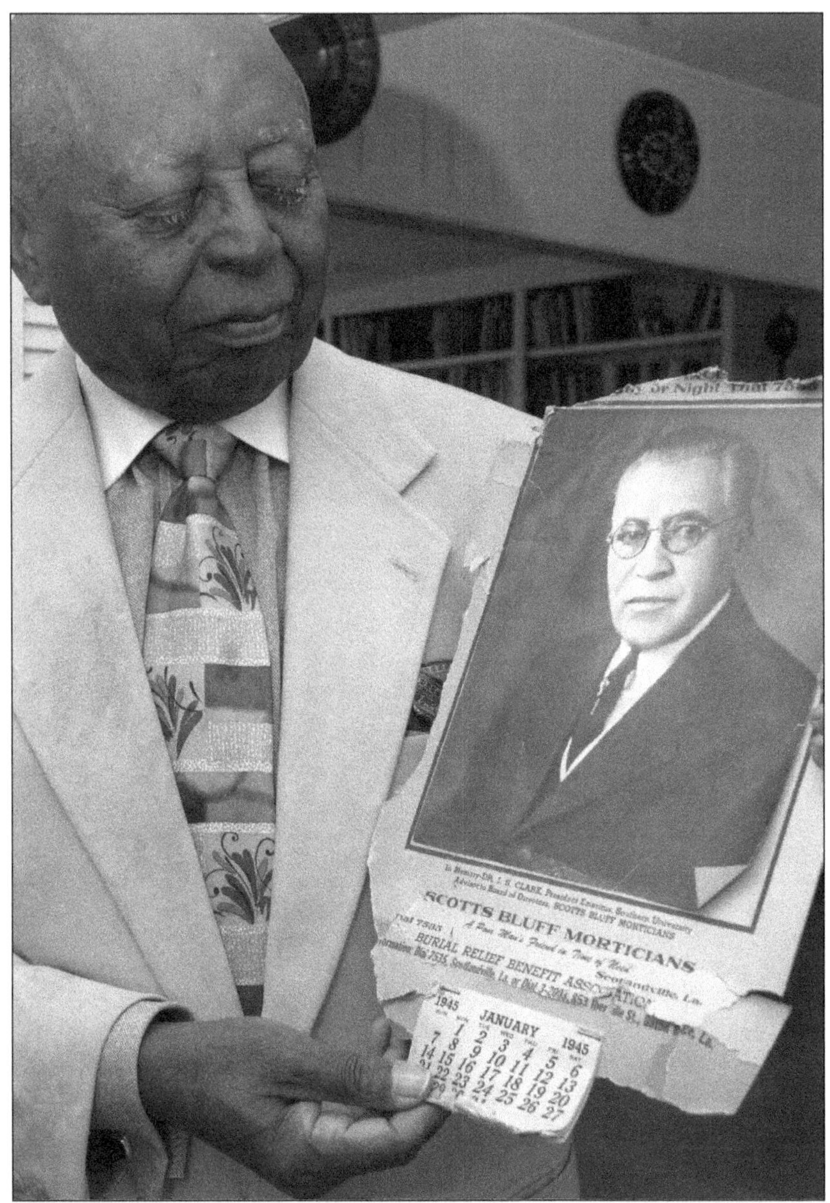

Scott's Bluff Morticians was opened in 1932 by owner-operator Mary Catherine Carlisle Meadors (1888–1982). In addition to offering funeral and burial services and transportation to hospitals and clinics, Meadors, who also worked in Southern's business office from 1920 to 1953, made her place of business available for meetings of black voter groups. According to a university historian, she was "the only black woman who went with the first Committee of Blacks to the City-Parish Government to ask for streetlights, black-topped streets and closed sewage in Scotlandville." Married to Hudson L. Meadors, the civic leader was a member and trustee of Camphor Memorial United Methodist Church; a member of Delta Sigma Theta Sorority, American Legion Auxiliary, Eastern Star, and YWCA; a founder of the Educators of Yesteryear; and a sponsor of a local Little League baseball team, the Scott's Bluff Dodgers. E.C. Harrison, a longtime university administrator, is pictured with a Scott's Bluff Morticians 1945 promotional calendar featuring a photograph of Southern's first president, Dr. J.S. Clark. (Courtesy of Christopher Rogers.)

Three

Churches

Leadership Opportunities and Support to Those in Need

An abundance of churches is a familiar sight in many American neighborhoods and Scotlandville is no exception. While the Baptist churches are historically high in numbers, followed by Methodist and Church of God in Christ, Scotlandville residents were diverse in their denomination preferences. As more families moved into the area, the Presbyterians, Catholics, and Episcopalians also founded places of worship.

In the Jim Crow South, the African American churches represented some of the first buildings that were erected through the collective financing and sweat equity of their founders. These were typically small groups of congregants who took great pride in their ability to "lean on the Lord" and "build His church." Church facilities ranged from often very modest to sometimes very grand. As more souls were saved and memberships increased, a one-room, wood-framed edifice on a small plot of land could develop into a brick, multidimensional complex, with additional acreage purchased for parking.

In churches, Scotlandville residents took on leadership positions as pastors, deacons, deaconesses, choir officers, ushers, Sunday school teachers and superintendents, and chairpersons of special committees. Fundraising and benevolent services added to the educational opportunities for church congregants.

According to Ruby Robinson Ennis in *Generations Recording: A Genealogical Findings and Memories of the Gaines and Robinson Families*, churches strengthened the residents' sense of community and fostered the concepts of cooperation and interdependence that enhanced the strength of neighborhood. And so it was in Scotlandville, as church members helped each other, inside and outside church walls, by supporting families and local businesses, providing opportunities for political and social attainment, and encouraging educational achievements.

The rich legacy of the African American churches of Scotlandville includes spiritual, benevolent, educational, and cultural enrichment for its members. From baby dedications and christenings, baptismal services, debuts, weddings, and funerals, the church ceremonies were significant parts of the lives of believers. Regardless of the religious denomination, this legacy was maintained and expressed, whether through preaching, singing, or sometimes, liturgical dance, in the uniquely distinctive African American worship experience.

Ten years after its annexation to Baton Rouge in the mid-1980s, the Scotlandville area was recorded as having approximately 30 churches.

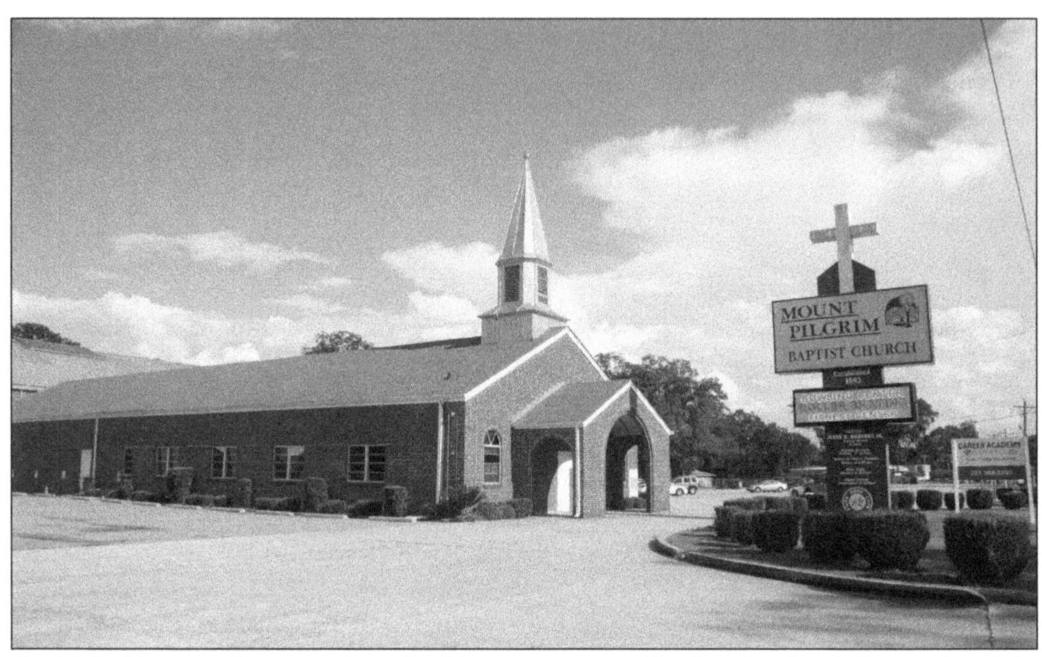

Established in a small wooden-frame building on an acre of land in Scotlandville purchased for $50 in 1893, Mount Pilgrim Baptist Church is now a multi-building brick complex with a 550-seat sanctuary, administrative offices, a kitchen, an education center, and a Family Life Center, all on the original site with additional parcels of land. The church was remodeled in 1924, destroyed by fire in 1926, and rebuilt in 1927. A new brick church was constructed in 1951, which has had a number of renovations and additions. A church cornerstone for the 1968 renovated building includes the names of the building committee members and deacons who were among the first families of Scotlandville, such as Eames, Early, Franklin, McGee, Sewell, Veal, Williams, and Wilson. (Both, courtesy of Steve Jarreau Photography.)

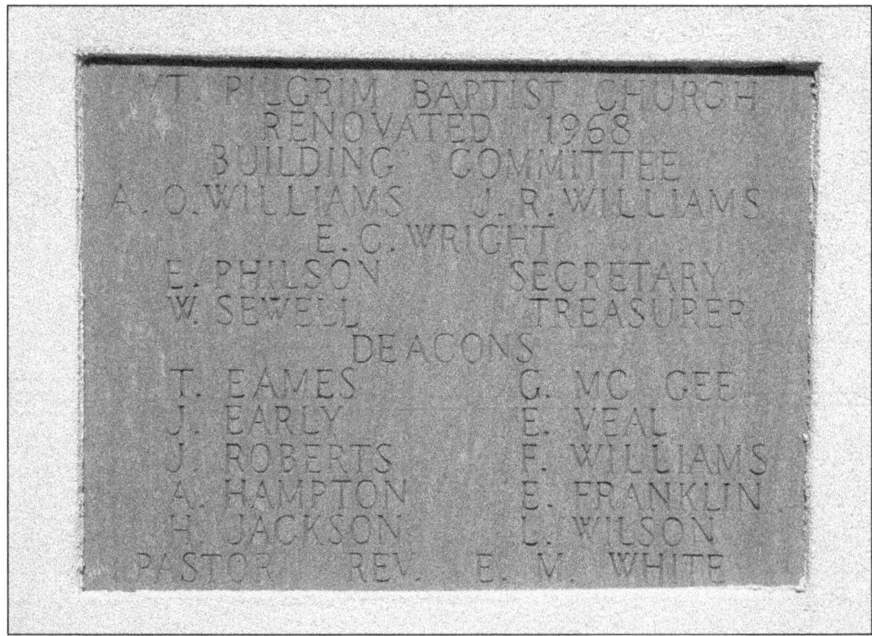

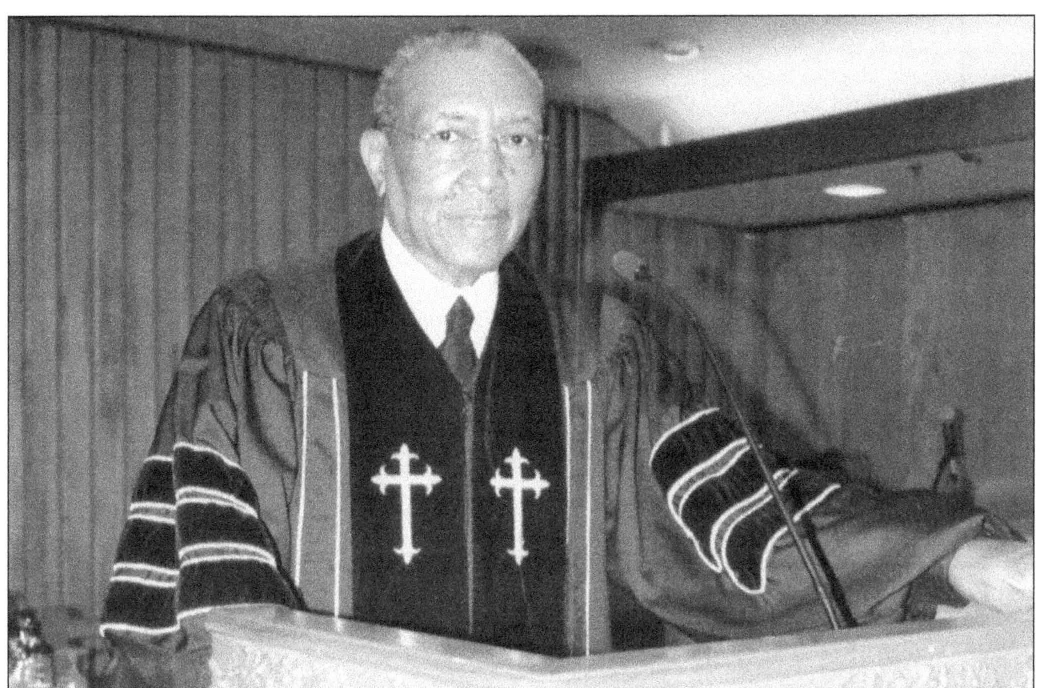

Elected by church members on January 16, 1984, Rev. Jesse B. Bilberry Jr. (above), a retired Southern University administrator, became Mount Pilgrim's eighth pastor. Bilberry, a native of Farmerville, Louisiana, earned a bachelor's of science in education from Southern University in 1951 and a master's of education from LSU in 1957. Following tenures as teacher and principal in high schools in North Louisiana, he joined the Southern University administrative staff in 1969 and retired the year he was named pastor. Subsequently, he served on the Southern University Board of Supervisors. The previous pastors were Rev. Harden Jackson (1893–1910), Rev. Pete Netter (1910–1914), Rev. J.M. Thomas (1914–1919), Rev. Richard W. Ball (1920–1964), Rev. Edward "Eddie" M. White (1964–1974), Rev. Joseph F. Richard (1974–1979), Rev. Frederick Powell (1980–1982), and Rev. Cornelious J. Hickman (right, interim pastor 1982–1984). (Both, courtesy of Peggy M. Wallace.)

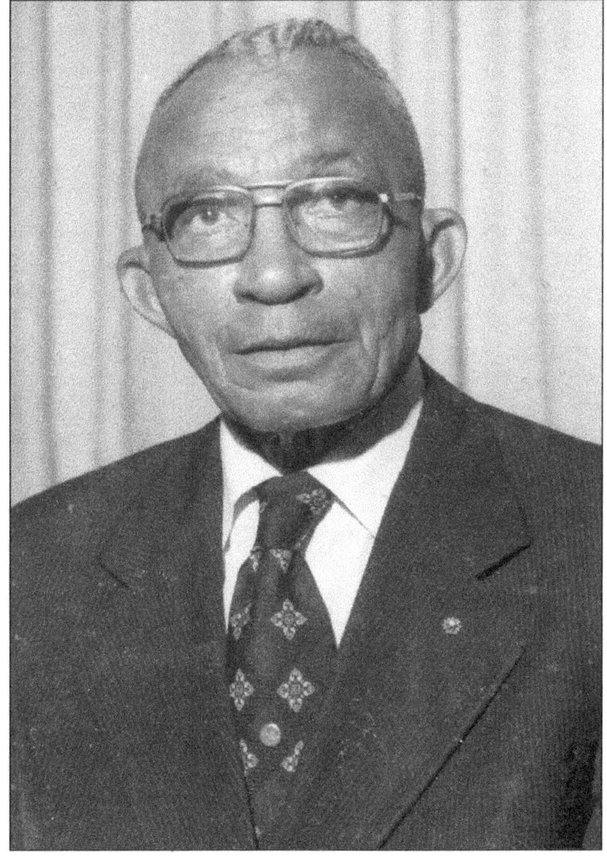

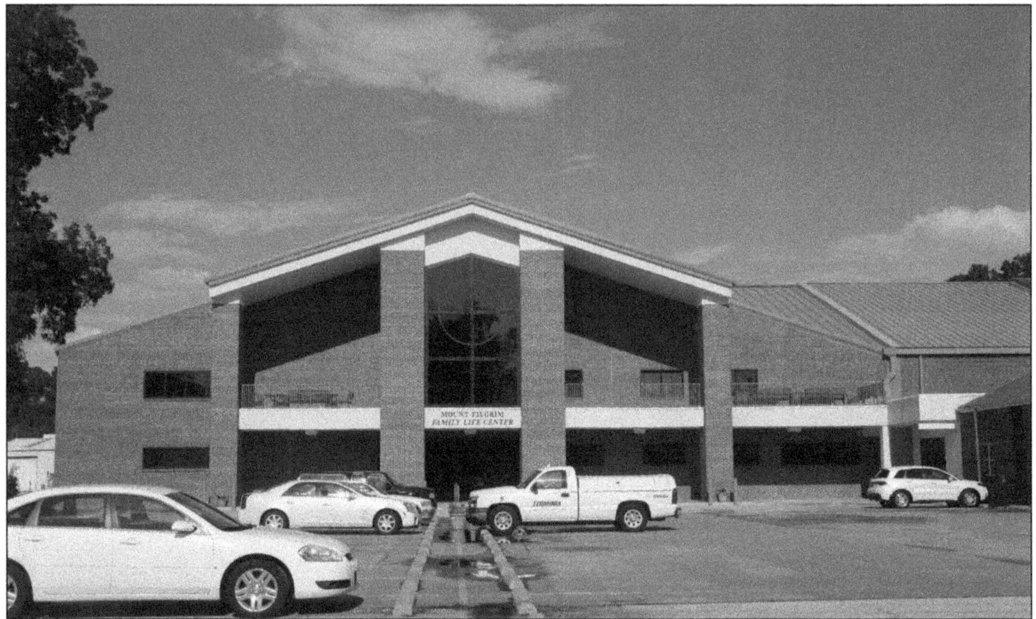

Mount Pilgrim's Family Life Center, which was completed in 2011, includes a gymnasium, bowling alley, skating rink, and expansive parking area for the more than 1,200 members and guests attending various activities held not only on Sundays but every day of the week. Mount Pilgrim's motto is "the church where everybody is somebody and Jesus Christ is the head." (Courtesy of Steve Jarreau Photography.)

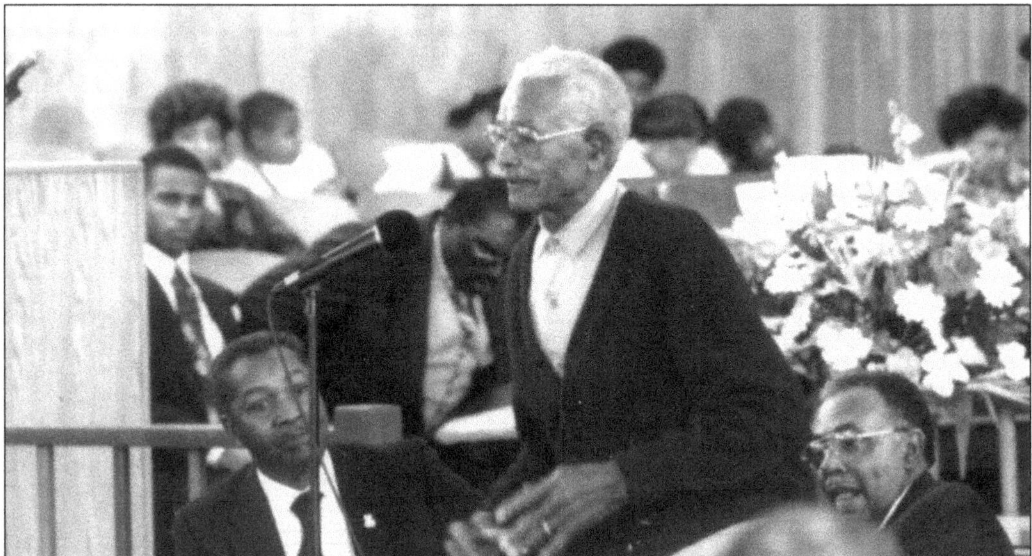

Deacons in the Baptist Church are men of faith serving and looking after the needs of the congregation. Here, Deacon Tom Eames speaks during the church's Fourth Sunday Testimony Service. Seated in the background are Deacon Nathaniel Roche and Deacon Albert Dixon. The church continues to embrace the public testimony that has been a longtime standard practice among Baptist churches. According to 1 Peter, chapter 3, "Always be prepared to give an answer to everyone who asks you to give the reason for the hope that you have. But do this with gentleness and respect." (Courtesy of Peggy M. Wallace.)

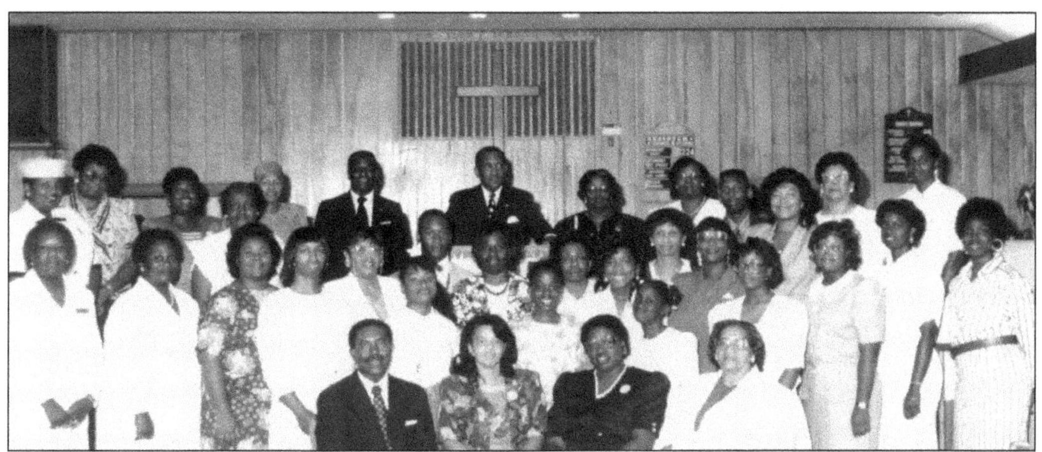

A Christian education program that typically focuses on children—although adults are encouraged to participate—vacation bible school (VBS) is held during the summer to connect children with the teachings of the gospel of Jesus Christ. The outreach is popular for fun-filled activities as participants learn songs that carry annual themes expressing the value of serving God. The Sunday school superintendent Edward M. White and Christian education leader Annie B. Knox organized the first VBS at Mount Pilgrim in 1955. Mount Pilgrim's VBS staff is pictured with Peggy Millender Wallace, VBS director. Peggy (sitting third from left), wife of Deacon Lawrence Wallace, has longtime family ties with the church and Scotlandville. (Courtesy of Peggy M. Wallace.)

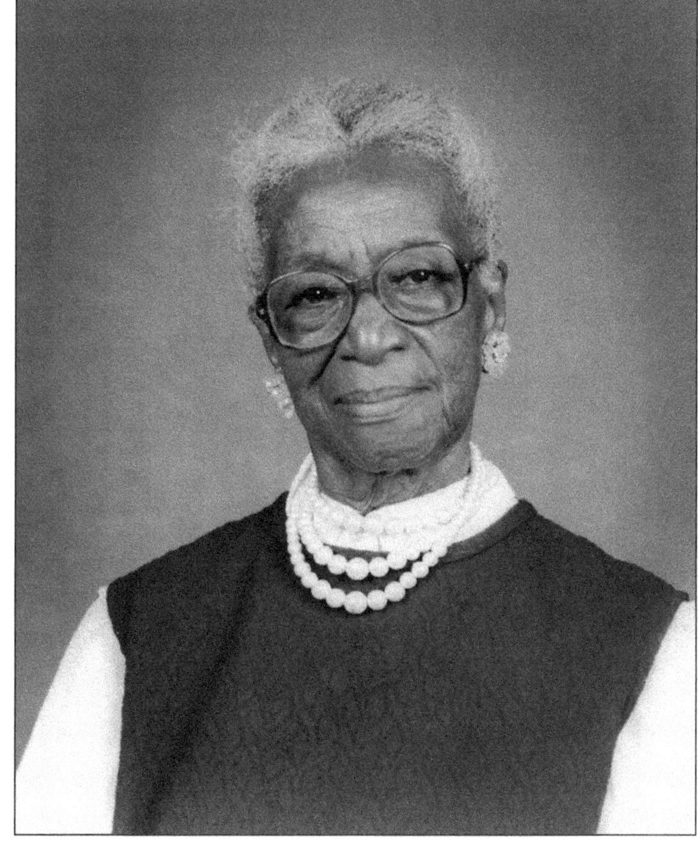

Listed on the church roster in 1928, Annie B. Knox has served as Home Mission president, Sunday school superintendent, and a worker in the Baptist Training Union and National Baptist Convention USA Inc. She also sang in the senior choir. In 1916, Knox was among the first graduates of Southern's two-year program. (Courtesy of Steve Jarreau Photography.)

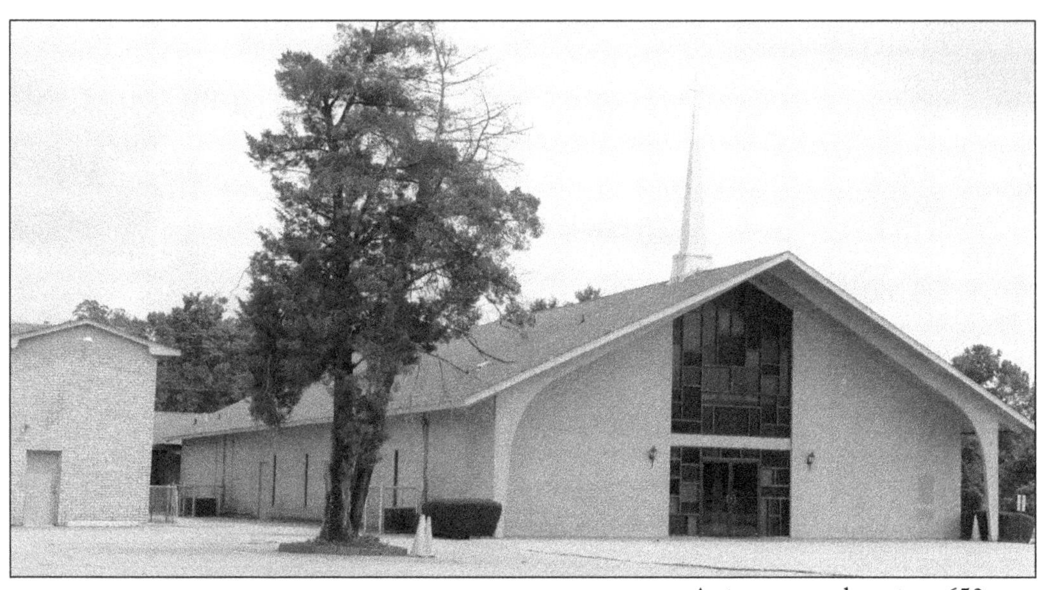

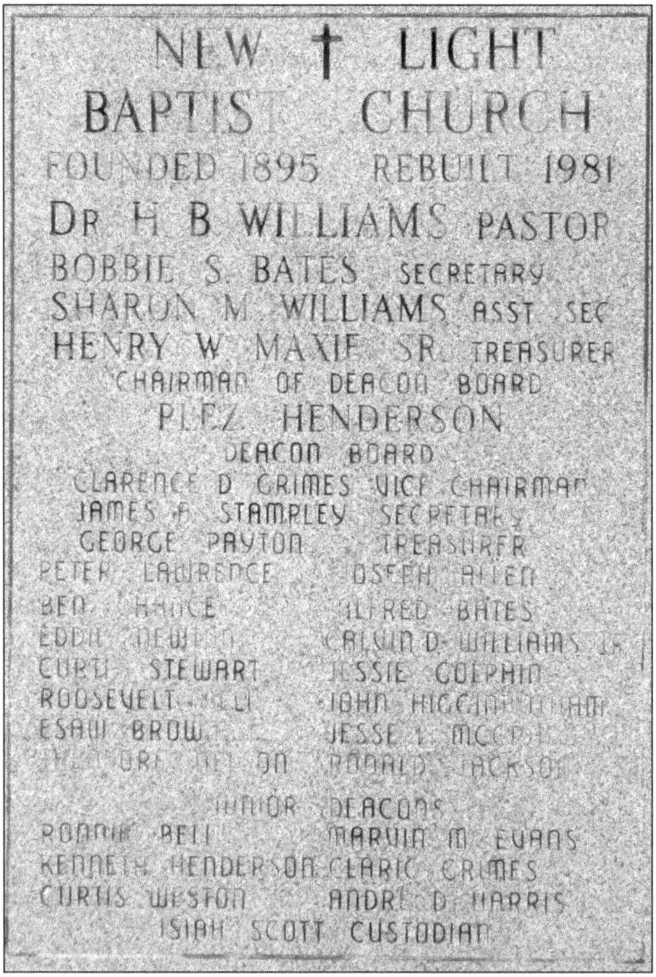

At its present location, 650 Blount Road, New Light Missionary Baptist Church, organized in 1895 and chartered in 1935, was led by the Reverend Tony Scott, a sugar cane farmer and founder and organizer of the church. Scott was married to Cicily Scott and was the father of nine children. In 1910, a storm destroyed the original church, which was rebuilt on Crane Street in Scotlandville. The rebuilding of the church in 1981 is recorded on this cornerstone, along with the members who led the effort. Dr. H.B. Williams was the pastor serving at the time. Williams preceded the current pastor, Rev. Gil Wright. Pastors before Williams and Wright were founding Pastor Scott, who served until 1921; Rev. Richard W. Ball, 1921–1923; Rev. J.P. Handy, 1923–1927; and Rev. Noah C. Chinn, 1927–1965. Ball and Handy were members of the first families of Scotlandville. (Both, courtesy of Steve Jarreau Photography.)

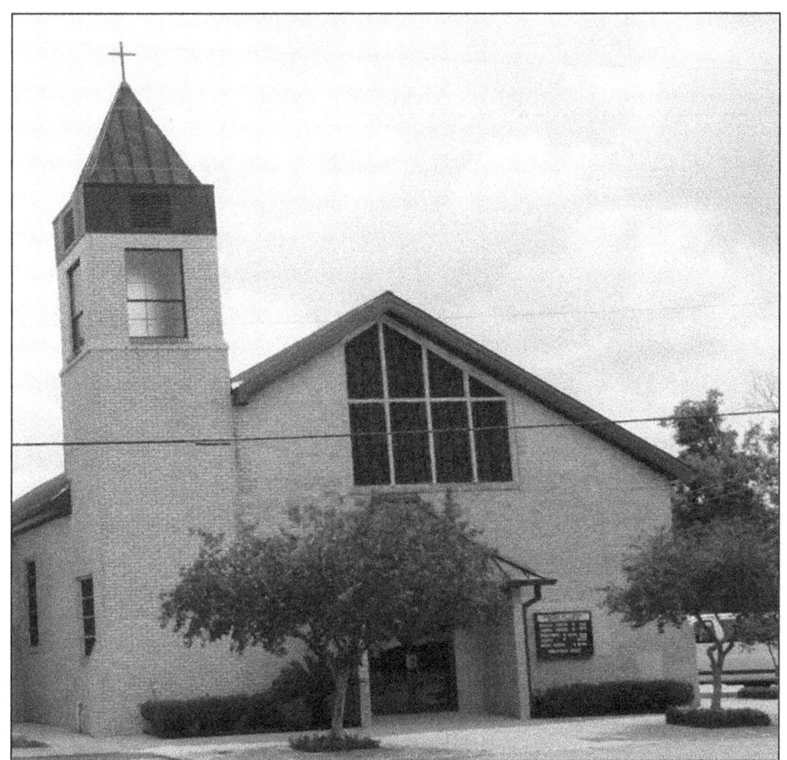

Mount Carmel Baptist Church, established in 1916 and renamed Greater Mount Carmel Baptist Church in 1951, is now located on Sora Street. The first services were held in the Odd Fellows Hall until Ernest O'Connor built the sanctuary in 1920. Pews and siding were added in the mid-1920s. A second edifice was constructed in 1939. An expansion was built in 1949, and an annex in 1962. The cornerstone on the rebuilt church (below) memorializes Greater Mount Carmel's third pastor, Rev. Lawyer Fields, and deacons who were among the first families of Scotlandville. (Both, courtesy of Steve Jarreau Photography.)

1962
MOUNT CARMEL
BAPTIST CHURH
PASTOR REV. LAWYER FIELDS
CHURCH OFFICIALS

NAME	POSITION
HENRY FRANKLIN	DEACON
FOSTER REESE ,SR.	"
OBIE VERNON	"
GEORGE LEWIS	"
FRED DAVIS	"
JOHN E. LABOYE	"
JOHN JAMES	"
WILLIE HAWKINS	SECRETARY

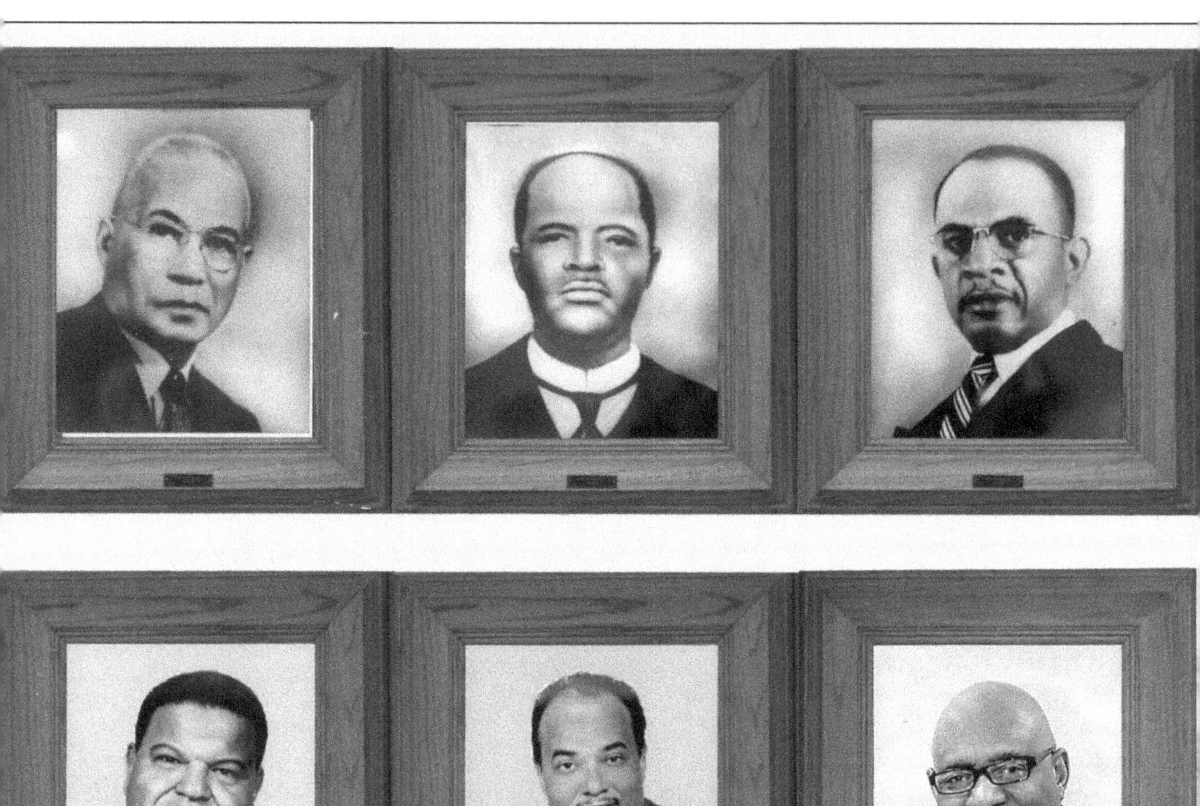

In a history of the Mount Carmel church written at the celebration of its 94th anniversary, six major periods were highlighted to present the major events and major "movers." These periods coincided in large part with the tenures of each pastor. They are Rev. Samuel Watkins, who served from 1919 to 1932, "The Genesis Period;" Rev. Louis Brown, 1934–1951, "The Building Period;" Rev. Lawyer Fields, 1951–1971, "The Period of Stability and Growth;" Rev. K. Edward Popleon, 1972–1992, "The Period of Expanding Capacity for Service," as well as "The Period of Outreach and Service;" and Rev. Fred Jeff Smith, 1992–2013, "The Period of Great Expectation and Spiritual Training." The current pastor, Rev. Clee Lowe, began his tenure in 2013. From left to right are (top row) Pastors Brown, Watkins, and Fields; (bottom row) Pastors Popleon, Smith, and Lowe. (Courtesy of Dianne Pullen.)

Deacon Wesley Elliot Gaines was one of the founders of Greater Mount Carmel Baptist Church. Gaines and his wife, Martha Scott Gaines, reared their 13 children in the church. Their sons were Edgar, Ernest, Harry, Wesley Jr., Mathew, Willie, and Henry Gaines and Lee Smith. The five daughters were Carrie and Tillie Gaines, Mary Bell Gaines Robinson, Berthera Elizabeth Gaines, and Myrtle Gaines Hill. (Courtesy of Dianne Pullen.)

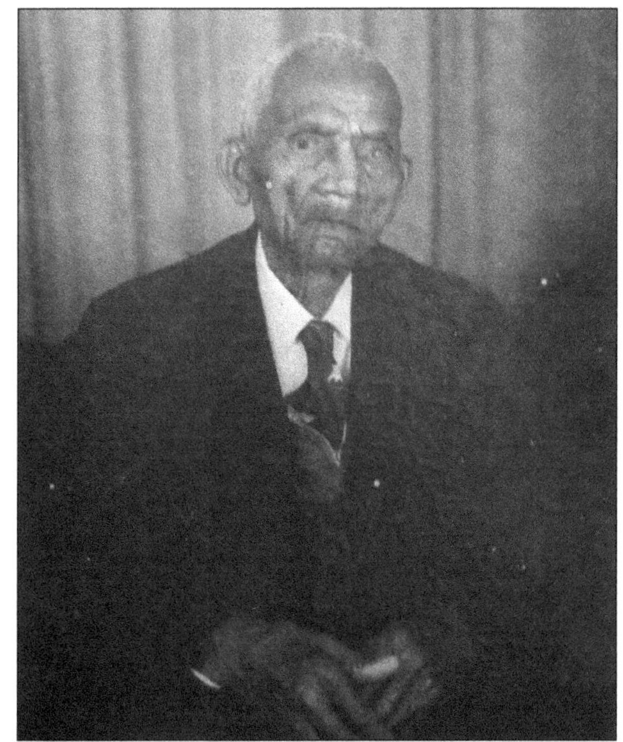

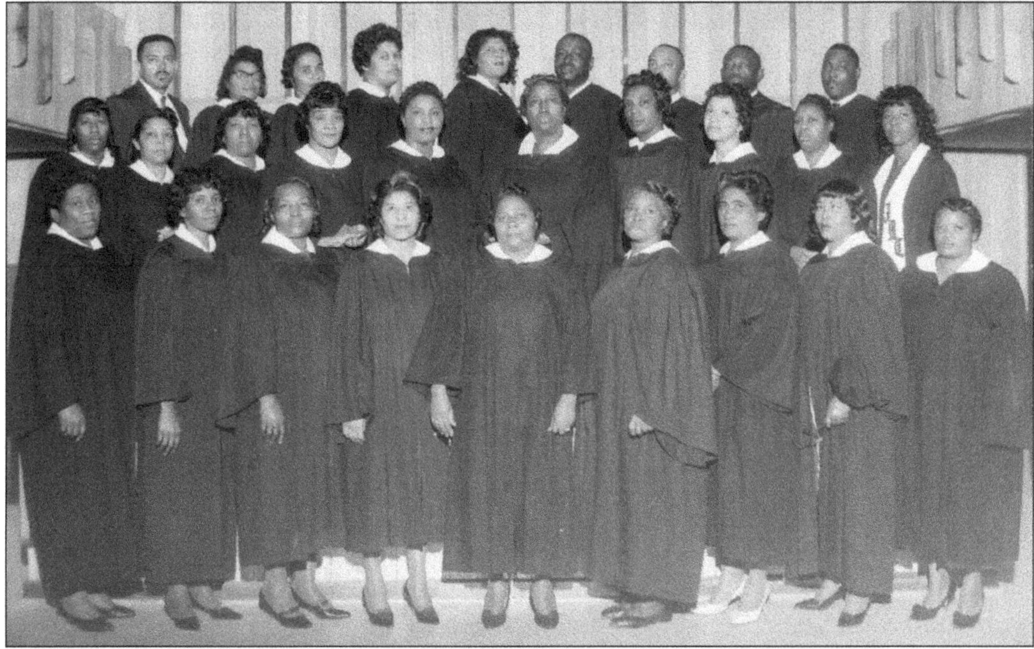

Many appreciate the value and beauty of church choirs in the worship experience. The melodies of choirs of Mount Carmel Baptist Church flow through the sanctuary and fall on the ears of congregants; the various church choirs are often named for the categories of their members, such as seniors, young adults, children, male-only, and women-only. Choirs like this one are the pride of pastors and members. (Courtesy of Dianne Pullen.)

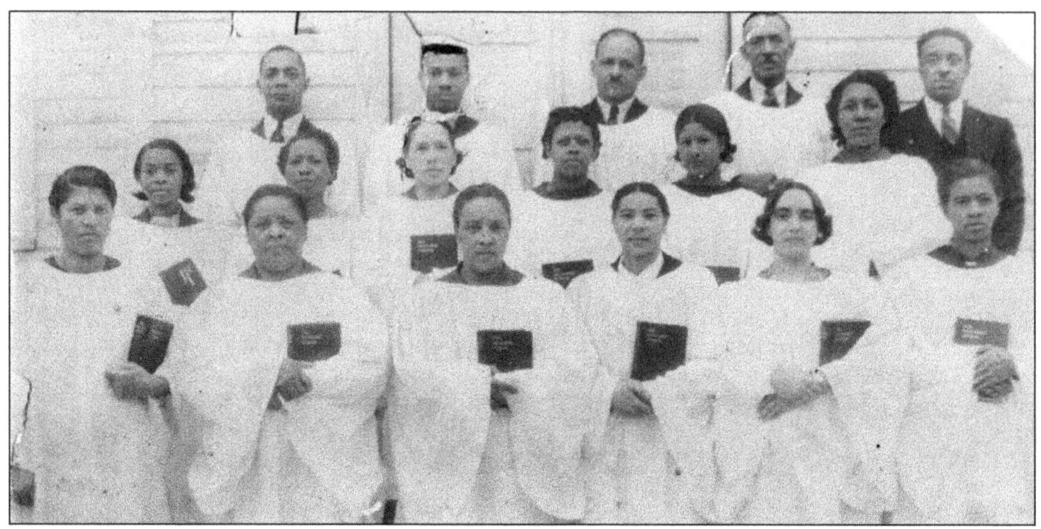

Founded in 1917, the first Methodist church in Scotlandville was given the name Taylor Colored Methodist Episcopal Church after its first minister, the Reverend Amos M. Taylor (1918–1922). A few years later, the name was changed to Camphor Memorial after Bishop Camphor. Founding members are featured on pages 21–29. Twenty ministers have served Camphor, including Rev. Mary Ann Robinson and Pastor Clifton C. Conrad Sr. The 1936 photograph above shows the Camphor senior choir. Pictured are, from left to right, (first row) Emma Robinson, Leslie Browne, Edna Kelly, Mable Rowley, Edith Langston, and Alvin Eames; (second row) Janie McClain, Emma Beshears, Bertha Harrell, Pearl Lewis, Mary Butler, and Rosa Carter, pianist; (third row) Sherman Flanders, Simon Lewis, O.M. Amacker, Hartzel Bradford, and T.W. Langston, who served as director for 43 years. A music professor at Southern, Langston was the arranger of the university's alma mater and fight song. The 1929 Sunday school class is pictured below. (Both, courtesy of Rhonda Crawford Stewart.)

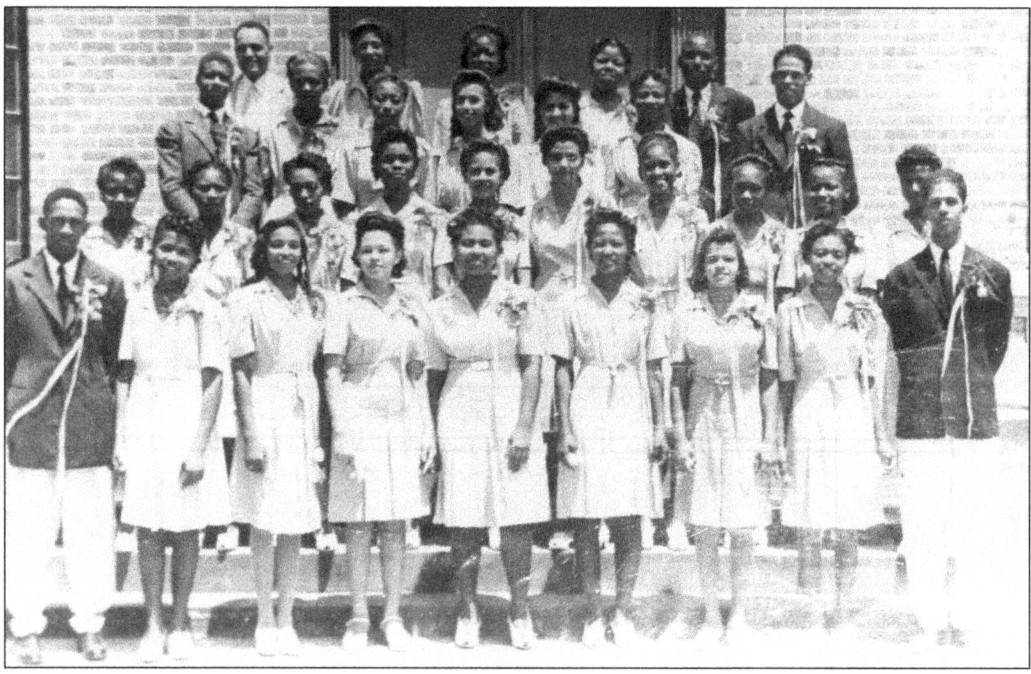

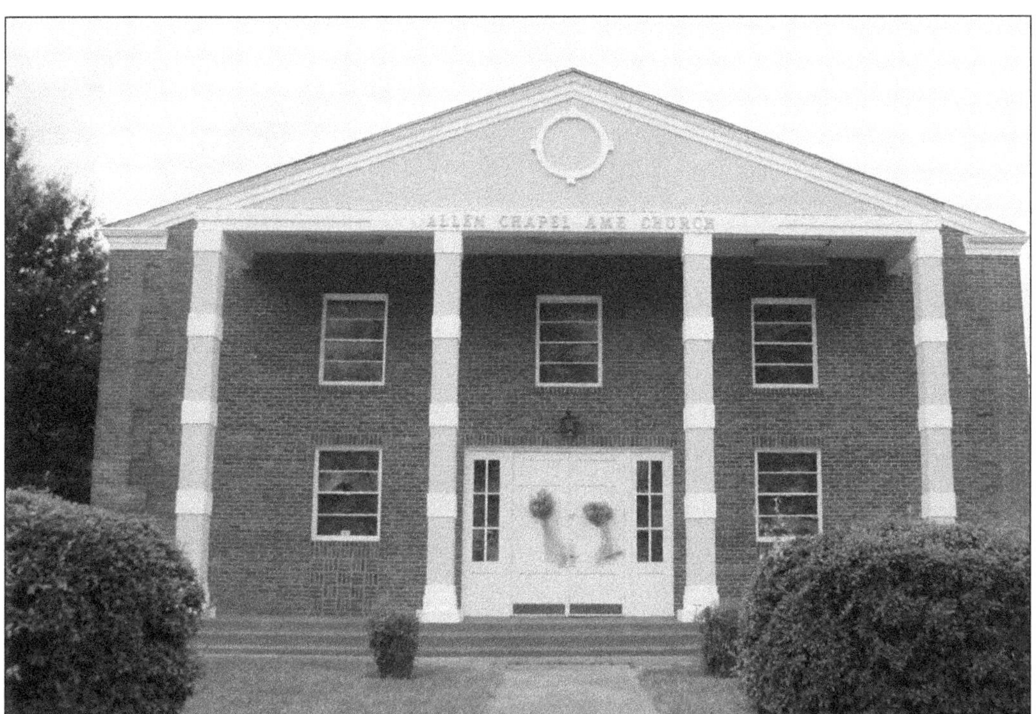

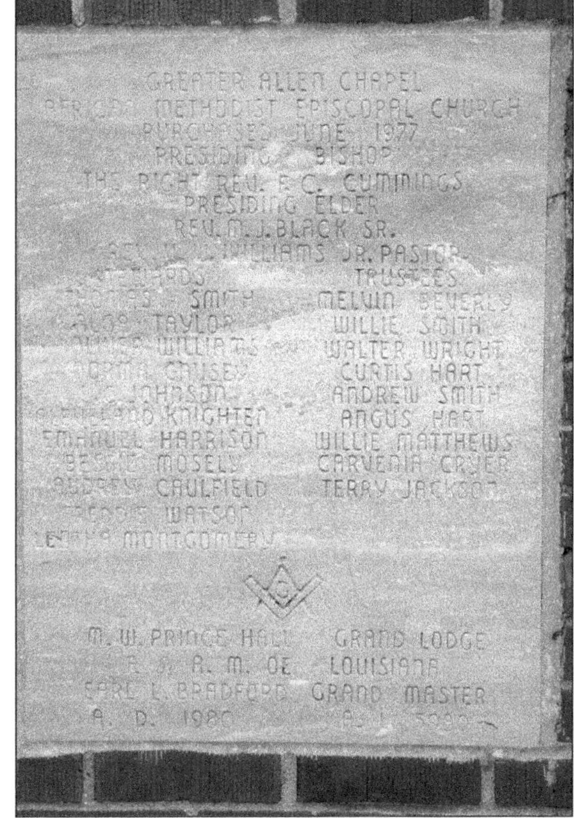

Under the leadership of the Reverend Bland Washington Sr., Greater Allen Chapel African Methodist Episcopal (AME) Church was purchased in 1977 at its current location, 6175 Scenic Highway, and continued the legacy of the work of Allen Chapel AME Church established in Scotlandville in 1921. From a small frame building erected on a donated parcel of land on Sora Street, poor draining, frequent flooding of the site, and, ultimately, a devastating storm that destroyed the building forced the church's first move to 1292 Cardinal Street in 1940. The Greater Allen Chapel Church building was upgraded to a stone facade in 1957. The 1977 cornerstone memorializes the stewards and trustees who were familiar names from the first families of Scotlandville. (Both, courtesy of Steve Jarreau Photography.)

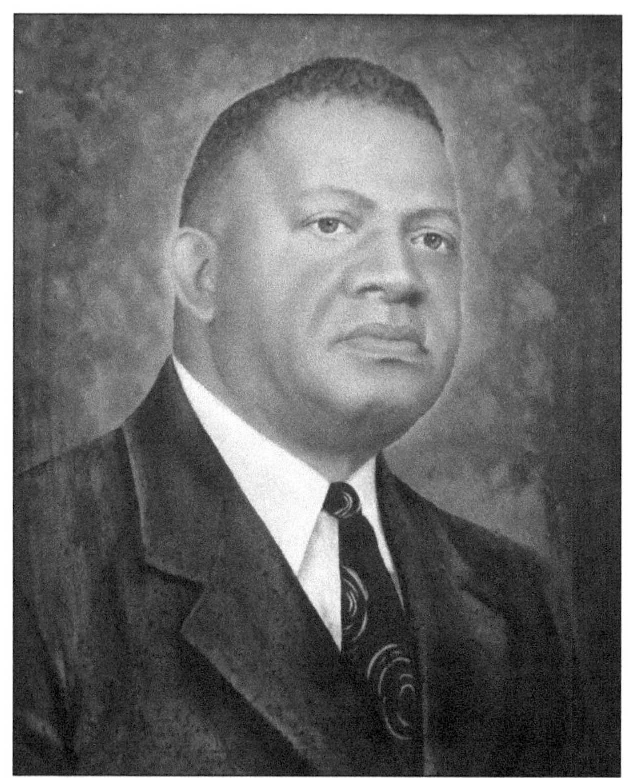

The Reverend John Rice Sr. (left), the founder and pastor of the First Presbyterian Church of Scotlandville on Rosenwald Road, was an Alabama native. In addition to the church, Rice established the third school in Scotlandville, a private grammar school referred to by local residents as "the Rice School." He and his wife, Theresa, who taught at the school, had one daughter, Theresa Rice Love, who became a professor of English at Southern University, and one son, John Rice Jr., who became the father of Condoleezza Rice, the first African American secretary of state. Below, Kathy Lemons and Rhonda Crawford play together outside First Presbyterian Church following a kindergarten graduation celebration. (Left, courtesy of Steve Jarreau Photography; below, courtesy of Rhonda Crawford Lewis.)

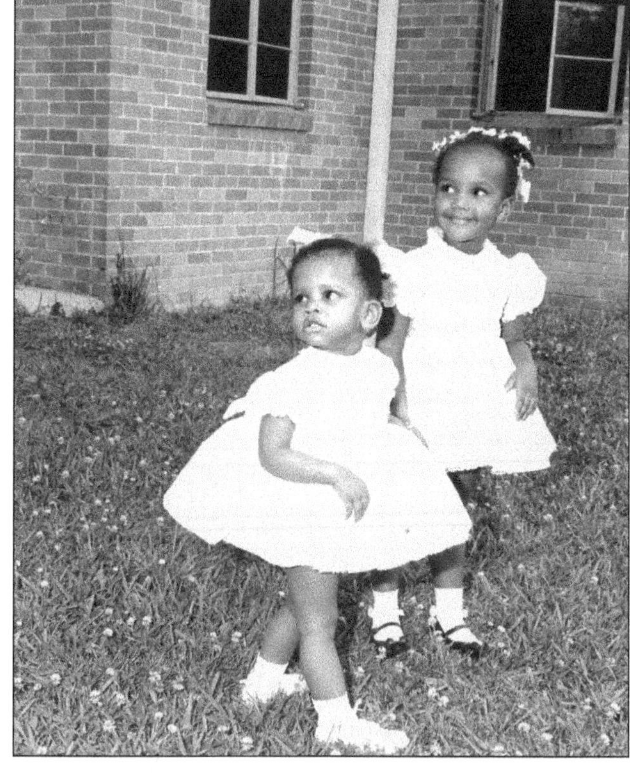

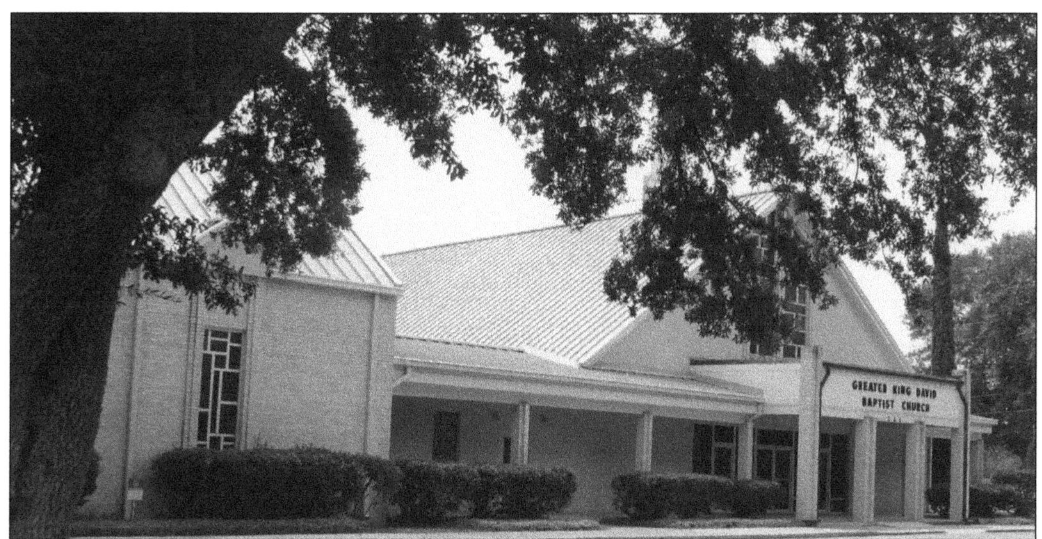

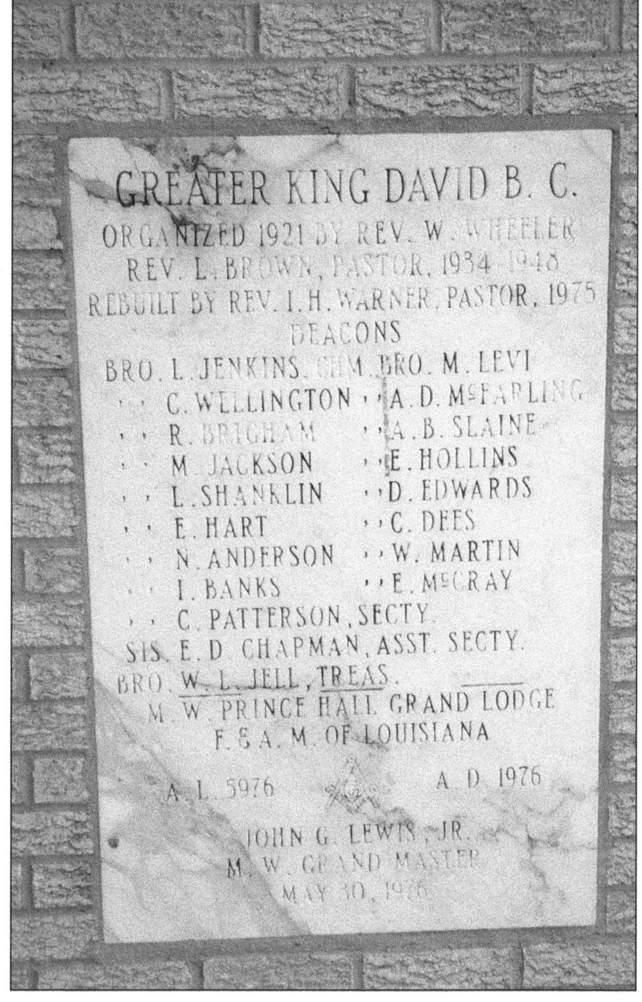

Established in 1922, Greater King David Baptist Church on Blount Road, located near the campus residential area of Southern University, has attracted a substantial number of student members. All five of the first pastors, Rev. Willie Wheeler, Rev. Joe Martin, Rev. A.D. Alexander, Rev. Louis Brown, and Rev. Isaiah H. Warner, are now deceased. The current pastor, Rev. John E. Montgomery II, was elected in 1988. Before the Martin Luther King Catholic Center in 1969, Wesley Foundation Methodist Student Center in 1974, and the T.J. Jemison Baptist Student Center in 1986 were established on the campus, students attended local churches exclusively not only for Sunday worship, but also for spiritual counseling, bible study, and denominational fellowship. (Both, courtesy of Steve Jarreau Photography.)

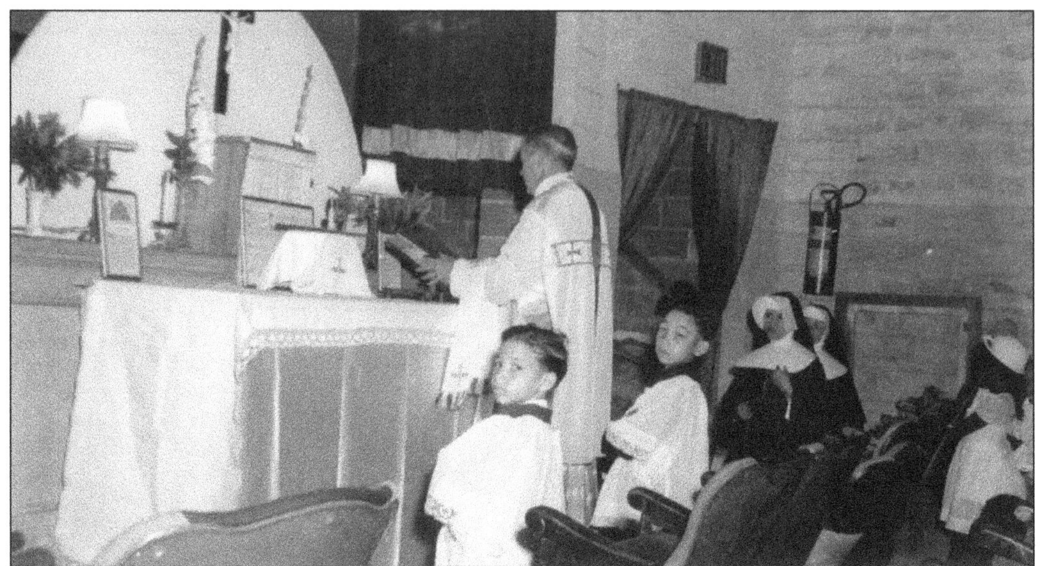

Although the Josephites fathers and sisters of Notre Dame had been working in the Scotlandville area for some time, until the early 1950s, the town's residents and the increasing number of Southern University faculty, staff, and students who were Catholic had only St. Francis Xavier Church of Baton Rouge as a place to worship. During the fall of 1946, Rev. Edward LeDoux, of the Society of St. Joseph, arranged with theater owner James Cook Sr. for Mass to be celebrated in the Scenic Highway movie house until a church in Scotlandville could be established. Pictured above, Mass is celebrated at Cook's Theatre on October 13, 1946. After a successful fundraising campaign and the volunteer labor of local builders, Immaculate Conception Catholic Church of Scotlandville, located on Curtis Street, was dedicated on December 13, 1953, pictured below. (Above, courtesy of Dr. James Carl Cook Jr.; below, courtesy of Archives of the Catholic Diocese of Baton Rouge.)

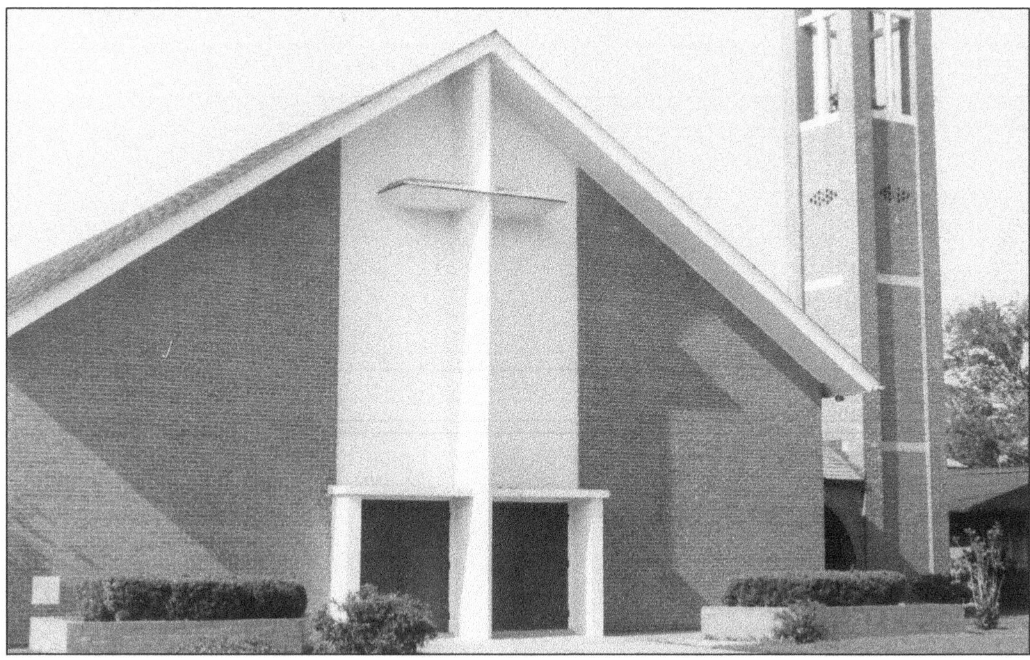

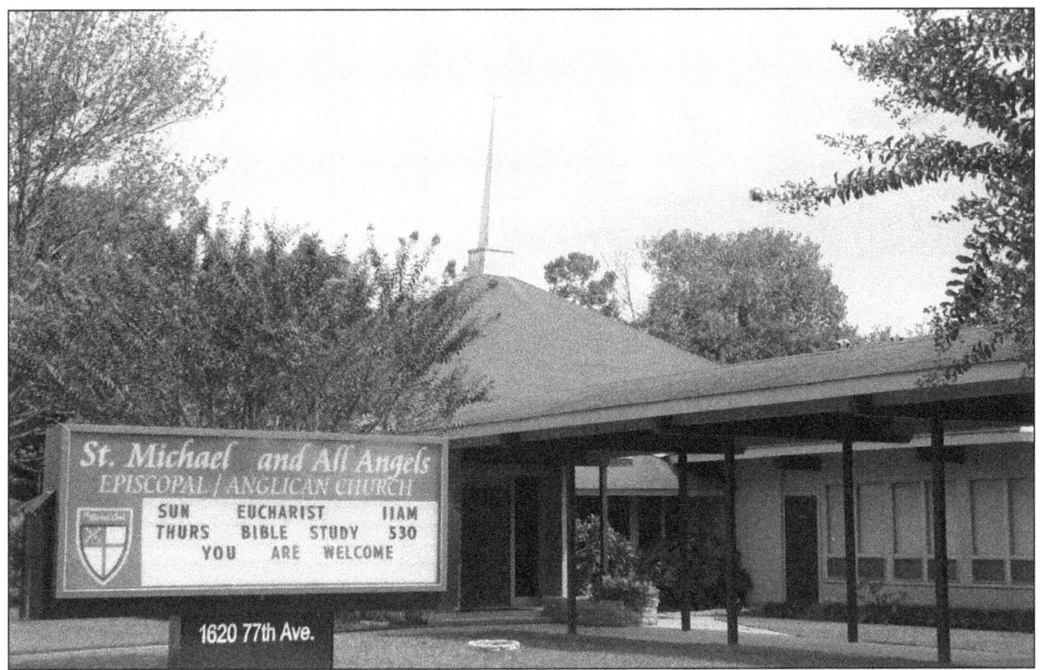

St. Michael and All Angels Episcopal Church, located in Scotlandville since the edifice was dedicated in 1970, is the third-oldest Episcopal church and the only predominantly black Episcopal congregation in the area. In 1941, a West Indies physician, Dr. H. Hornes Huggins, and Southern University instructor Elsie Lewis were concerned that because of segregation, black Episcopalians had no formal place to worship. They discussed the situation with the provost at St. James Episcopal Church in Baton Rouge. The bishop of the Diocese of Louisiana met with Dr. Huggins and a group at SU to outline plans for a church. Saint Michael's Church was organized in 1941 and formally recognized as a mission the next year. A church day care center (below), designed by communicant and architect Henry Thurman of Scotlandville, was opened in 1986. (Above, courtesy of Steve Jarreau Photography; below, courtesy of Helen Gist.)

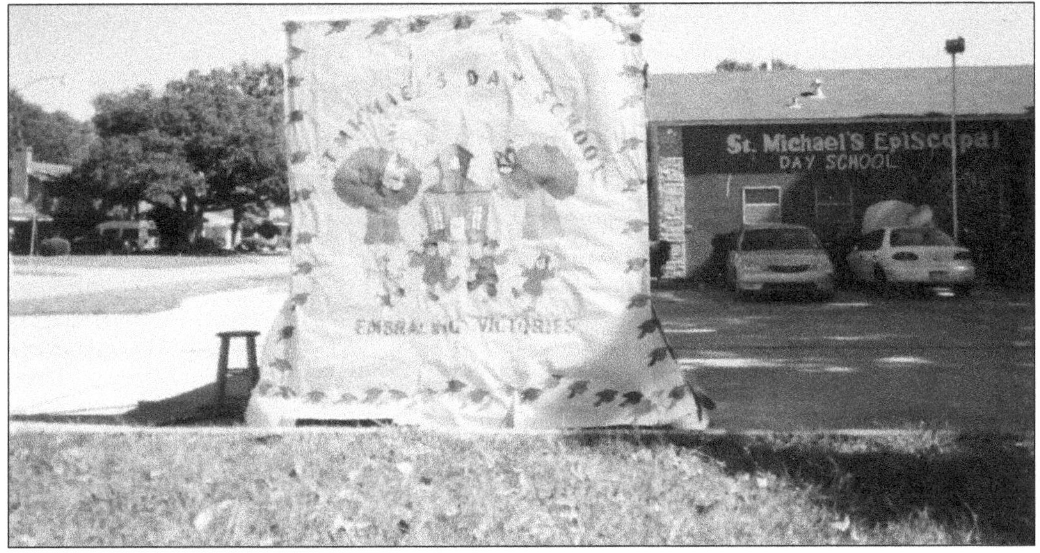

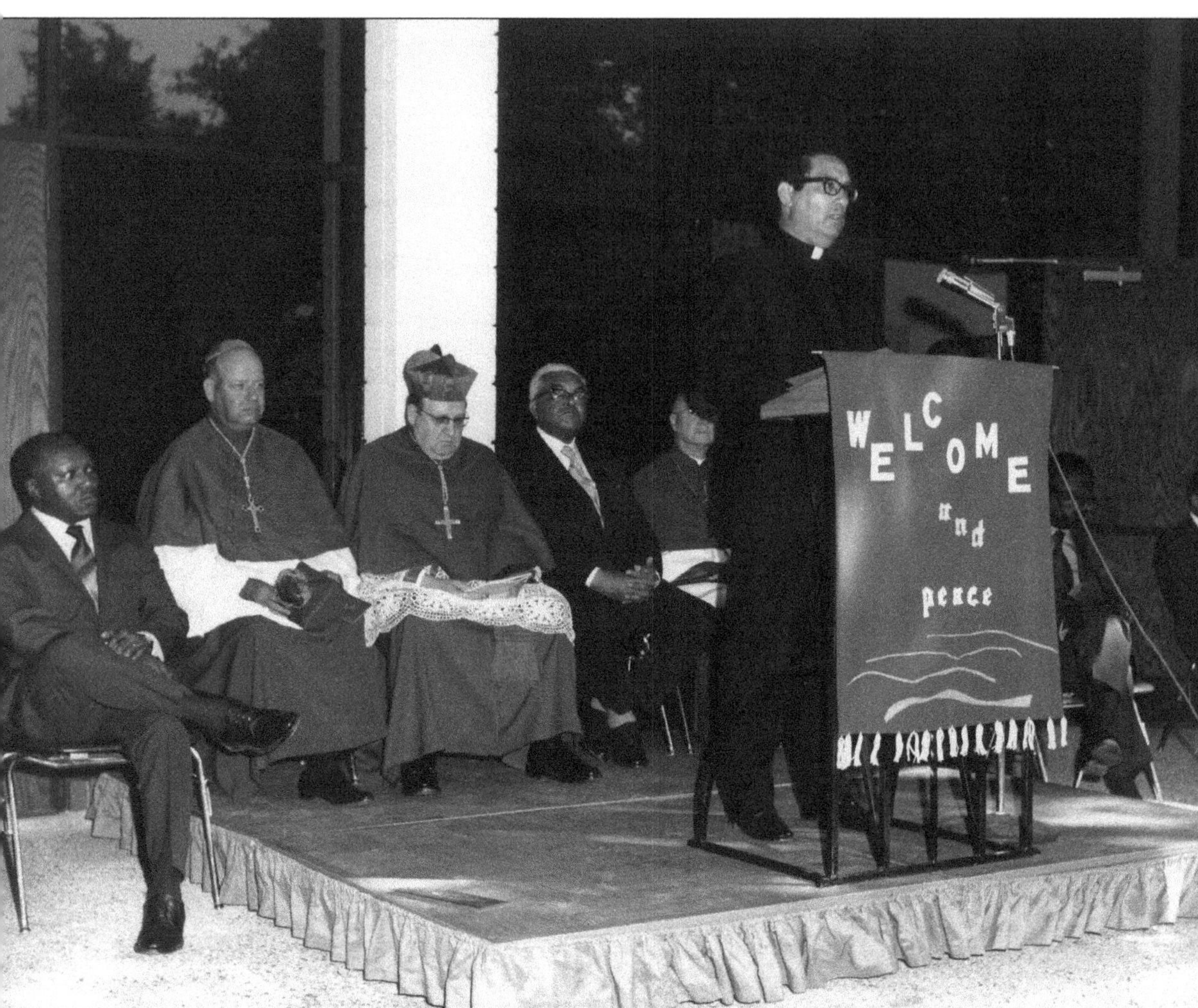

Prior to the construction of what was then called the Newman Center in 1969, Father Rawlin B. Enette celebrated Masses with the 1,500 Catholics at Southern in the moot courtroom of the law building. Thanks to land donated by a university official, the Newman Center was staffed by the Josephites. It was renamed the Martin Luther King Jr. Catholic Student Center, and in 1984, was staffed by the Jesuit fathers, who continue to serve at the center today. Pictured are participants at the inauguration of the Martin Luther King Jr. Catholic Center in 1970, including Southern University president G. Leon Netterville, on stage, third from left. (Courtesy of Archives of the Catholic Diocese of Baton Rouge.)

Four

Education
The Ability to Stand Tall in the Walk of Life

According to Southern University's Felton G. Clark, African Americans migrated to Scotlandville in the early 1900s to acquire the skill sets and the educational development that would enable them "to stand tall in the walk of life."

Churches in Scotlandville, with the help of congregants, missionary societies, Northern charities, and state and federal funding, served as some of the first sites for academic training then and continue to do so today. However, one of the main benefits of living in Scotlandville was being able to get a good education from Southern University and A&M College model training school, forerunner of the Demonstration School and the Southern University Laboratory School. The laboratory school was a teacher preparatory school (also called training and practice school), which was organized by the university for students in the first through eleventh grades.

The Julius Rosenwald Fund, established in 1914 by a Sears, Roebuck, and Company executive, administered the rural school building program for African American children throughout the South. Funds from this program assisted the demonstration school at Southern University and helped establish the Scotlandville Rosenwald School. The fund required matching contributions from local communities. Residents held fundraisers, donated land, and helped build the school.

In the mid-1940s, the East Baton Rouge Parish School System built the first school for black residents, Scotlandville Negro Elementary, with local taxpayer funding; it was located on the site of the former Rosenwald School. With the community's growth in population, the parish school system constructed other elementary and secondary schools between the 1950s and 1970s.

Southern's first president, Dr. J.S. Clark, traveled the state telling African American parents, their children, and community leaders that "the school was always for community improvement; therefore, the college must grasp every opportunity to serve, to cooperate with, and enlighten the community."

It proved wiser for some African Americans to move to Scotlandville and get an education than it would have been for them to stay where they were. The emerging black consciousness movement of the 1960s in resistance to racial oppression seemed to match Clark and the university's message, which emphasized self-reliance, cultural pride, economic uplift, and community betterment.

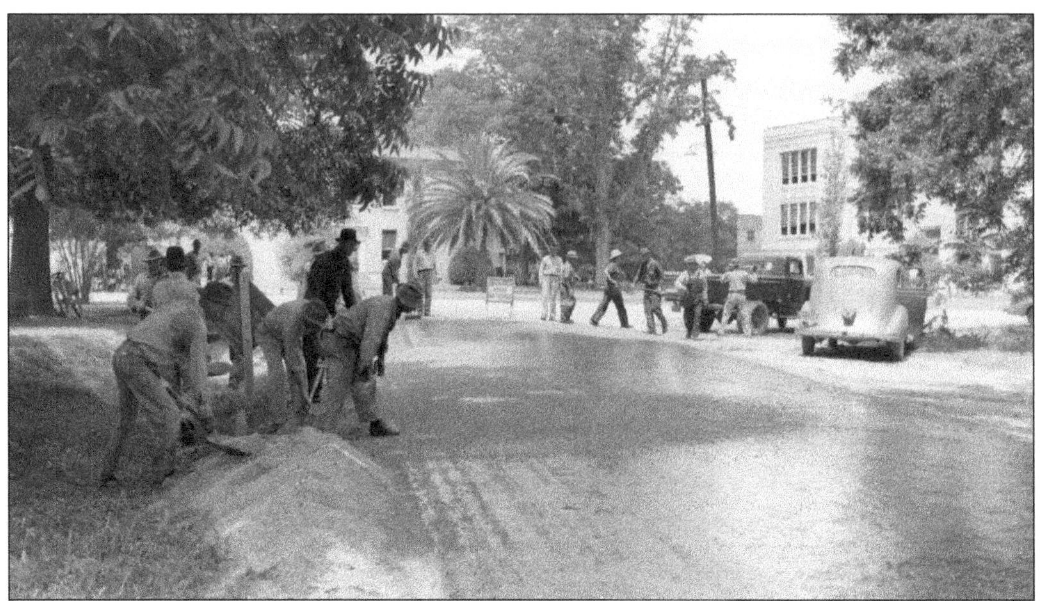

In the early 1920s, all academic subjects were taught in this Academic Building, which also housed faculty offices, a contract post office, and a small vendor's stand in the basement and the Counseling and Career Center on the second floor. Dr. William H. Wethers I, a physician who served the campus during the early years, planted the palm tree adorning the front lawn. Workers are shown working on a street near the building. Improvements to the campus were supported through funds of the WPA program. (Courtesy of the Louisiana State Library.)

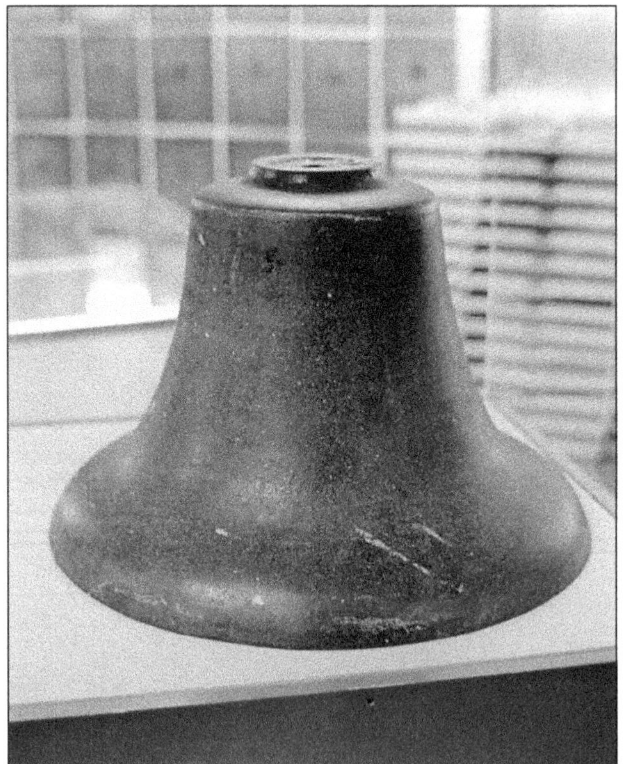

Plantation relics found at the opening of the campus are a printing machine, potbelly stove, and this bell, now on display in the university's John B. Cade Library. Speaking of the bell during his annual Founders' Day address often brought tears to the eyes of Dr. F.G. Clark. The same bell that the master used to wake slaves was then being used to wake students. Once representing oppression, it now was the symbol of liberation. (Courtesy of Naville J. Oubre.)

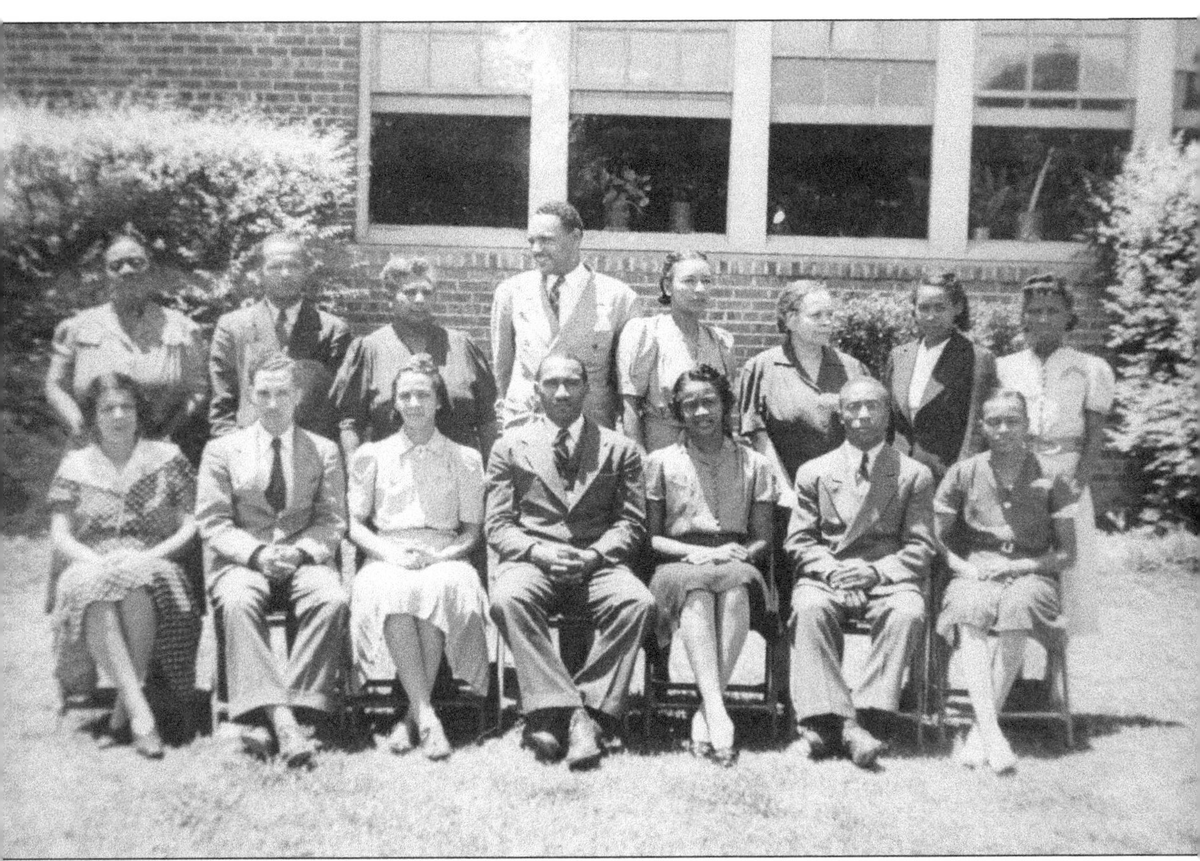

Dr. J.S. Clark knew that a strong training school should be established to prepare Southern University students enrolled in the teacher preparation program. The university administration carefully selected the faculty and administration for the Southern University Laboratory School from among accomplished, dedicated educators. This group photograph was taken in the late 1940s. Standing, third from left, is Alice Almira Boley, a former university instructor (1916–1942); she was principal from 1942 to 1958. A six-story coed residential facility is named for her in honor of her 42 years of service. Others pictured are, from left to right, (sitting) Sarah David Mack, noted author Frank Yerby, Margaret Walker Stewart, Dr. William Gray Jr., secretary Sophronia Stanley Steele, Lincoln Harrison, and Lesley Solete Banks; (standing) Ernestine Jones George, coach Cliff A. Purnell Sr., Boley, SU junior division dean Harrison D. Lawless, librarian Myrtle D. McLeod (see page 77), Mamie Bronson, Eula Patty Smith, and C. Beck Holmes. (Courtesy of Southern University Lab School Archives.)

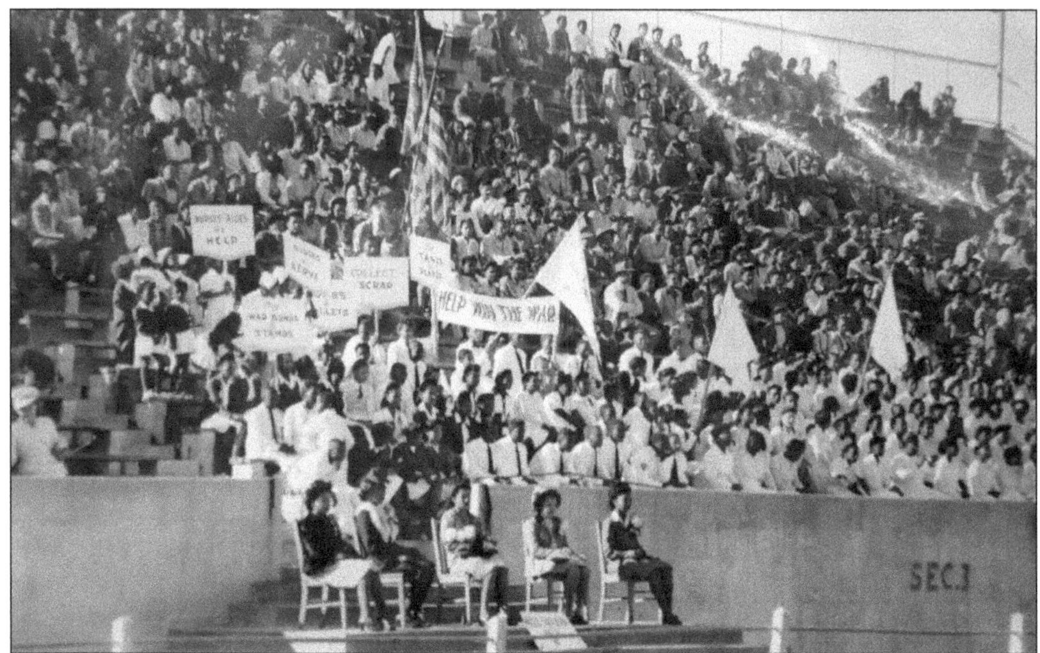

Miss Southern Lab and her court are seated on a platform before the crowd during a homecoming game. Attendees in the stands show support for the football team, as well as the war effort. Students and the band were seated directly behind Dr. Felton G. Clark and university administrators in section 3 on the 50-yard line. (Courtesy of Southern University Laboratory School.)

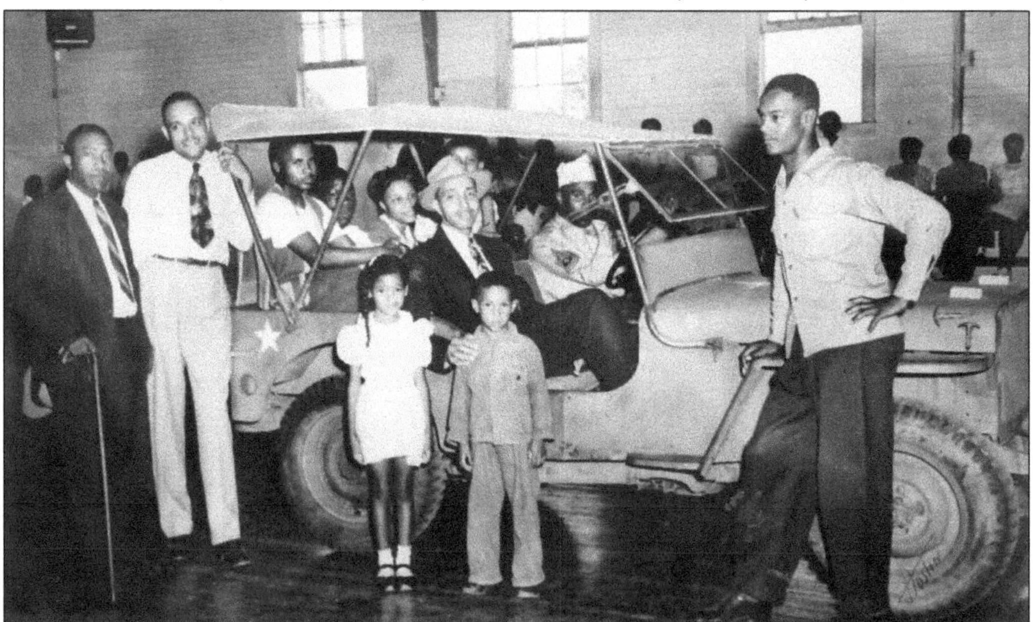
In a salute to the military of World War II, Dr. Felton G. Clark is shown entering a sporting event (seated on the front passenger side of the jeep) surrounded by students, parents, and a driver, who was a member of the military. A position as the president's driver was a coveted campus job for young men. Neither Dr. J.S. Clark nor his son Dr. F.G. Clark drove himself while on official university business. (Courtesy of Southern University Laboratory School.)

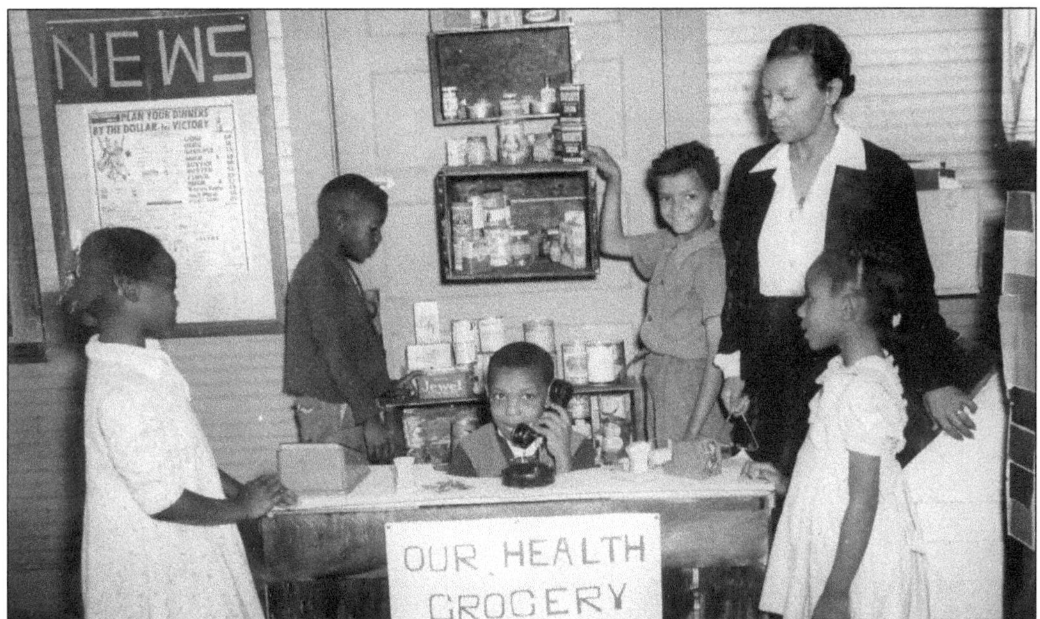

Myrtle Daughtery McLeod was hired in 1922 as critic teacher for the model training school. McLeod, who taught grades first through third for more than 30 years, is pictured above with her "little persons," who, on this day, were studying a unit on "healthy eating." Her husband, Jeremiah William McLeod, was hired the same year as the Farm Shop supervisor and teacher trainer. (Courtesy of Southern University Laboratory School.)

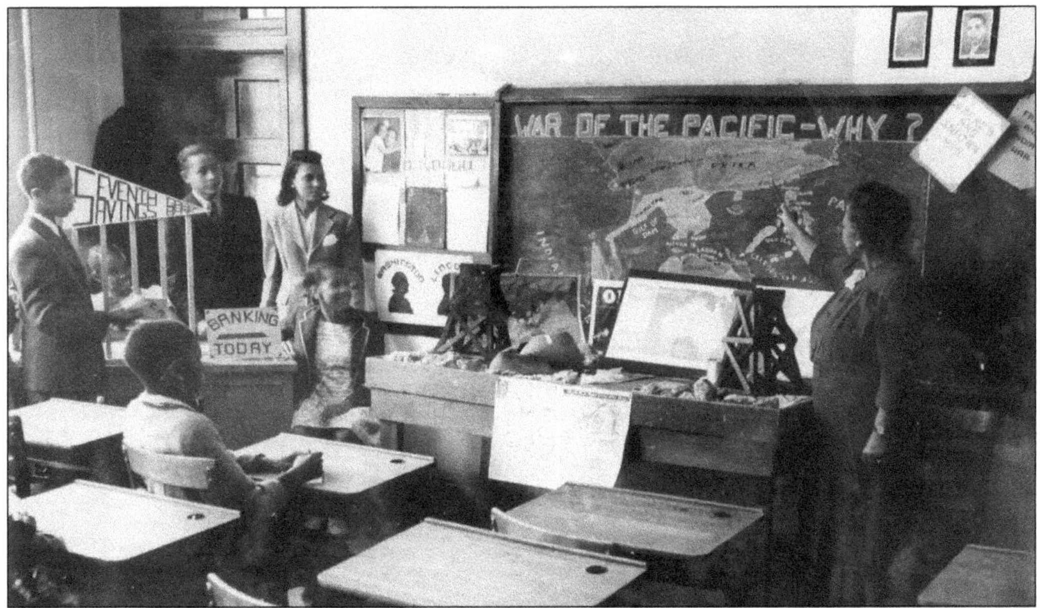

Classroom visual aids indicate that lab school students enrolled in this class are being taught lessons on thriftiness and patriotism. At right, the Seventh Savings Bank was named for the age of the second graders who are being instructed on banking principles and financial literacy. Their teacher also discussed the effects of the economy and the United States' role in the Pacific during World War II. (Courtesy of Southern University Laboratory School.)

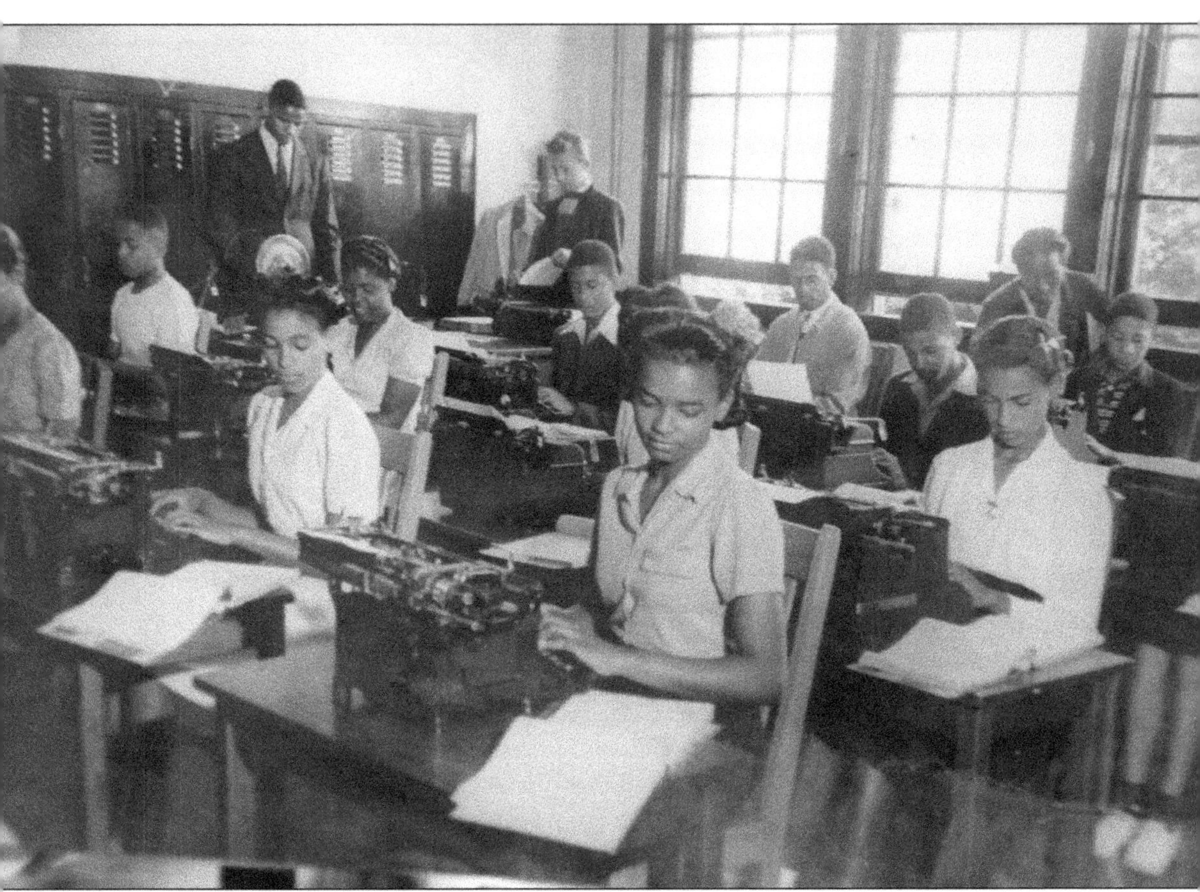

There was no gender stereotyping in typing classes during the 1940s at Southern Lab. Female and male students were both enrolled in these classes. Additionally, the instructor and practice instructor pictured here are both males. Military servicemen returning from World War II had learned typing and were able to teach this skill back home as school instructors. (Courtesy of Southern University Laboratory School.)

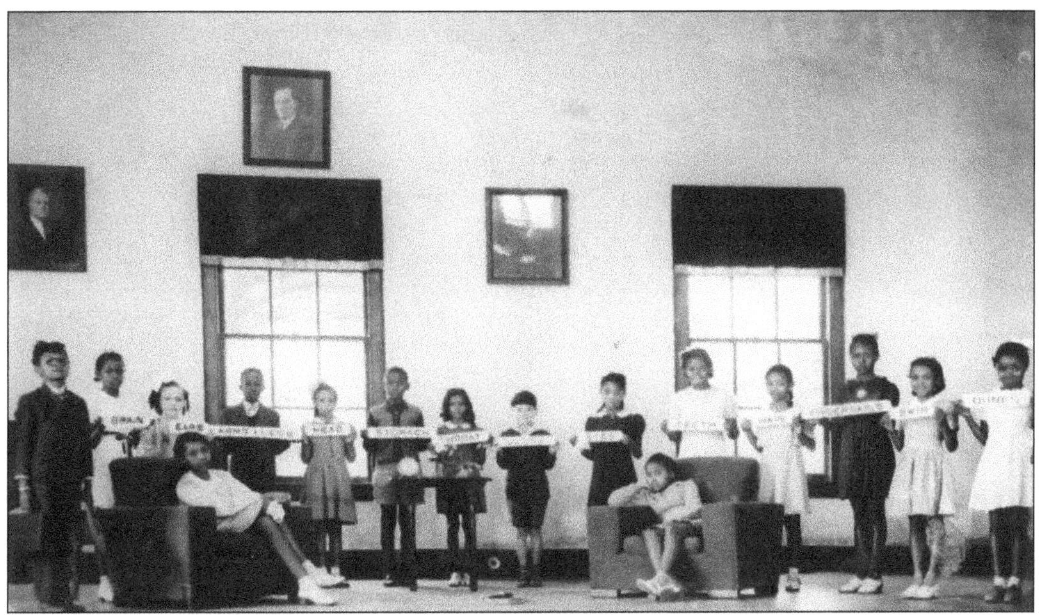

Laboratory School students show what they have learned about the human body in an anatomy class presentation. Visitors to the campus are no doubt more fascinated with how much the children are learning than perhaps their peers. In this early 1940s photograph, the student coach on the far left seems to have decided to honor Dr. J.S. Clark. Imitation is the highest form of flattery. The Lab School administration and teachers highlighted the importance of library time for the impact it had on student achievement. The longtime school librarian, Mamie Bronson, was an essential employee in improving teacher effectiveness and student growth. Bronson is pictured with the faculty on page 75. (Both, courtesy of Southern University Laboratory School.)

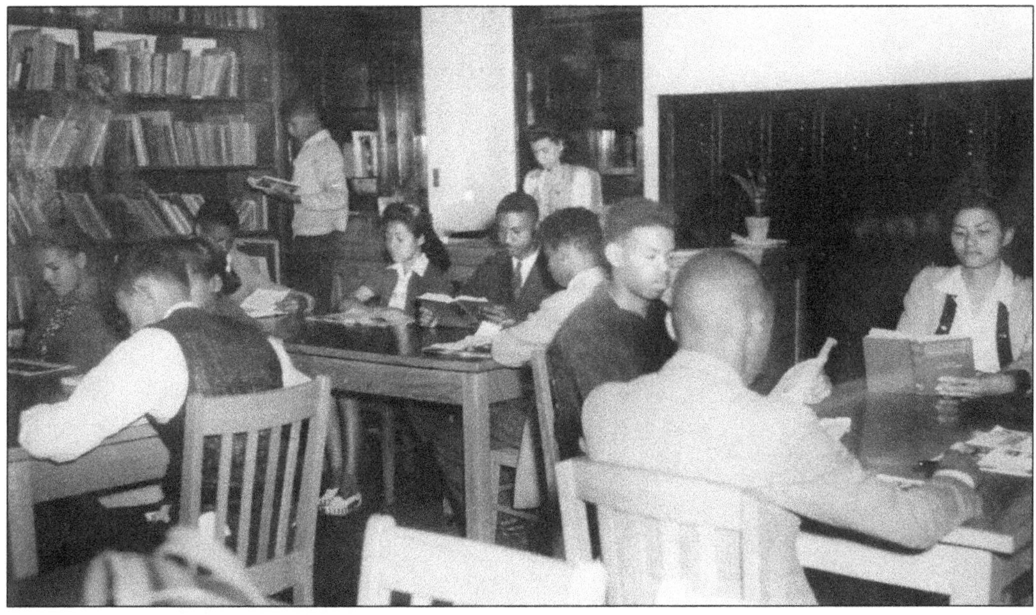

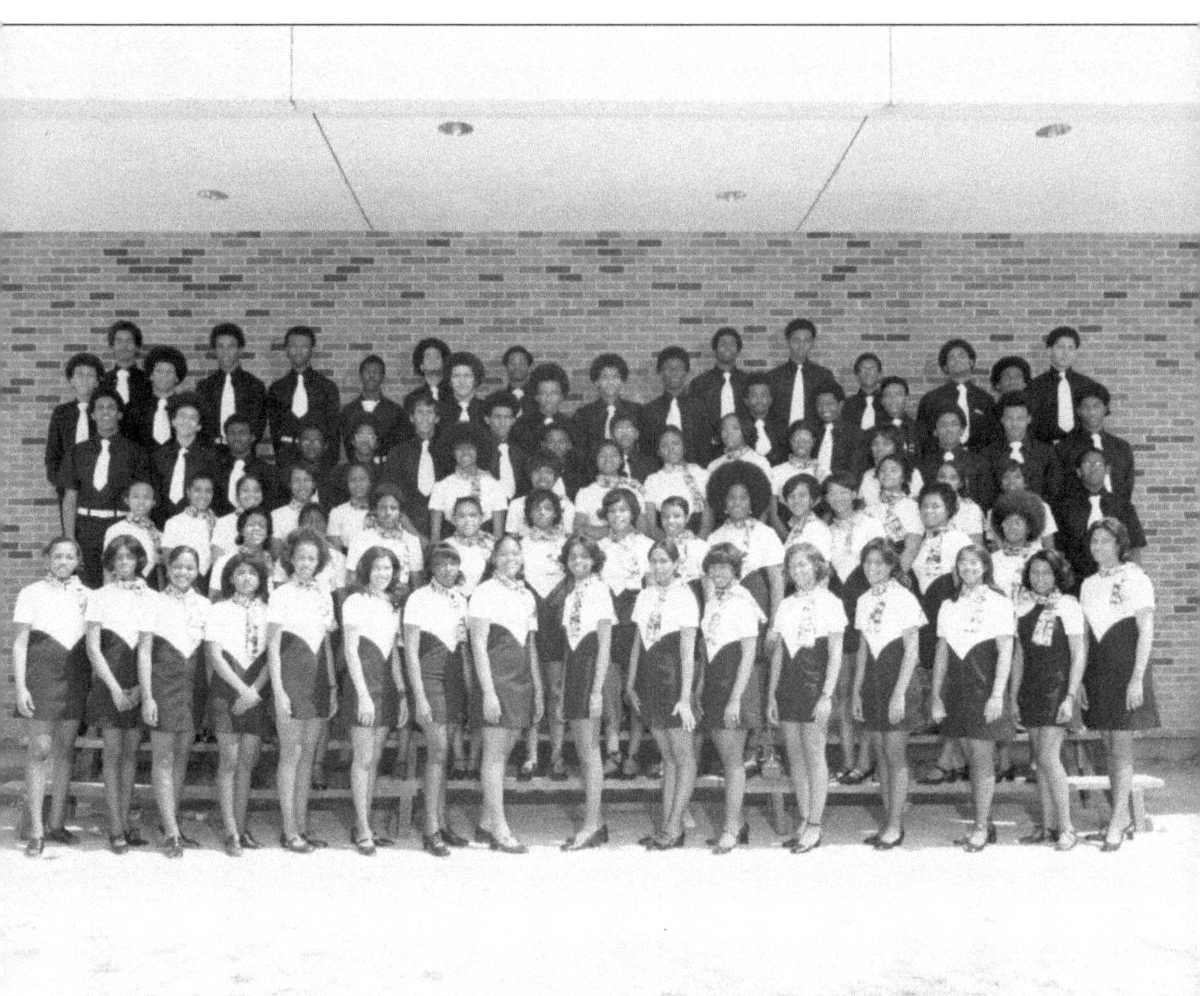

The 1971–1972 SU Laboratory School Choir Sweepstakes Award district champions are pictured here. From left to right are (first row) Sharon Albert, Candace Hebert, Karmeise Henderson, Lisa McCurthy, Kathy Walker, Vallory Simms, Seleria Matthews, Eleanor Wilcox, Mildred West, Tonya Vincent, Muriel Felder, Karen Redd, Audree Greggs, Eugenia Cardoza, student teacher Ladricia Priuel, and teacher Lyndia Mims Williams; (second row) Joycelyn Harrison, T. Turner, C. Riley, Sharon King, Janice Harrell, T. Johnson, M. Spann, C. Montgomery, Rhonda Crawford, Karlene Crawford, Linda Veal, Janice Jenkins, Anita Levy, Renee Mozee, A. White, and G. Robinson; (third row) D. Amacker, Lynette Virdue, Glynnis Major, Jo B. Ward, Jan Hall, Valerie Eunice Moore, Cheryl Yvette Anderson, Patricia Woods, C. Montgomery, Urlecia Cooks, B. Hebert, Sheila Sims, Paul Poydras, Gregory Handy, and Phillip Hawkins; (fourth row) A. Johnson, Reginald Kiper, M. Wilcox, Rodney Reese, Danny Jones, John Wilson, T. Jefferson, Arnold Johnson, Jerry Cole, Eric Smith, and Alvin Batiste; (fifth row) Huel Perkins, Lowell Major, David Geralds, R. Wheelock, Lawrence Wallace, Ron Hall, Russell Kelly, Gerald Wilson, Henry Griffin, Konrad Dawson, E. Polk, Eugene Coates, Joe C. Randall, A. Hebert, Anthony Lombard, C. Overstreet, and Ted Jemison. (Courtesy of Muriel Felder Haysbert.)

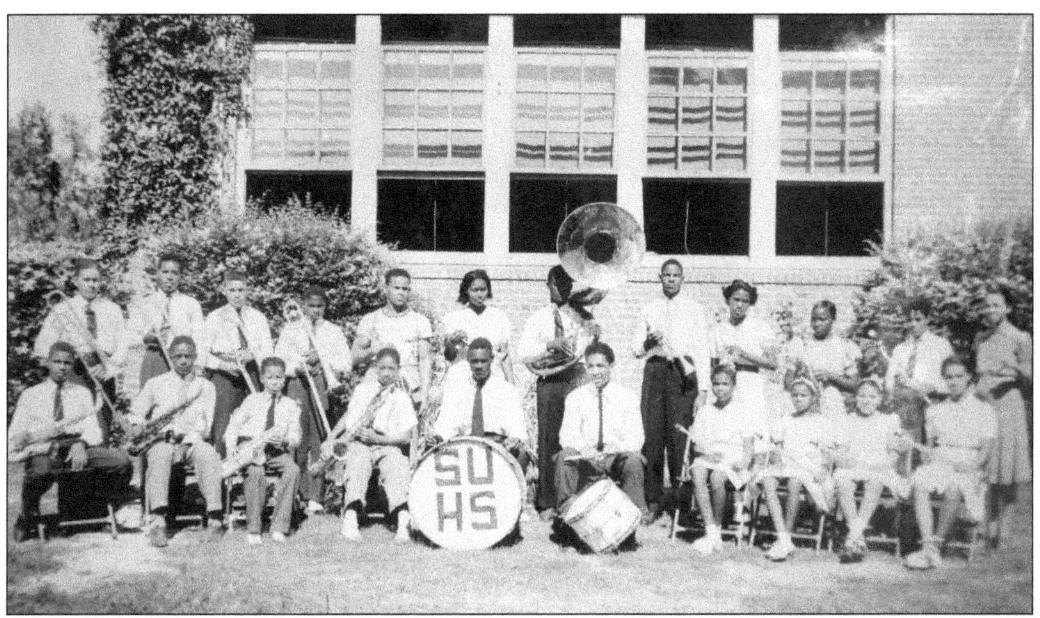

The Lab School band of the late 1940s, 1950s, and early 1960s was under the direction of Ludwig Freeman (1933–2013). Freeman also served as the university's band director from 1965 to 1968 after the retirement of the band's first director, T. Leroy Davis (1947–1964). The second director of the Lab School band was a 1948 Southern grad, Isaac Greggs, who led the band to a number of championships. Dr. Greggs would also direct the world-renowned Southern University band, dubbed the "Human Jukebox," during his tenure from 1969 to 2005. (Above, courtesy of Southern University Laboratory School; below, courtesy of Muriel Felder Haybert.)

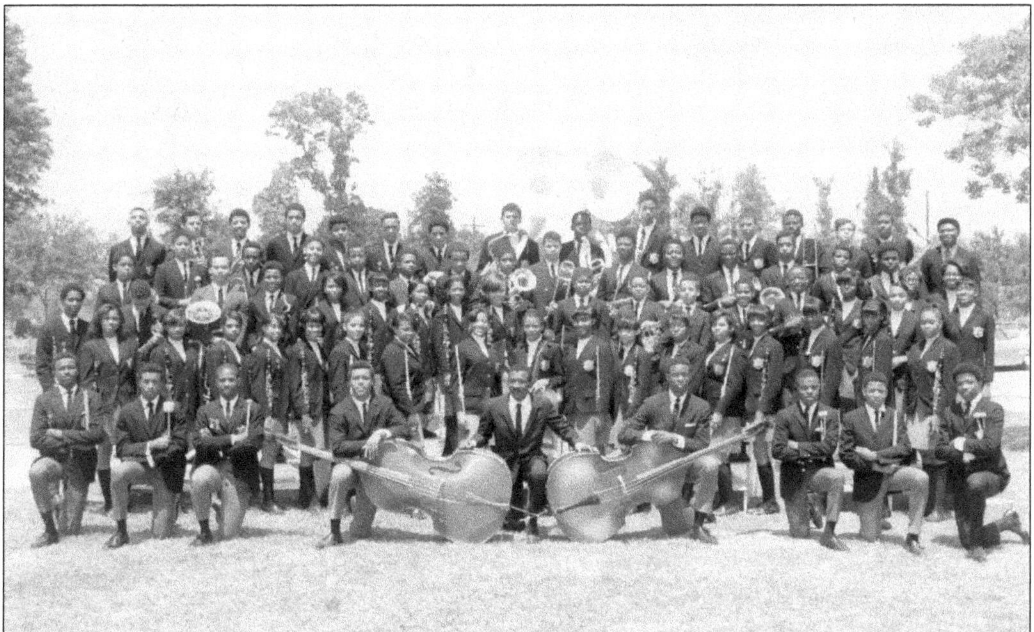

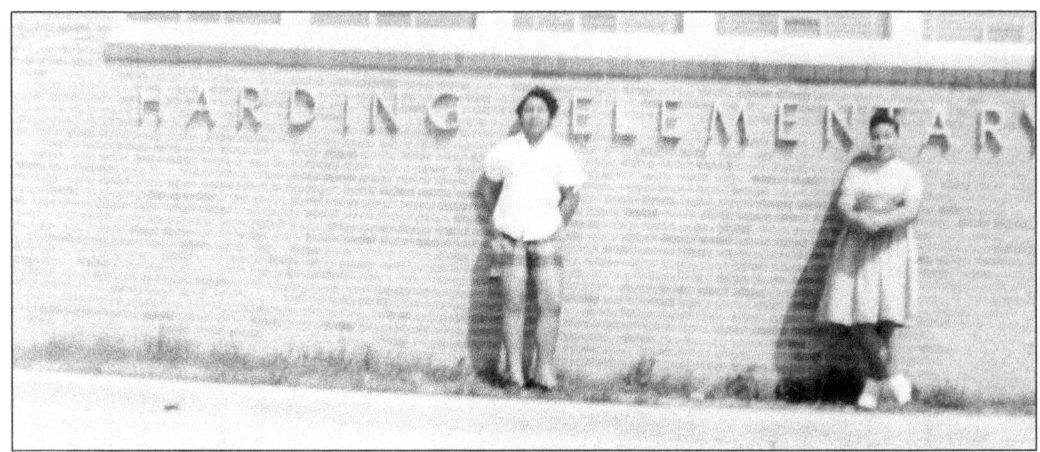

The first public school built in Scotlandville by the East Baton Rouge Parish School System was North Scotlandville Elementary in 1950–1952. The "old" school became South Scotlandville Elementary. Later schools in the community built by the parish were the first junior high school in 1952, which later became Scotlandville Junior-Senior High; Harding Elementary, which replaced South Scotlandville, in 1956; Progress Elementary in 1959; Scotlandville Senior High, the first high school, in 1960, which later was named Scotlandville Magnet High; Crestworth Middle, in 1968; Ryan Elementary, in 1969, and Crestworth Elementary, in 1973. Pictured above, Marjorie Ann Green (left) is shown with her sister Sandra Marie Green, both students at Harding Elementary. Below, Marjorie appears in an "Indian operetta" held at Scotlandville Junior-Senior High. Her costar in *Dawn Boy* was Theodore Martin. Teacher and coach Walter Banks directed the show. (Both, courtesy of Marjorie A. Green.)

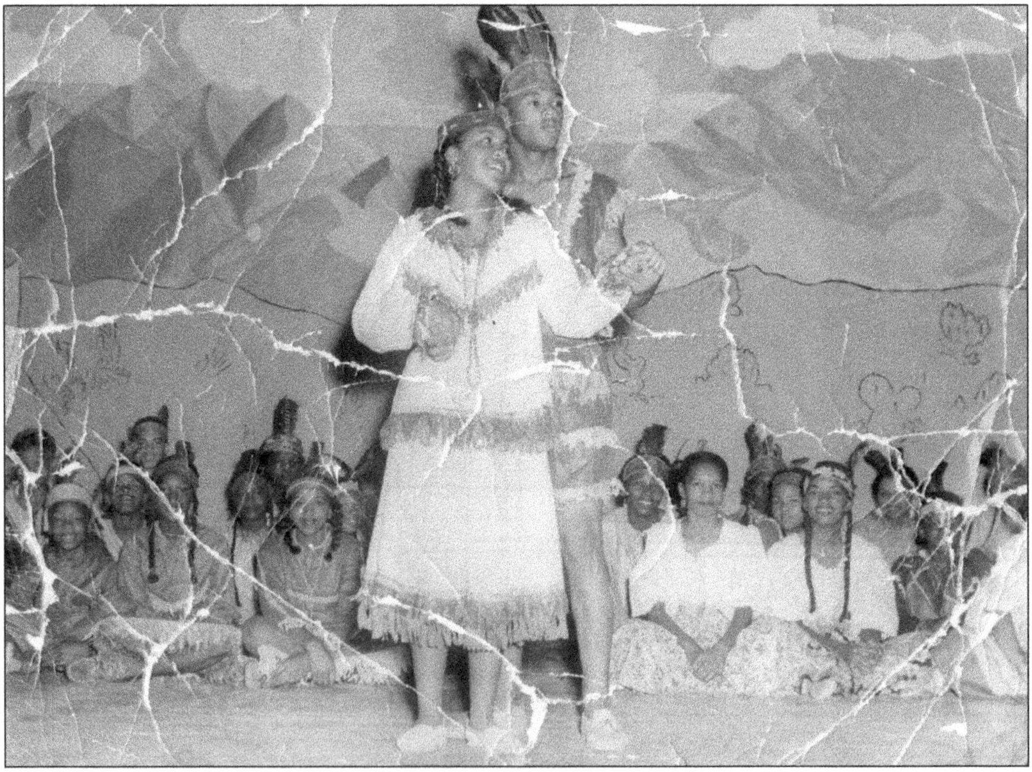

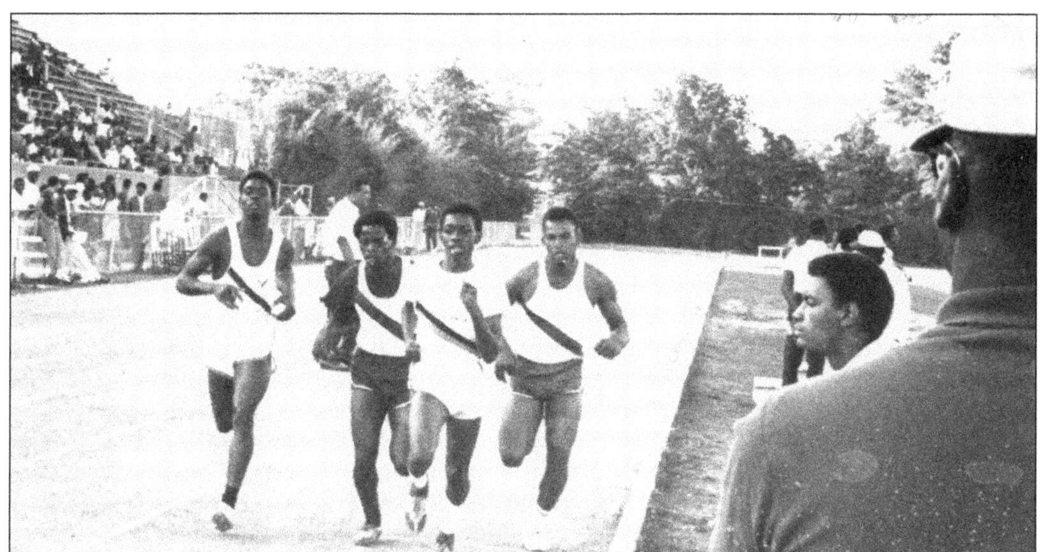

Melvin "Kip" Holden, second from right, is ahead of his competitors in this track and field meet. As a long-distance runner in high school, Holden acquired his nickname from Kip Keino, the Kenyan runner who won medals in the 1968 and 1972 Olympics. John B. Cade Jr., a former Scotlandville High School teacher who taught Holden for three years, remembers Holden as also having a talent for organizing students. (Courtesy of Mayor-President Melvin "Kip" Holden.)

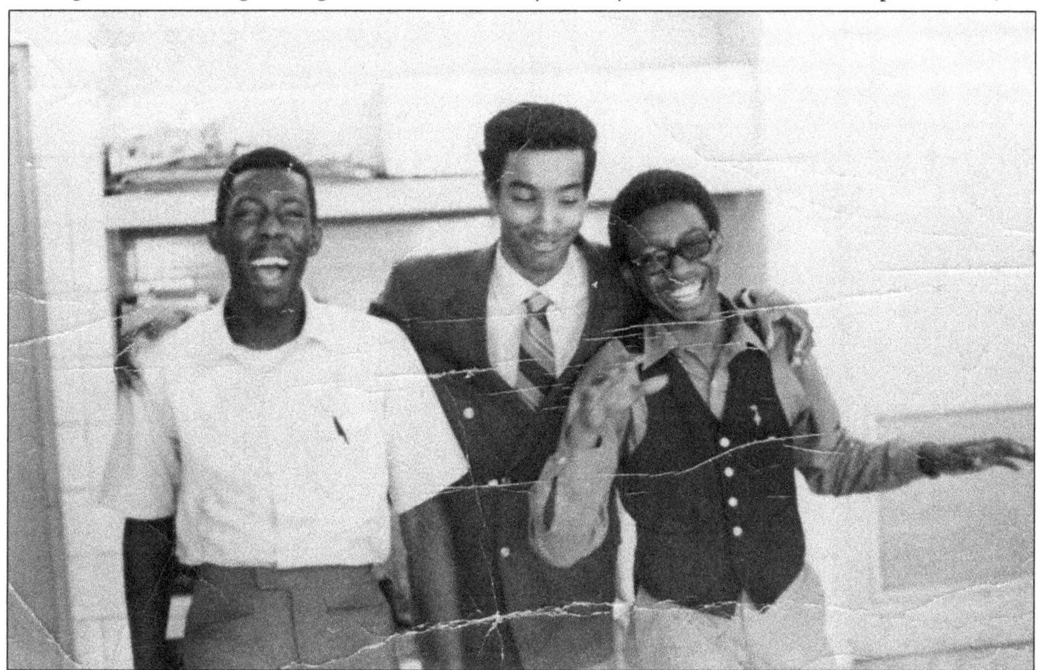

From left to right, best friends Larry Caulfield, Harleen Ivey, and Kip Holden navigated the junior and senior high school days with fun, finesse, and style. Holden's senior memory book noted Harleen "Sonny Boy" Ivey II as the "most popular boy" and Kip as the "best boy dresser" and the student with "the most brains." While wishing his friend luck in the future, Caulfield wrote: "Character is the real foundation of all worthwhile success." (Courtesy of Mayor-President Melvin "Kip" Holden.)

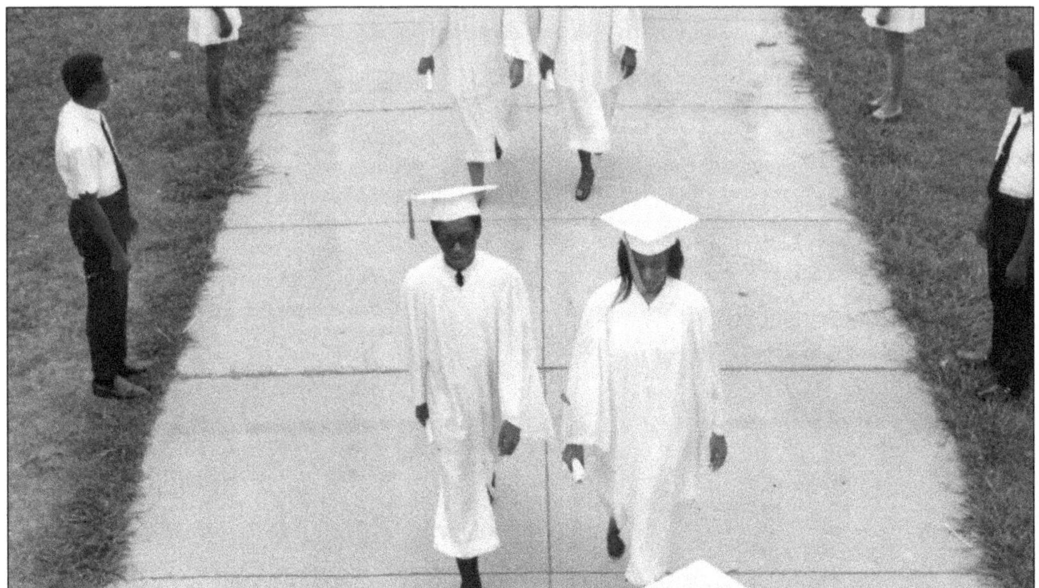

Celebrating their educational attainment was on the minds of the 1970 graduates of Scotlandville High School. The new high school at 9870 Scotland Avenue opened in 1960. There had been a junior high school, which opened in 1952 and expanded a grade a year until its first high school graduating class in 1956. In 1970, the school was legally desegregated, although the student population remained predominantly black. Honor graduate Kip Holden is in the foreground at left. (Courtesy of Mayor-President Melvin "Kip" Holden.)

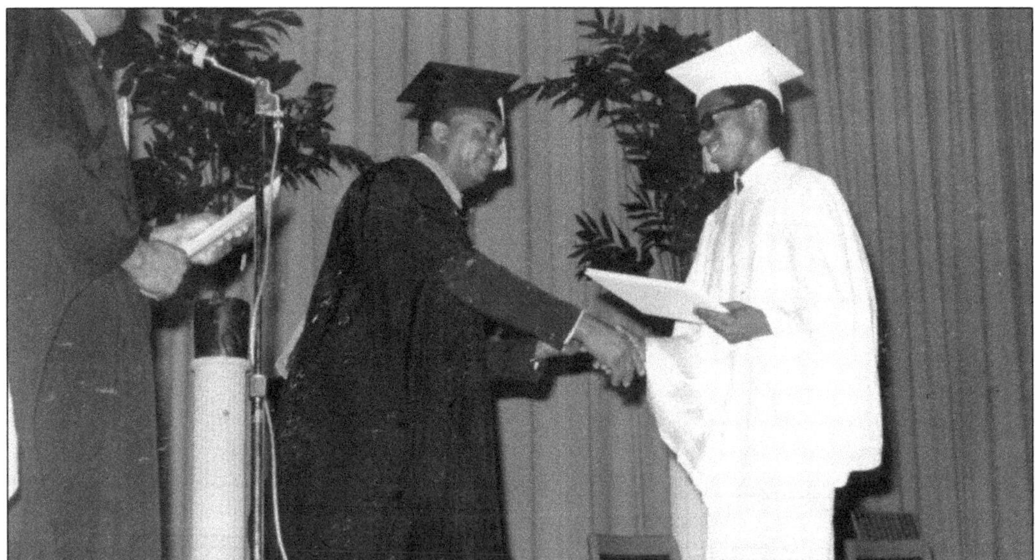

Principal Robert West congratulates honor graduate, star athlete, and student leader Melvin "Kip" Holden, son of Rosa May Rogers and Curtis Holden, during the 1970 commencement exercises. Holden would later earn a bachelor's degree in journalism from LSU in Baton Rouge (1974), a master's in journalism from SU (1982), and a juris doctorate from SULC (1985). He also completed formal education at the National Institute of Trial Advocacy and the Oxford University Round Table in England. Read more about his career achievements in chapter seven. (Courtesy of Mayor-President Melvin "Kip" Holden.)

Blanche Barker Felder (1921–2013) sits with students at the Louisiana School for the Deaf. In addition to teaching, Felder directed the school's junior choral group. A native of Franklinton and longtime resident of Scotlandville, Felder was a graduate of Alcorn State University and Gallaudet University in Washington, DC, and active in a number of civic, social, and religious organizations. She was a member of Delta Sigma Theta Sorority, Phi Delta Kappa, and the Louisiana Retired Teachers Association. (Courtesy of Muriel Felder Haysbert.)

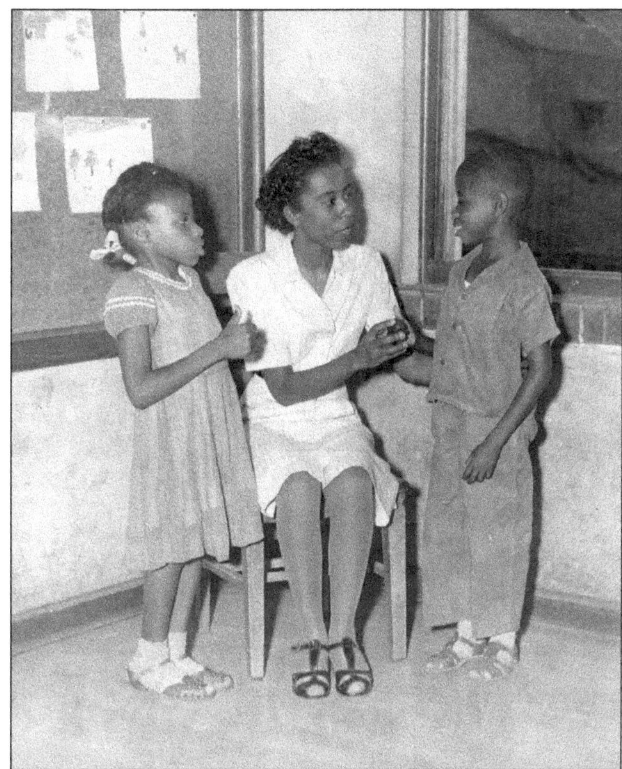

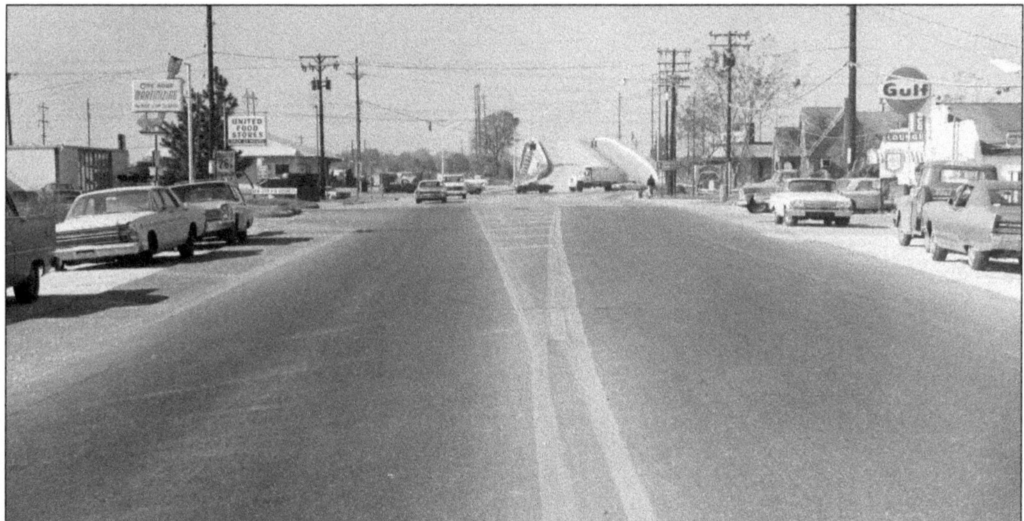

From 1914 to the 1970s, Swan Street at Scenic Highway provided the only entrance to Southern University. A second entrance at Mills Avenue did not solve what had become a major problem. Railroad cars when passing or stopped on the tracks just east of the campus blocked pedestrian and vehicular traffic to and from Southern. Students argued that such long waits were causing them to be late for or miss classes. More problematic was the inability to get on and off campus in case of emergencies. After several demonstrations and writing campaigns, their voices were heard. The Harding Boulevard overpass was approved and constructed. Today, it is the most-traveled route to the university. (Courtesy of Louisiana State Library.).

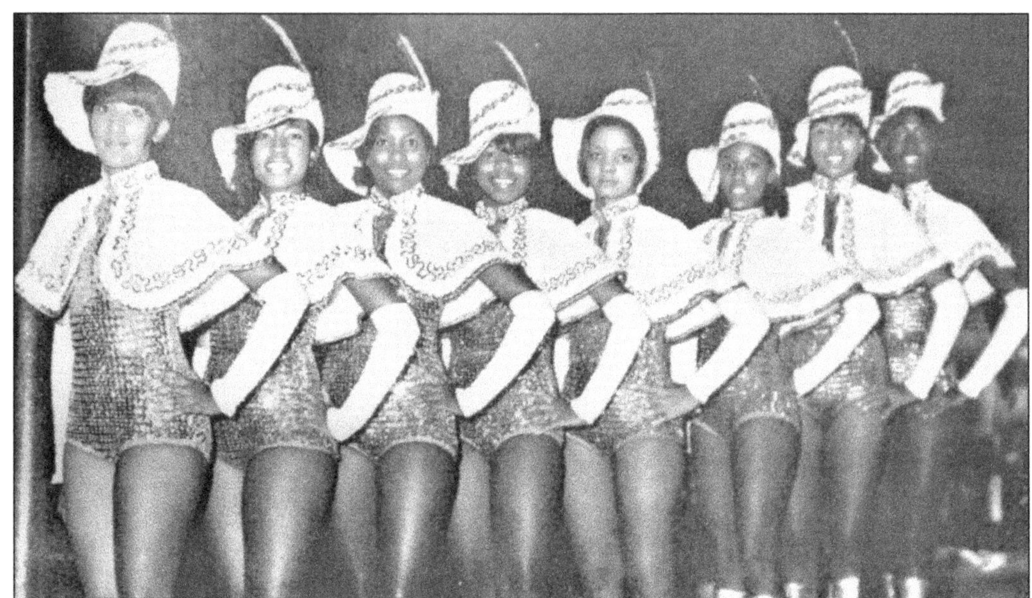

Band director Isaac Greggs selected organizer/choreographer Gracie Nell Franklin Perkins and the original eight members of the Southern University Dancing Dolls, a group of female student dancers that "added pizzazz" to his all-male band. Posing in costume for a 1969 photograph, original members are, from left to right, Niehma "Betty" McDonald Lowe, Theta Batiste Augustus, Gail Leggins Gaines, Lois McFarland Gattis, Linda Watson Mitchell, Brenda Mack, Mauretta Wailes Hurst, and Sara Moody Thomas. (Courtesy of Gracie Perkins.)

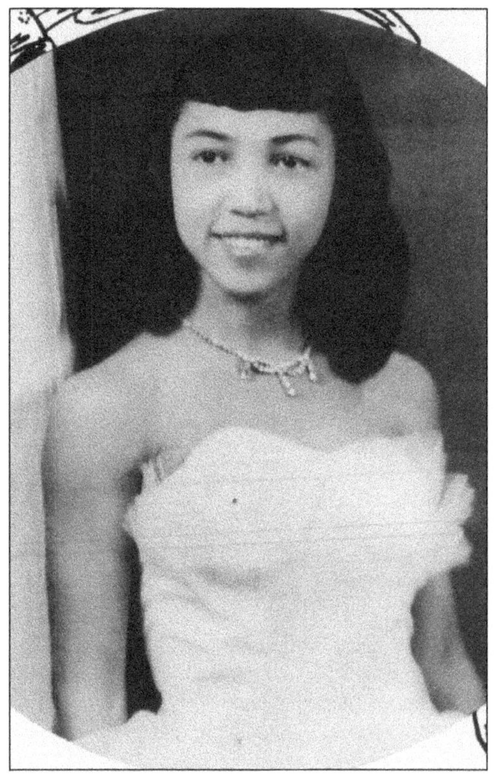

In 1951–1952, Delores Kelly was elected the 21st Miss Southern by the university student body, becoming the third Scotlandville native to wear the crown. Other Scotlandville residents chosen for this coveted title were Corrine Maybuce (1939–1940), Earline LaMotte (Bradford) (1933–1934), Myrtly A. Richard (Joyner) (1959–1960), Carrie Bailey (Johnson) (1962–1963), and Betty J. Reese (1974–1975). After graduating from Southern, Delores moved to California and became a teacher. (Courtesy of the Archives Department/John B. Cade Library/ Southern University and A&M College.)

At right, Monroe, Louisiana, native Donald Carlye Wade (1935–2012) earned a bachelor's degree in history and master's degree in school administration from Southern. In 1970, Wade became the second executive director of the Southern University Alumni Federation, serving for more than 25 years. He is credited with creating the Miss Bayou Classic Pageant and the Annual SU Alumni Round-up. His wife, Beverly Dixon Wade, is retired dean of the SU Honors College. Below, Navy veteran Huel D. Perkins (1924–2013), a Scotlandville resident, graduated from Southern with highest honors in 1947 and earned master's and PhD degrees at Northwestern University in Evanston, Illinois. Perkins wrote Southern's fight song in 1951. This humanitarian taught music at Southern for 27 years. Continuing his career as an administrator and faculty member at LSU in 1979, he was named professor emeritus of humanities in 1989 and was awarded an honorary Doctor of Humane Letters in 2005. (Right, courtesy of Peggy M. Wallace; below, courtesy of Thelma S. Perkins.)

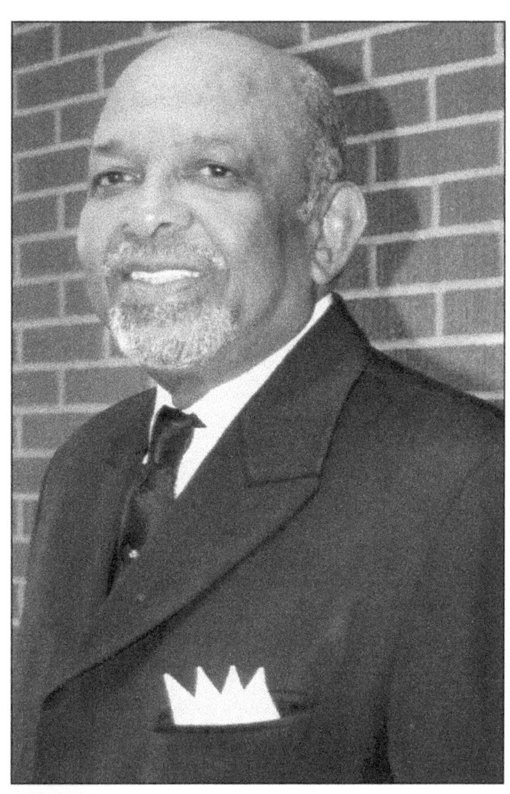

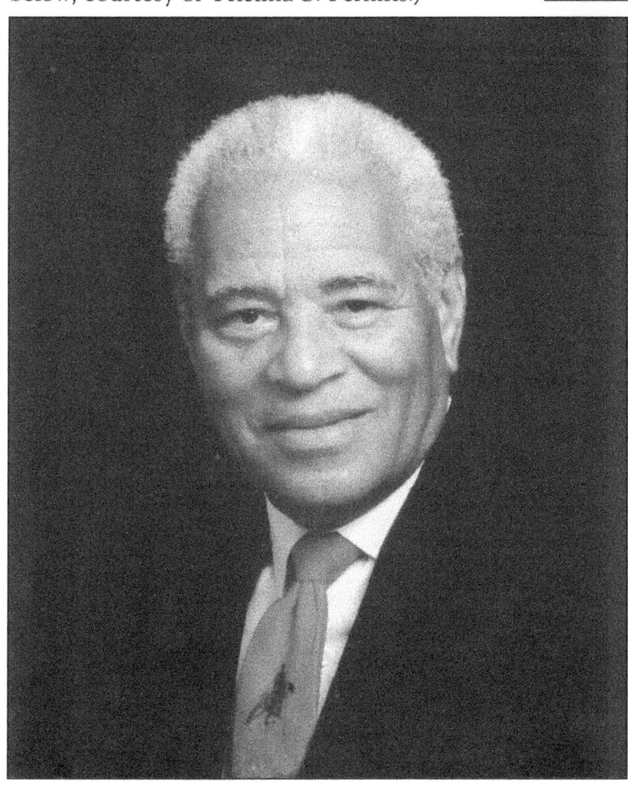

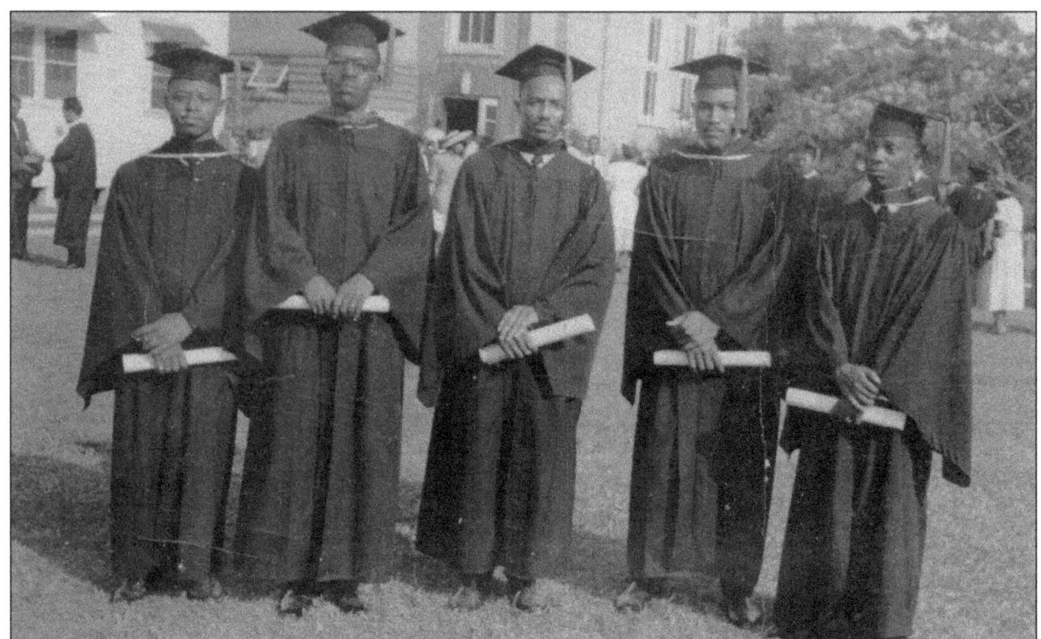

With their commencement, members of the Southern University Law School's first graduating class in 1950 became much-needed additions to the legal arena. Pictured are, from left to right, noted civil rights attorney Alex L. Pitcher; 30-year Internal Revenue Service professional Leroy White; educator Ellyson F. Dyson; Shreveport civil rights attorney and educator, former dean of SU School of Law, ad hoc justice of the Louisiana Supreme Court, first Southern University System president, and former SU Board of Supervisors member Jesse Stone; and New Orleans attorney Alvin B. Jones. Not pictured is New Orleans attorney St. Elmo Johnson. Pictured below making a class presentation is Mary Gloria Lawson, the first female law graduate; in June 1956, she was the first African American woman admitted to the Louisiana Bar. Seated behind her to the left is fellow 1956 graduate Revius O. Ortique Jr. of New Orleans, who became the first African American elected to the Louisiana Supreme Court. (Both, courtesy of the Southern University Law Center.)

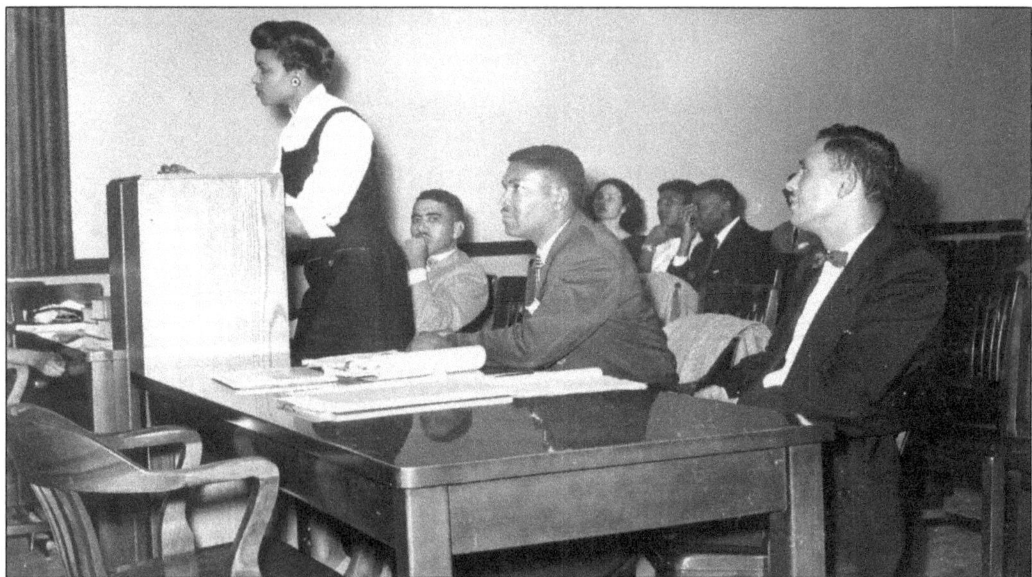

Jazz clarinetist Alvin Baptiste (1932–2007) cofounded the jazz studies program and taught at his own jazz institute at Southern. Well-known musicians who studied under him included Henry Butler, Herman Jackson, Randy Jackson, and Branford Marsalis. In addition to albums that he produced, he played with Cannonball Adderley and Wynton Marsalis. He performed extensively in Europe, Africa, Canada, and the United States. (Courtesy of Louisiana State Library.)

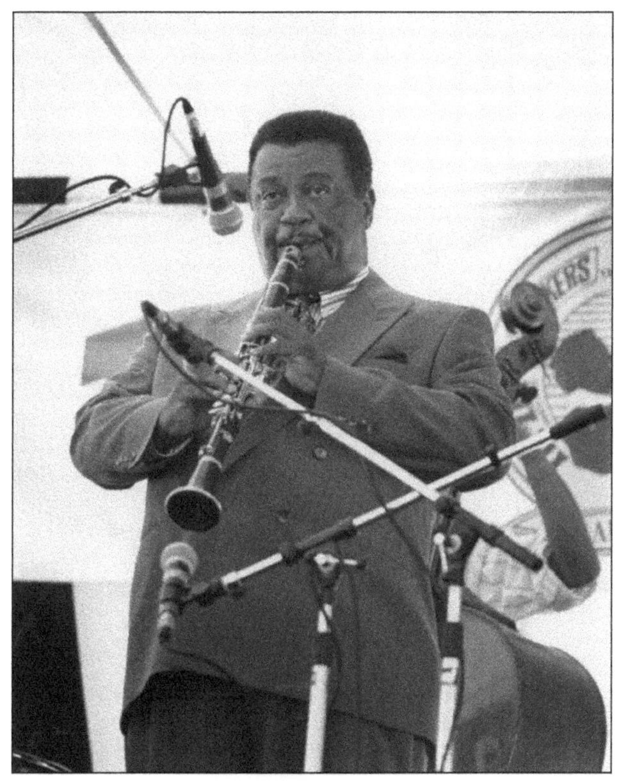

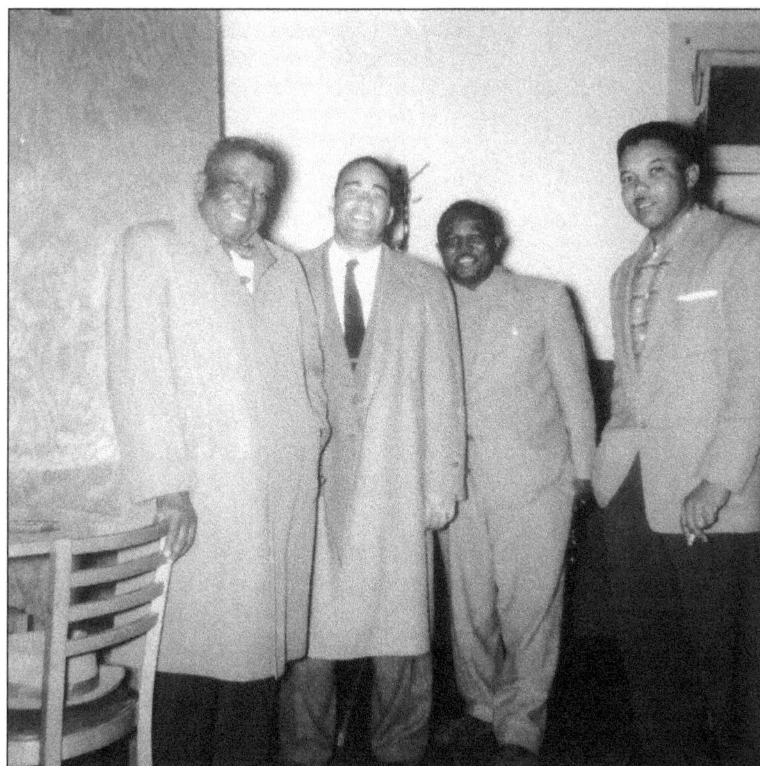

Head football coach and athletic director from 1936 to 1961, Arnett William "Ace" Mumford led the Jaguar team to a 169-57-14 overall record, won or tied for 11 Southwestern Athletic Conference and five Black College national championships, and produced 35 All-Americans. The university football stadium bears the name of the 2001 College Football Hall of Fame inductee. Mumford is pictured at far left, with fans including Southern graduate Carl Ford, at far right. (Courtesy of Dr. James Cook Jr.)

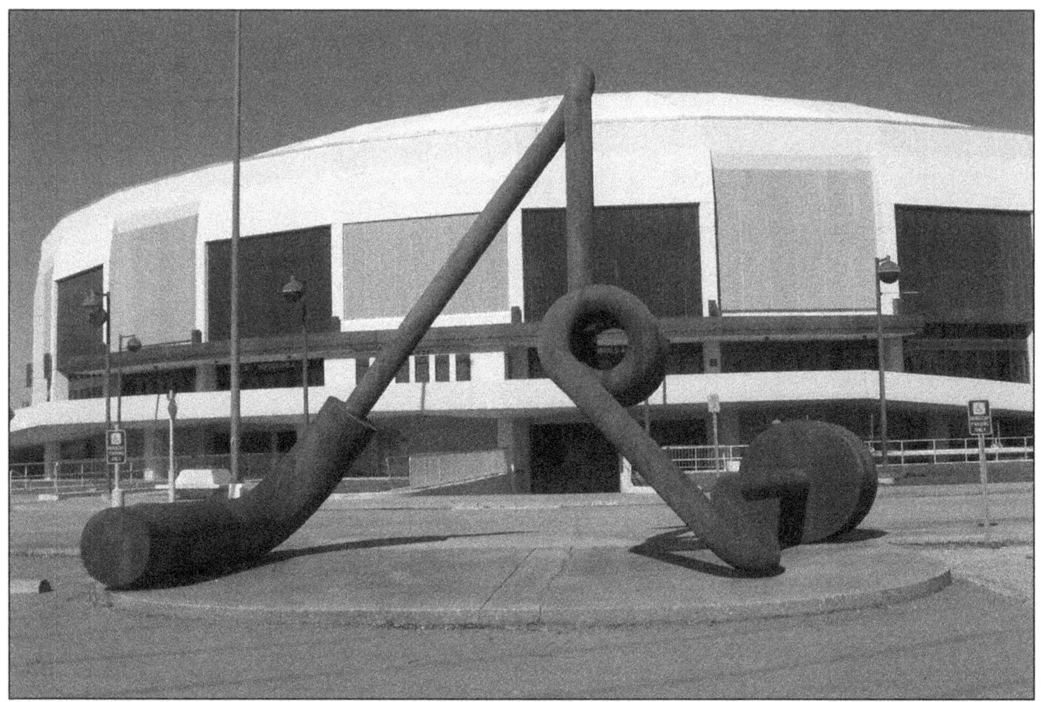

In 1913, Dr. J.S. Clark stood with his son on the bluff looking over the land that stretched to the Mississippi River and described his vision for Southern. Felton said, "I don't see any university out there." Dr. Clark challenged his son to use his imagination and said, "One day Southern will stretch from the Mississippi River to the railroad tracks." SU Professor Al LaVergne's sculpture displayed at the south entrance of the Felton G. Clark Activity Center, located just west of the tracks, represents this vision coming to fruition. It is interpreted by some as representing freedom, lifting and climbing despite obstacles, and togetherness. The class of 1947 donated this historical marker posted on the bluff in memory of Pinckney Benton Stewart Pinchback, who authored the bill in the Louisiana legislature that created Southern. (Both, courtesy of Naville J. Oubre.)

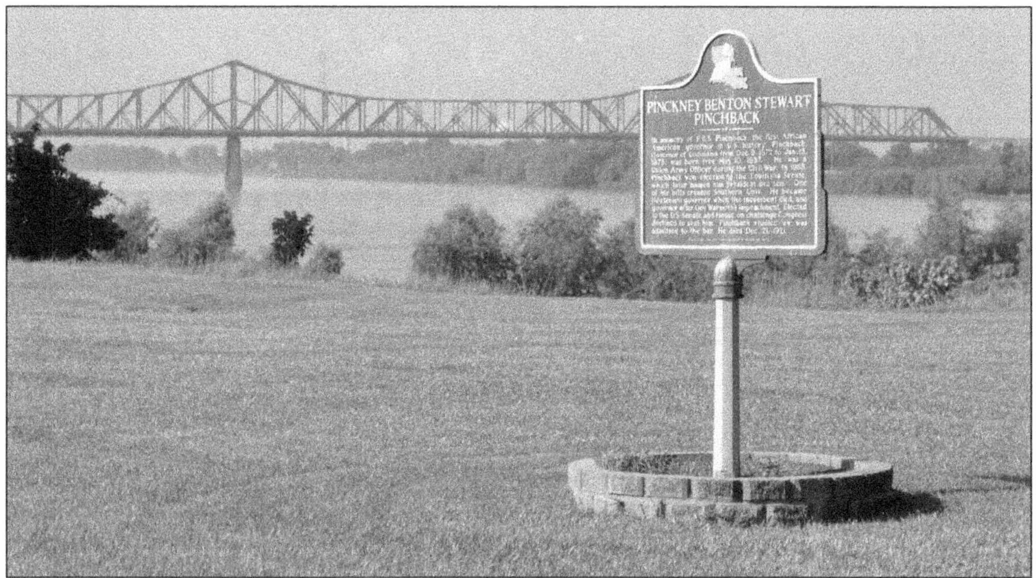

Five

Social and Civic Organizations

Celebrations, Pastimes, and Service

Booker T. Washington once said, "In all things that are purely social we can be as separate as the finger, yet one as the hand in all things essential to mutual progress." The social impact of Jim Crow laws prohibited the participation of black residents with social and civic organizations founded by white residents. It did not deprive black residents of civic and social programs of concern to themselves, for throughout African American communities, like Scotlandville, networks and associations were established as a way to encourage and promote culture, heritage, traditions, and expectations for the building and maintaining of community life.

These organizations, often with national or statewide affiliations, provided professional networking opportunities, leadership and involvement in civic issues, socialization and entertainment, financial support and mentoring, promotion of special interests and creative endeavors, and efforts of giving back to the community.

Often, these groups were established initially as an outgrowth of the church, and were known as "benevolent societies." They were partnerships between Southern University and the Scotlandville community for civic engagement. Later, they were black affiliates of white-only organizations for social, civic, and professional assignation.

These organizations joined in the ongoing relay to create a neighborhood that was clean, safe, economically viable, and a decent place to rear children.

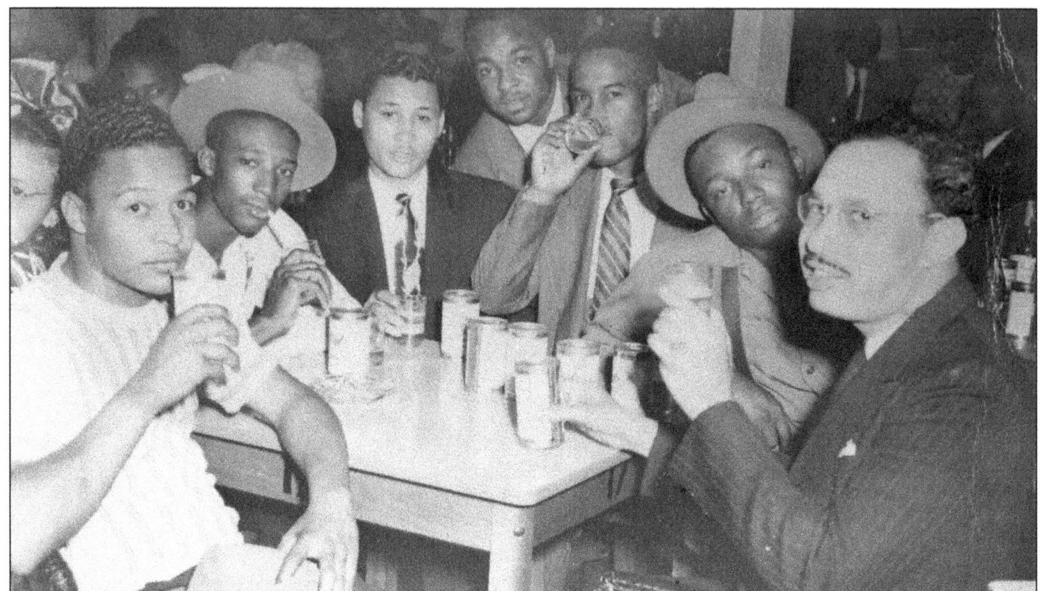

This group of lifelong friends frequently enjoyed an evening of conversation and beverages. Members of the first families of Scotlandville are among those pictured; they are, from left to right, Charles Jackson, "Tout" William, John E. "Pool" Simms, Freddie Jackson, and Henry Franklin Jr. When Tout left Scotlandville and made his home in Chicago and Charles moved to Klamath Falls, Oregon, the get-togethers became reunion celebrations during the holiday seasons. (Courtesy of Vallory Simms Hills.)

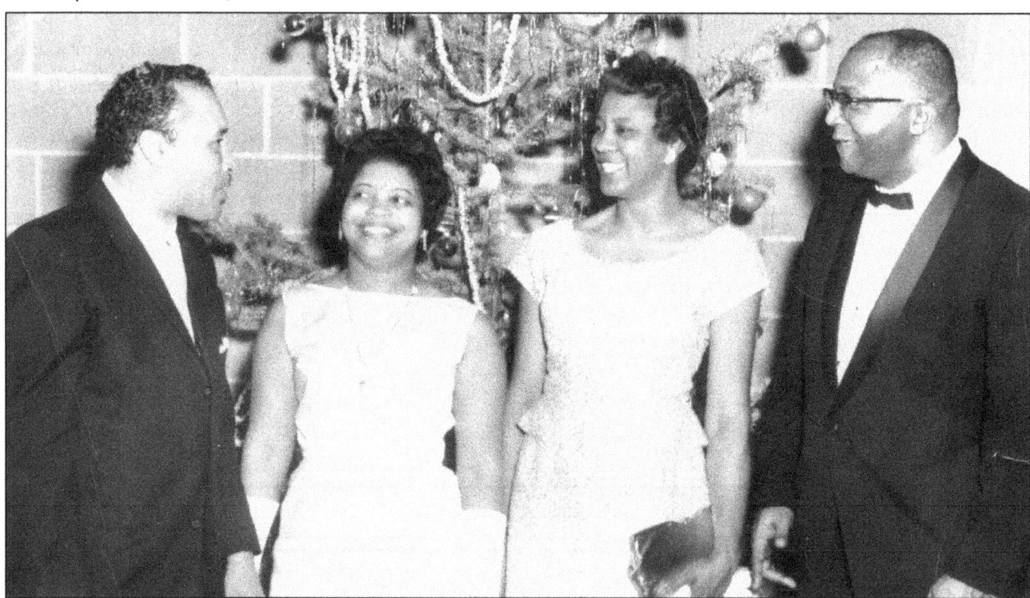

A Christmas social was hosted by, from left to right, John E. "Pool" Simms, Evelyn Handy Simms, Dorothy Robertson, and her husband. Robertson left Scotlandville after graduation from Southern University and made her home in Chicago. She introduced her husband, a native of Chicago, during his first trip to her hometown. Dorothy's parents were Emma and G.B. Robertson. Her father was one of the first black employees hired by the Standard Oil Company. (Courtesy of Vallory Simms Hills.)

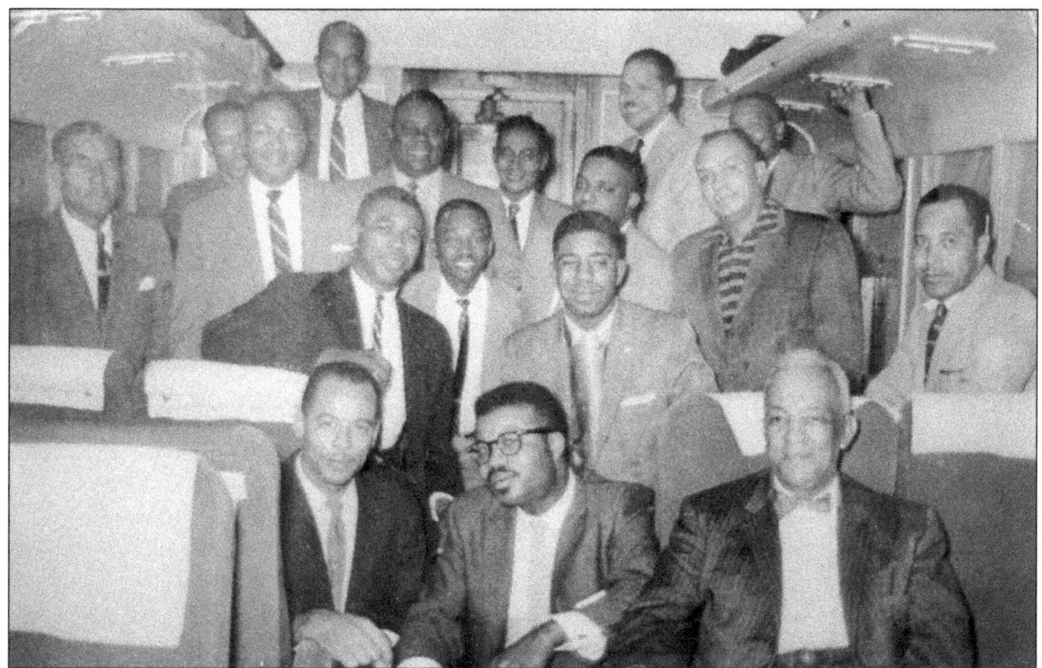

Professional men organized chartered bus trips for social outings and networking opportunities to events like football games, fraternity functions, and group activities. Among the businessmen in this photograph are (first row) Henry "Dickey" Thurman, left, and Dr. Raymond Baranco, right; (second row) Dr. Dupuy Anderson far right; (third row) Samuel Jenkins, far left, and Horatio Thompson, far right. (Courtesy of Phyllis White.)

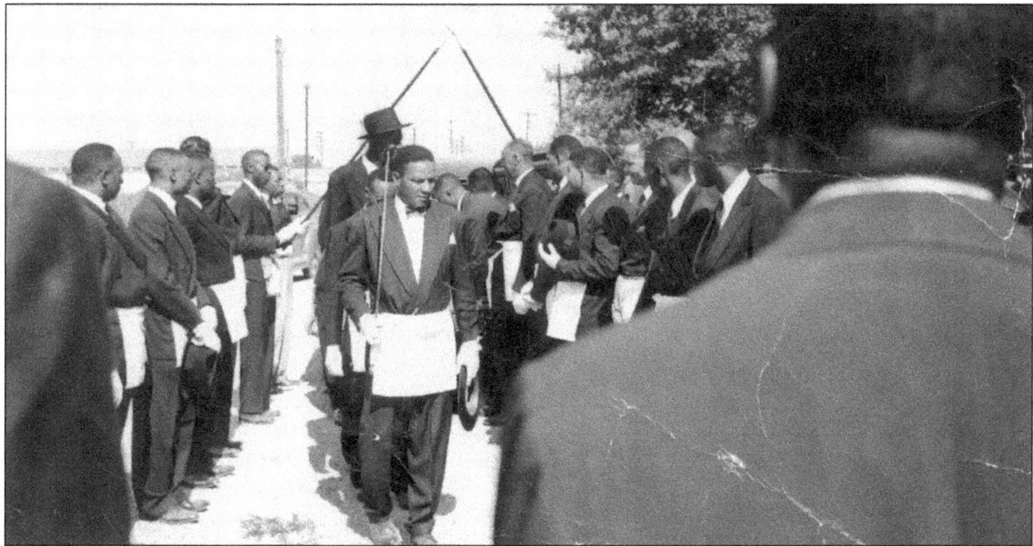

Prince Hall Freemasonry has had a longstanding tradition in the African American community. When excluded from existing Masonic and Grand Lodge communities because of racist Jim Crow laws of the past, black men organized the Prince Hall Masons to promote fellowship, Christianity, and social respectability, while standing against slavery and white supremacy. Scotlandville Masons are pictured engaged in their ritual regalia of aprons, collars, and hats on a major thoroughfare in the central business district. (Courtesy of Vallory Simms Hills.)

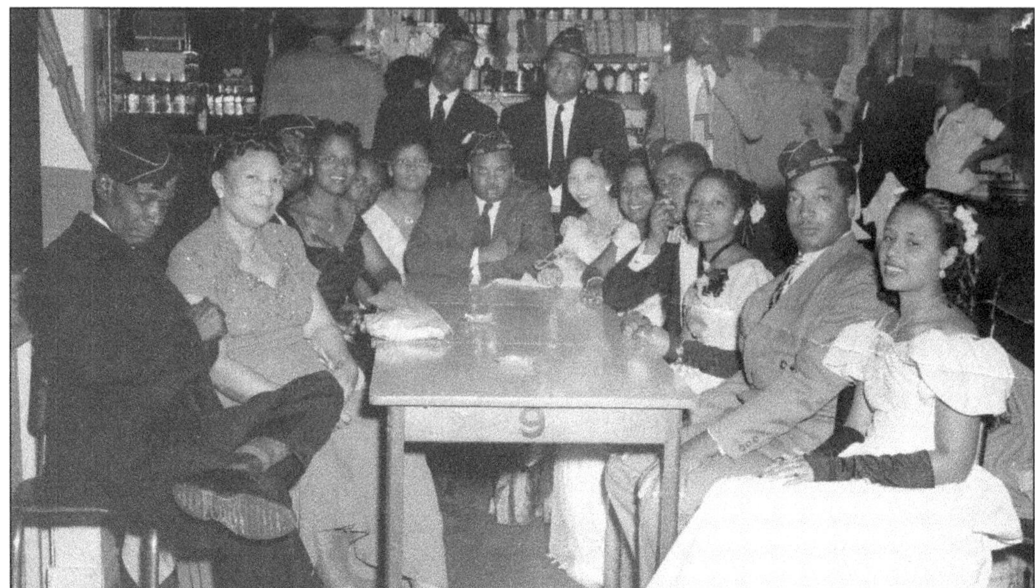

The Charmette Social and Civic Club hosts an annual Christmas dance held at the Masonic lodge on Rosenwald Road in Scotlandville. Among the partygoers are the beret-wearing military members of the Bonnette-Harrison American Legion Post No. 502 of Scotlandville, including the group's charter commander, Nathan L. Lewis. Post No. 502, chartered in August 1947, was named for Curtis Bonnette and Otis Harrison, who were killed in World Wars I and II respectively. (Courtesy of Julia Bradford Moore.)

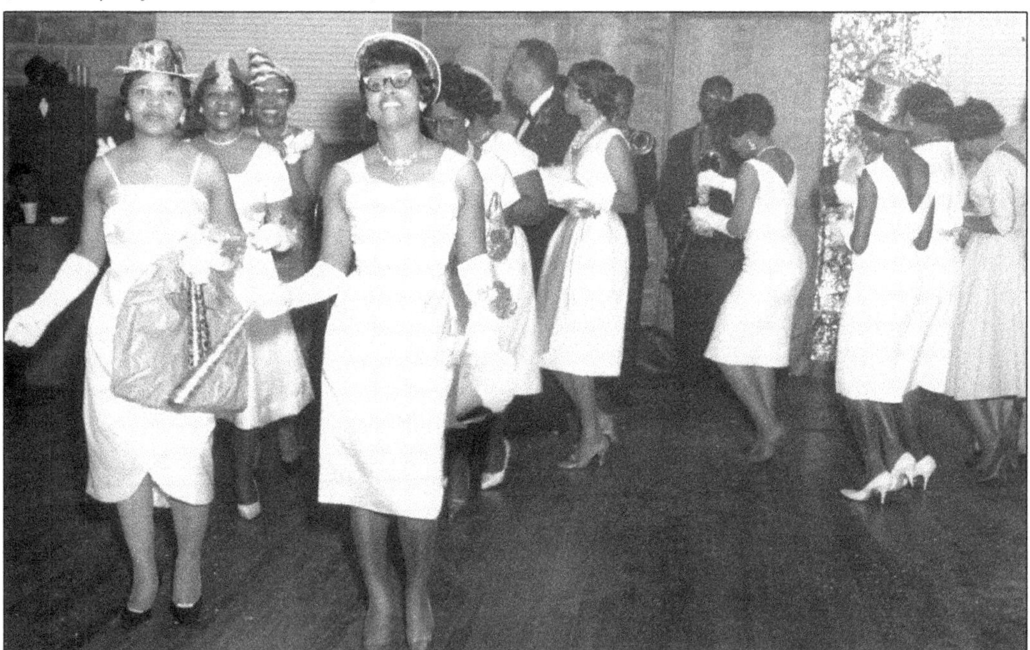

Members of the Charmette Social and Civic Club enjoy a line dance at their New Year's dance held at the Masonic lodge. Among the revelers are, from left to right, (first row) Fannie Hayes Dunn Terrell and Gloria Murray Handy; (second row) Eula Jackson Barnes and Jannie Murray Cox; (third row) Annie Pearl Williams. (Courtesy of Vallory Simms Hills and Chaz Handy.)

New Orleans has been a favorite convention destination for Prince Hall Shriners. Lillian and Percy L. Jackson of Scotlandville enjoy the festivities and the fellowship of their co-members from throughout the country at the Shriner's Ball, an annual charity event. (Courtesy of Lillian S. Jackson.)

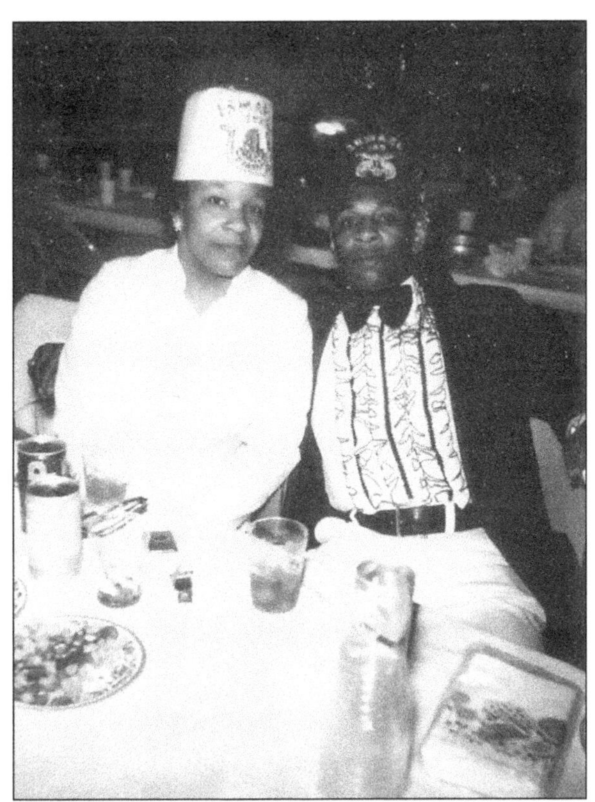

Members of the Twilight Lodge No. 166 Free and Accepted Masons of Scotlandville pose for an official photograph during the formal meeting for election and installation of officers. Percy L. Jackson, seated fourth from left, is the worshipful master of the group. The 92-year-old Masonic group annually distributes Thanksgiving baskets to families in need throughout the community. Historically, African American Masons have supported and promoted a number of educational and civil rights efforts for community improvement. (Courtesy of Lillian S. Jackson.)

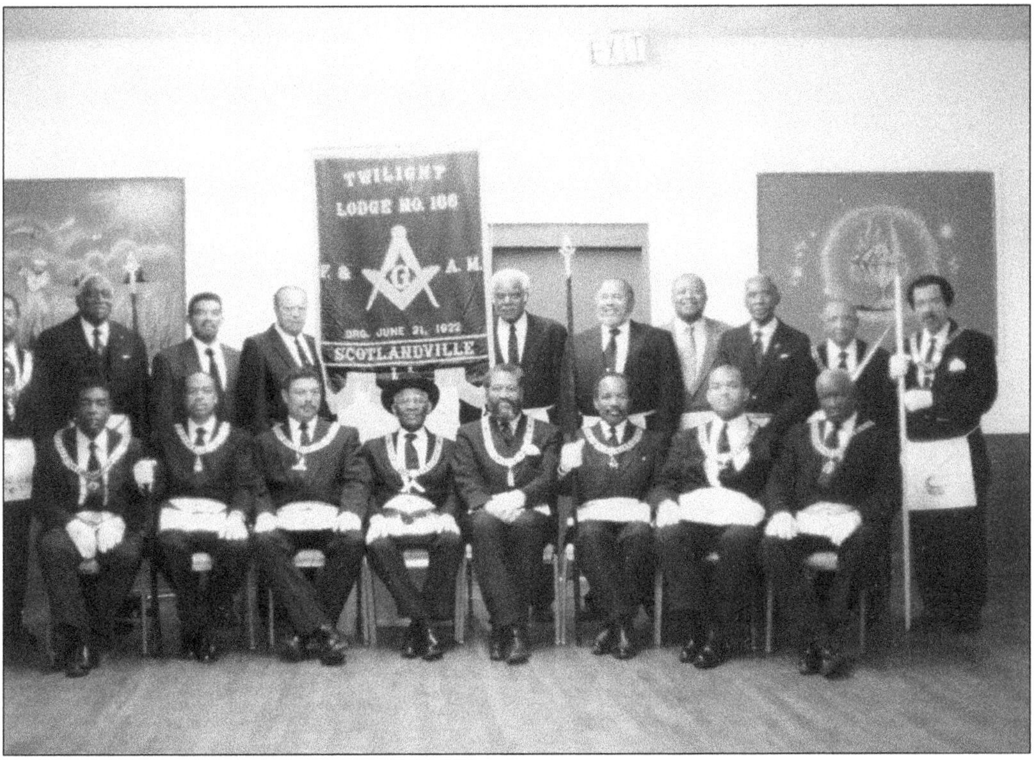

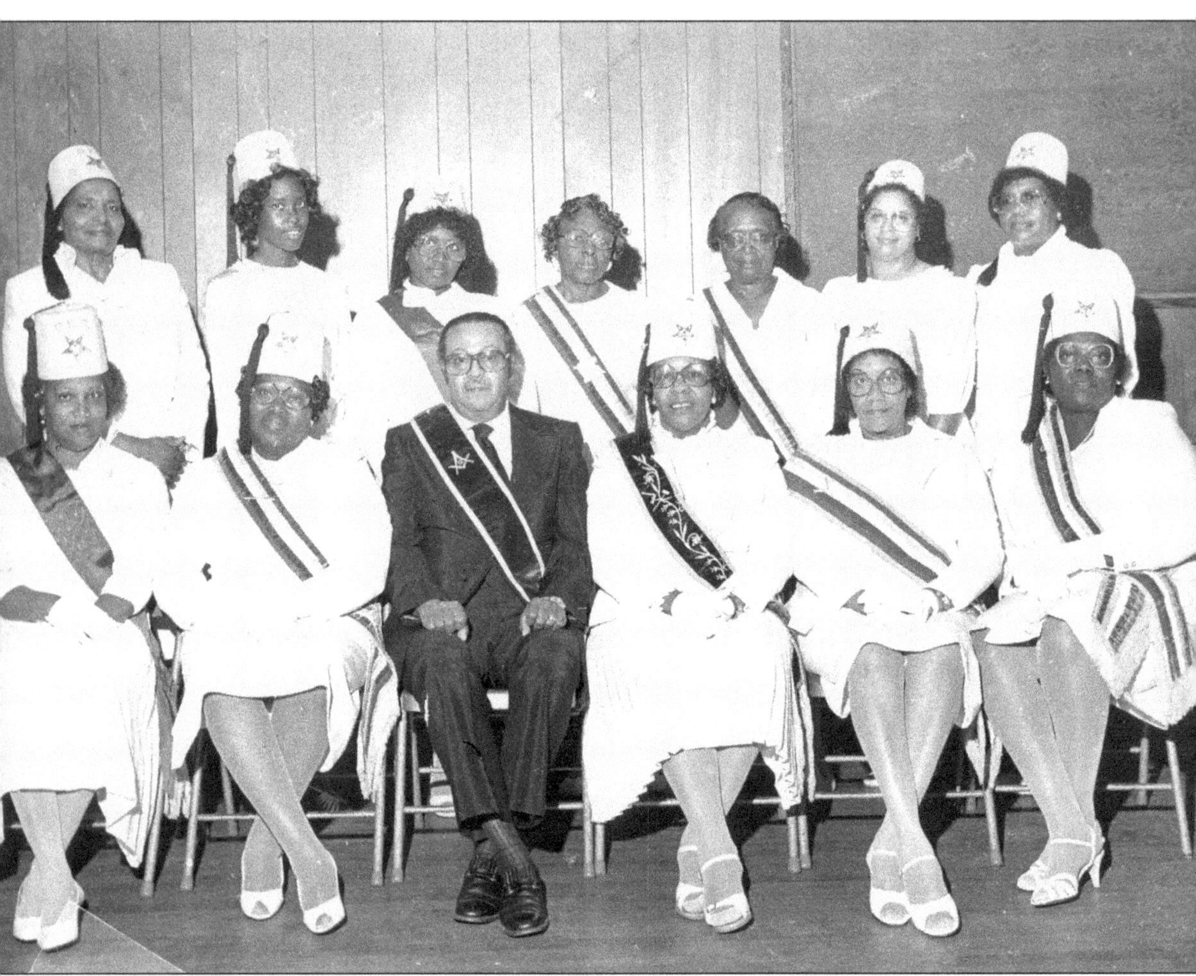

The Order of the Eastern Star, a fraternal organization open to men and women, promotes character-building lessons such as obedience, justice, charity, and faith and trust in God. Members of the Pride of Scotlandville Chapter No. 11 OES-PHA PM 60-96 are pictured with supervising officer Worthy Patron Otis D. Stewart and presiding officer Worthy Matron Lillian S. Jackson, seated third and fourth from left. (Courtesy of Lillian S. Jackson.)

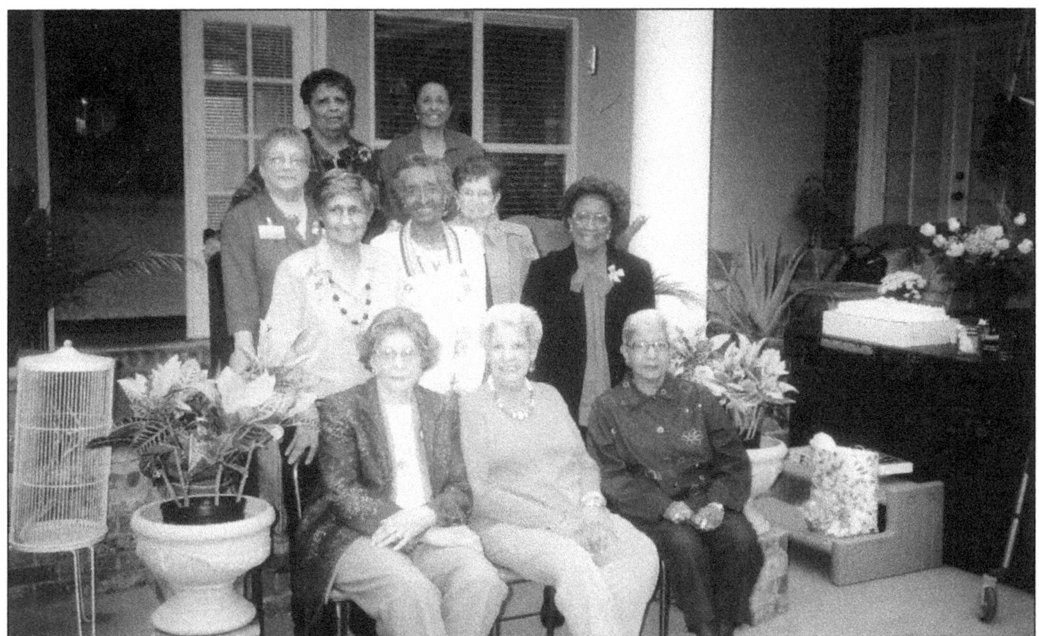

The Junior Matrons Club, a social club for young married women, was founded in October 1941. The founding president was educator Marjorie Dumas Lawless (1920–2007), of Natchez, Mississippi, the wife of Dr. Harrison "Didy" Lawless Jr., dean of Southern's Junior Division. An annual debutante ball was held to introduce members' and their friends' children to society. Later, proceeds from the ball went to the NAACP. The Matrons (the group dropped "Junior" as members matured) also provided financial support to the Girl Scouts and Boy Scouts of America, Sickle Cell Anemia Foundation, YWCA and YMCA, Good Samaritan's Good Fellows, and the DeBose National Piano Competition Foundation. Members pictured below are, from left to right, (sitting) Nona Gray, Dorthal Wailes, Bernadine Rucker, Naomi David, Melba Simmons, Sadie Keel, and Eva Williams; (standing) Alice Washington, Thelma Perkins, Dorothy Fleet, Rozina Wiggins, Jannie Cox, Lena Lockhart, Marian Morgan, Catherine Kraft, Claire Harvey, Inez Boston, Celestine Jemison, Alice Wilson, Meryl Hedgemon, Rachel Coleman, Avis White, Veraldine Bernard, Daisy Rucker Winbush, Thelma Tacneaux, and Earline Williams. (Both, courtesy of Mada McDonald and Thelma S. Perkins.)

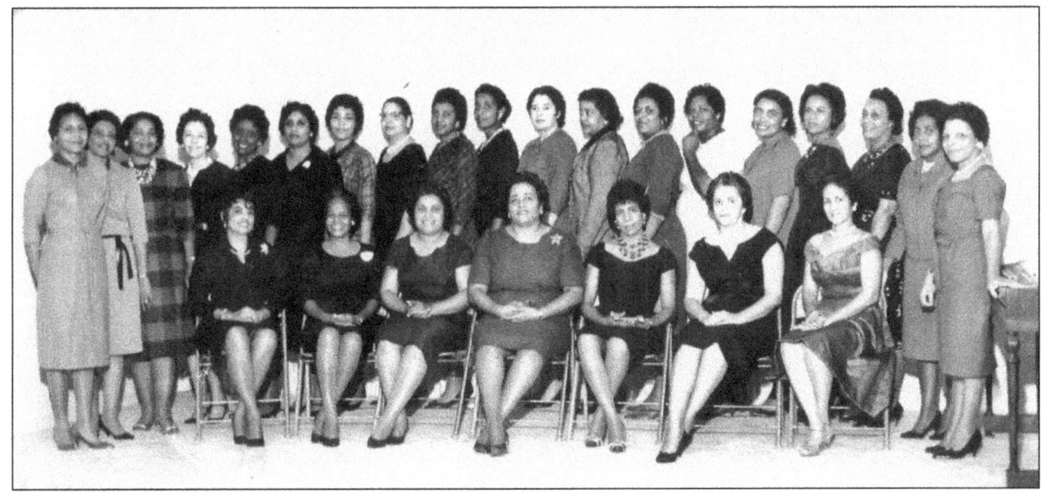

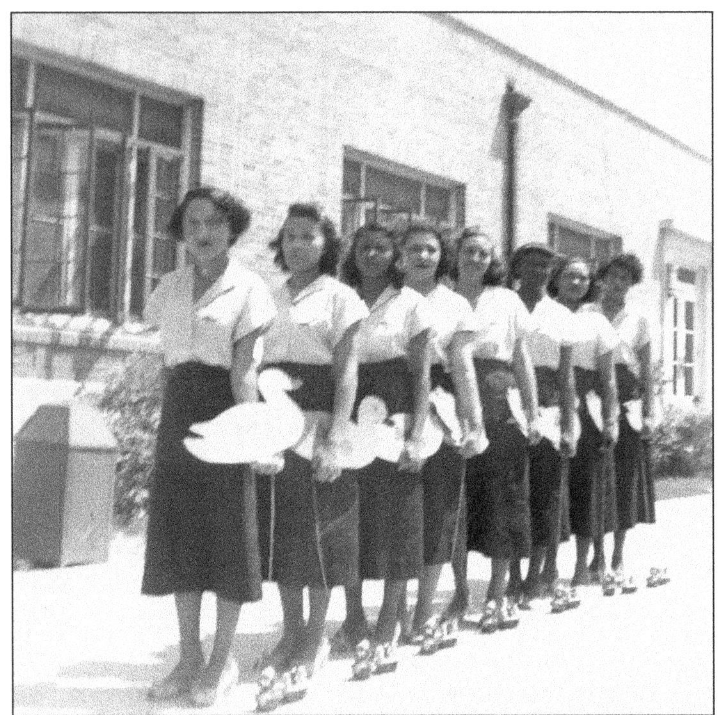

The Alpha Tau Chapter of Delta Sigma Theta Sorority was founded on June 30, 1934, on the SU campus. This chapter's seven charter members, Edith P. Balton, Zolee M. Jones, Sadie O. Keel, Sophronia Stanley Steele, Ozelle M. Taylor, Rosa L.G. Wallace, and Lucille J. Weiss, organized to serve the needs of the campus and surrounding area. The group is now one of more than 900 chapters in the United States and abroad. The white wooden ducks carried by this group of Deltas connote the duck stage within the membership pledge process. (Courtesy of Lillian S. Jackson.)

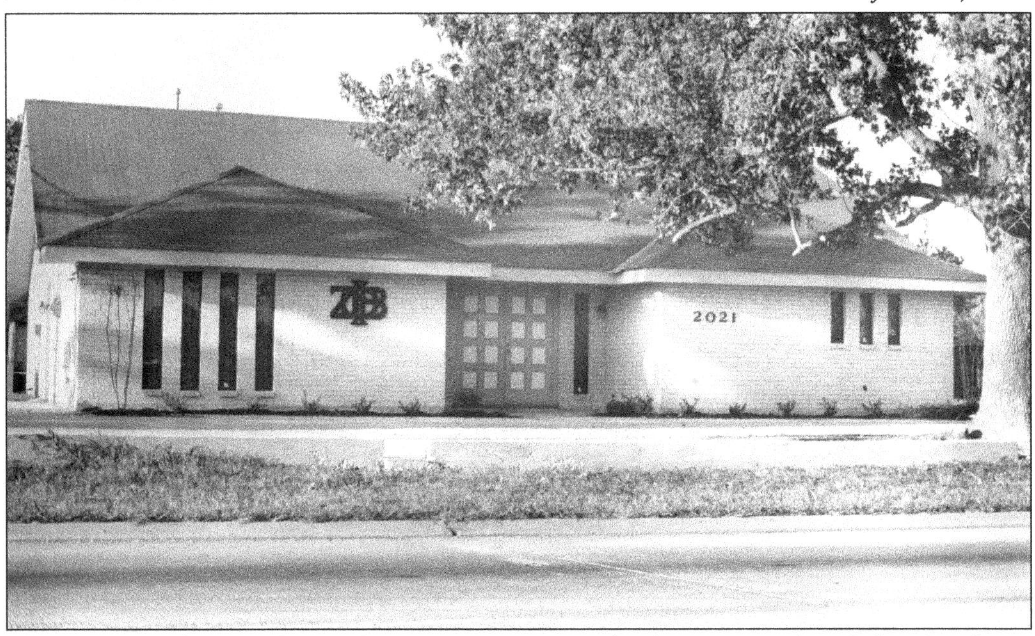

The Mu Zeta Chapter of Zeta Phi Beta Sorority was the first sorority founded at Southern, and established the first sorority house, pictured here, on Harding Boulevard. Several of the chapter's major projects and annual activities include the Stork's Nest, a program of workshops and clothing gifts for young expecting mothers; Z-Hope; Community Thanksgiving Dinner; Christmas food boxes; Fifth Grade Student Recognition Program; and Taste Fair. Proceeds from the sorority's Blue Revue Extravaganza fund scholarships and other charitable activities. (Courtesy of Geraldine A. Simms.)

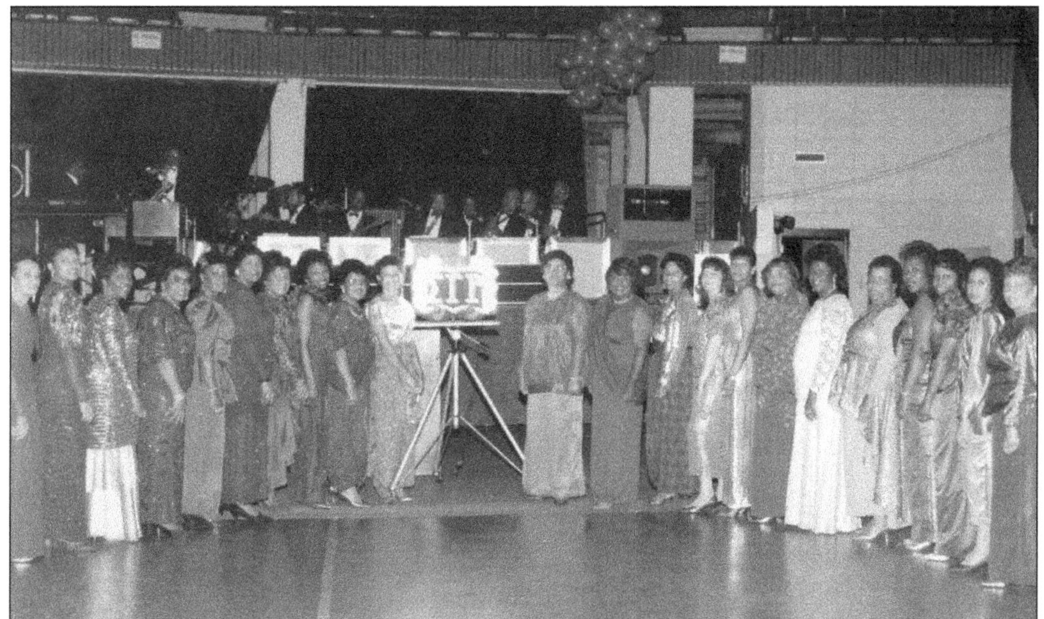

Founded in 1945, Mu Sigma Chapter is among more than 500 chapters internationally of Sigma Gamma Rho Sorority. The national chapter was founded in 1922 at Butler University in Indianapolis, Indiana. Mu Sigma sisters are pictured during the annual debutante ball, an activity that highlights the group's commitment to giving back through supporting activities of public service, leadership development, and educating youth. (Courtesy of Lillian S. Jackson.)

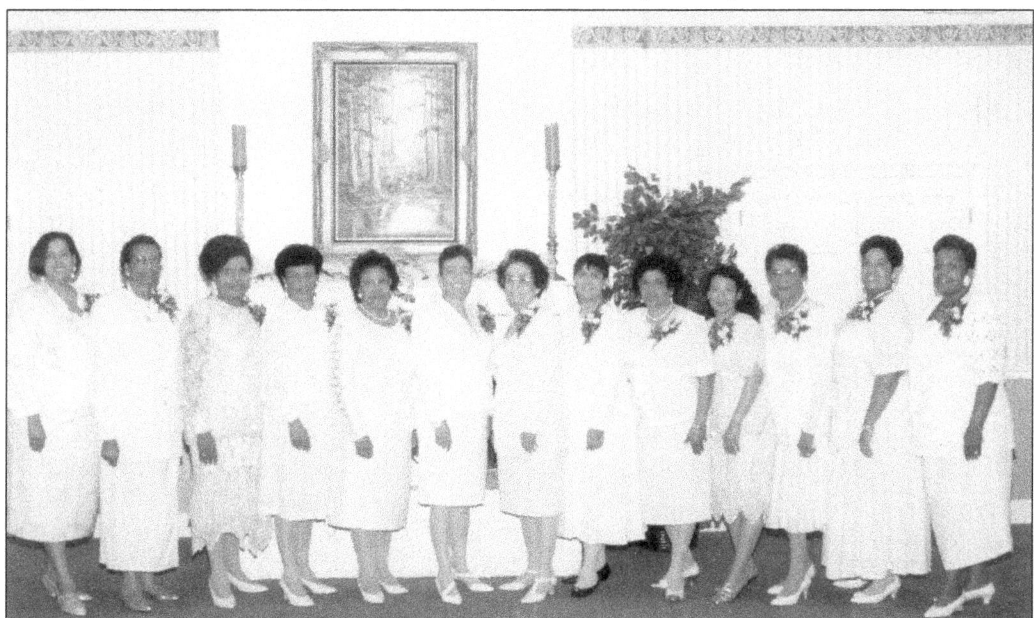

Pictured at their annual Christmas party are two active members of the twelve charter members of the Pearls Civic and Social Club: Rosemary Stacia (fourth from left) and Bertha R. Stewart (seventh from left). Members take turns hosting monthly meetings to discuss politics, the economy, and society in general. They also plan service activities such as community workshops, food giveaways, and attending various university programs. (Courtesy of Lillian S. Jackson.)

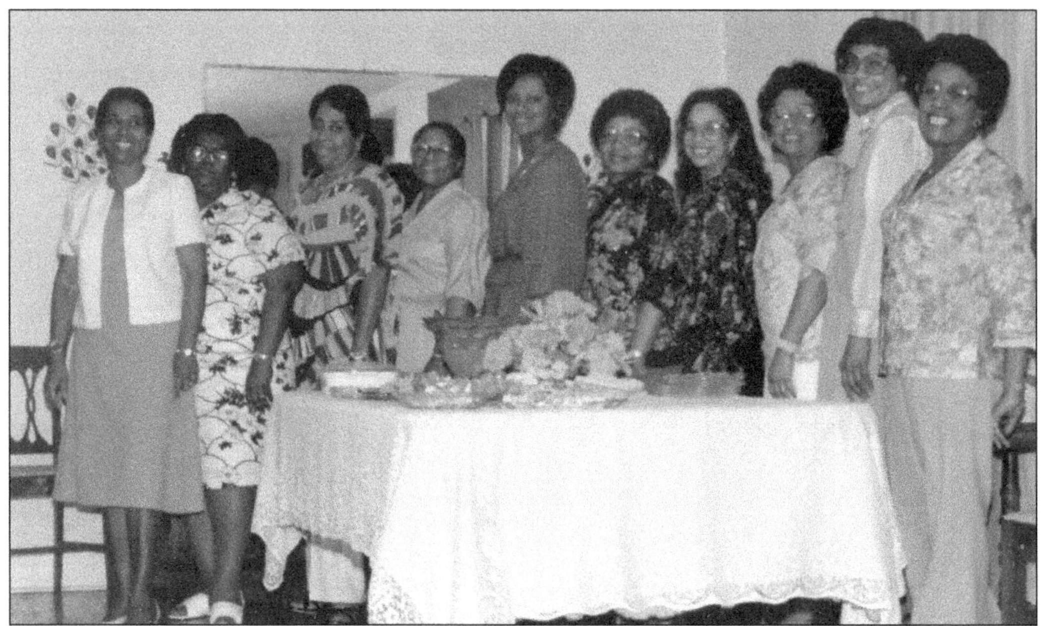

Childhood friends and Lab School classmates initiated the Women of Elegance Social and Civic Club to socialize with each other and provide assistance to the community. Pictured at a regular monthly meeting are, from left to right, Blanche Felder, Helen Grant, Lena Armstead, Eula Barnes, Willie Dean Mars, Fannie Dunn Terrell, Audrey Jackson Nabors, Gloria Handy, Willie B. Webber, and Jannie Cox. (Courtesy of Lena Armstead.)

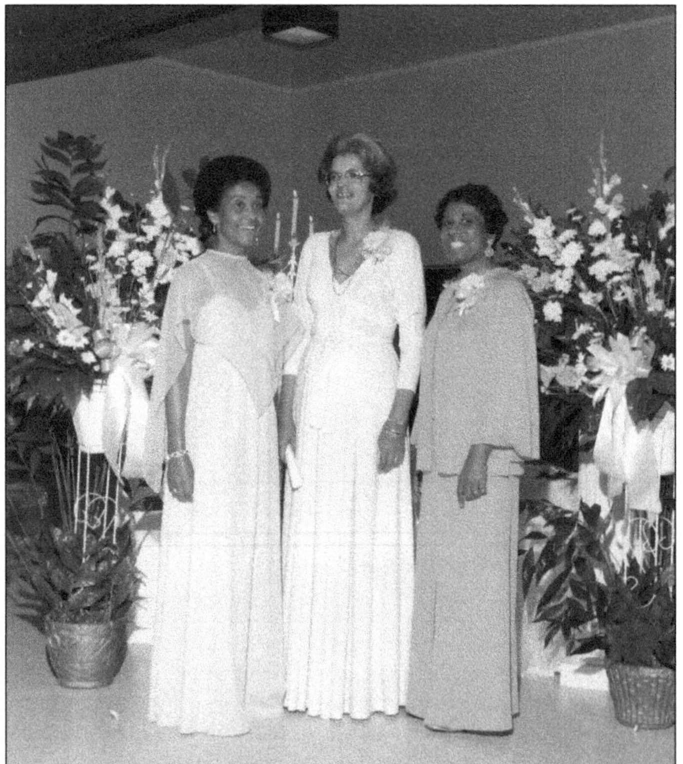

Engagement parties and wedding showers were often held in private homes and public venues in the community. Guests were welcomed and entertained by hostesses like these Southern Heights subdivision friends and neighbors (from left to right) Louise Brown, Hazel Stewart, and Blanche Felder. The three display their exquisite style and flair for putting on formal social events. (Courtesy of Muriel Felder Haysbert.)

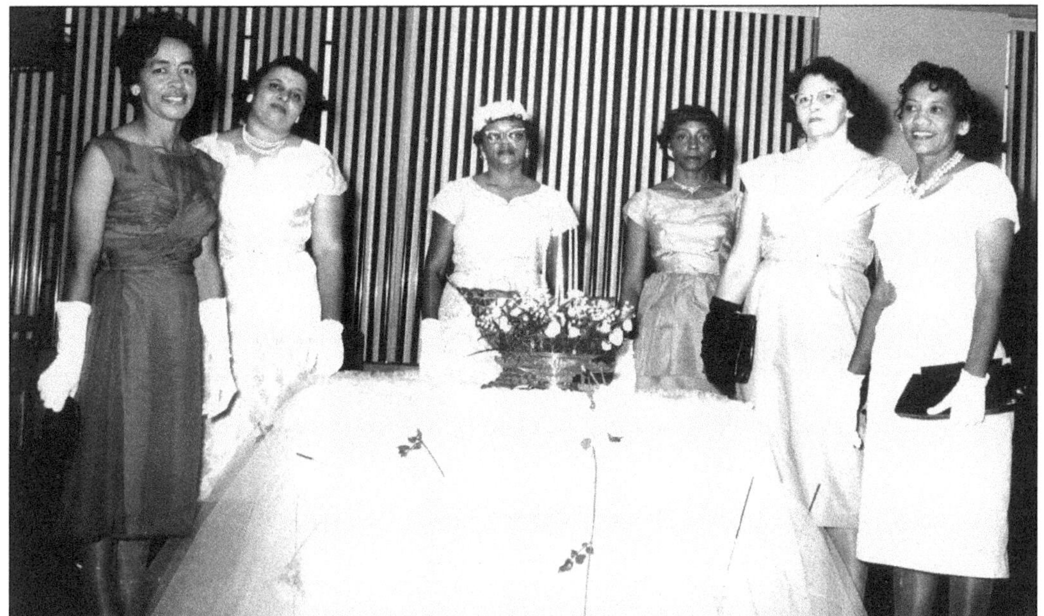

Cultural expressions are learned and preserved through the arts. Educational programs and private lessons encourage artistic excellence, and performances foster community bonding. Children of Scotlandville residents took piano lessons at the Ashford Music Studio. Southern instructor G. Kellogg also taught lessons on campus. Proud mothers are pictured at a reception after a piano recital, where their children were the stars of the show. (Courtesy of Doveal Essex.)

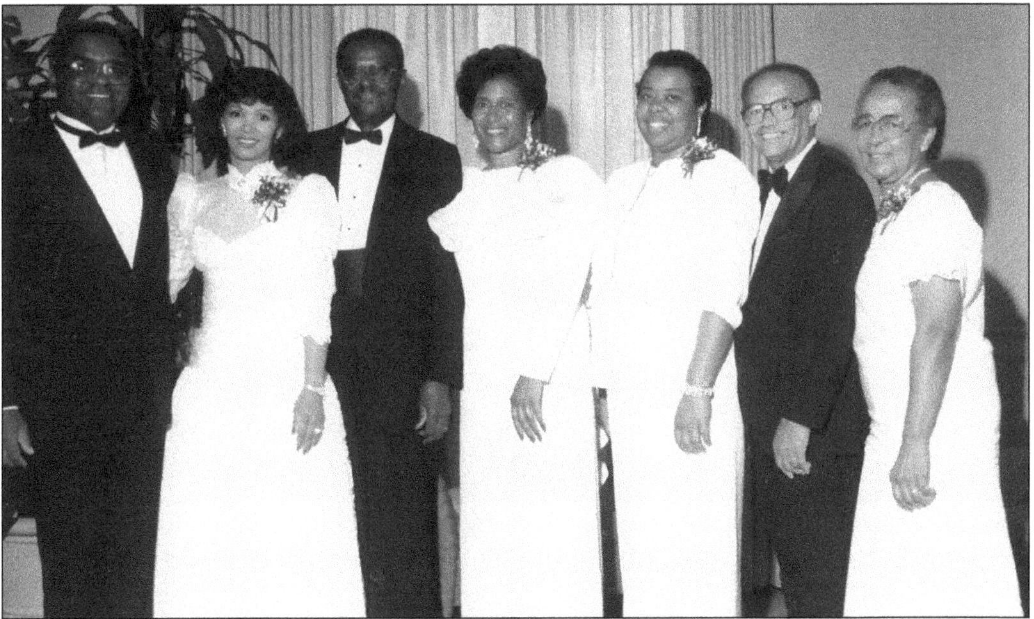

The Links Inc. is one of the nation's oldest and largest women's volunteer/nonprofit service organizations committed to cultural and economic development in the black community. The Baton Rouge Chapter of the Links was chartered in November 1964. Pictured are, from left to right, members installed in 1987 and their husbands: Roy and Effie Carter, Obie and Eula Mae Massingale, Dr. Helen Hedgemon, and Henry and Doveal Essex. (Courtesy of Doveal Essex.)

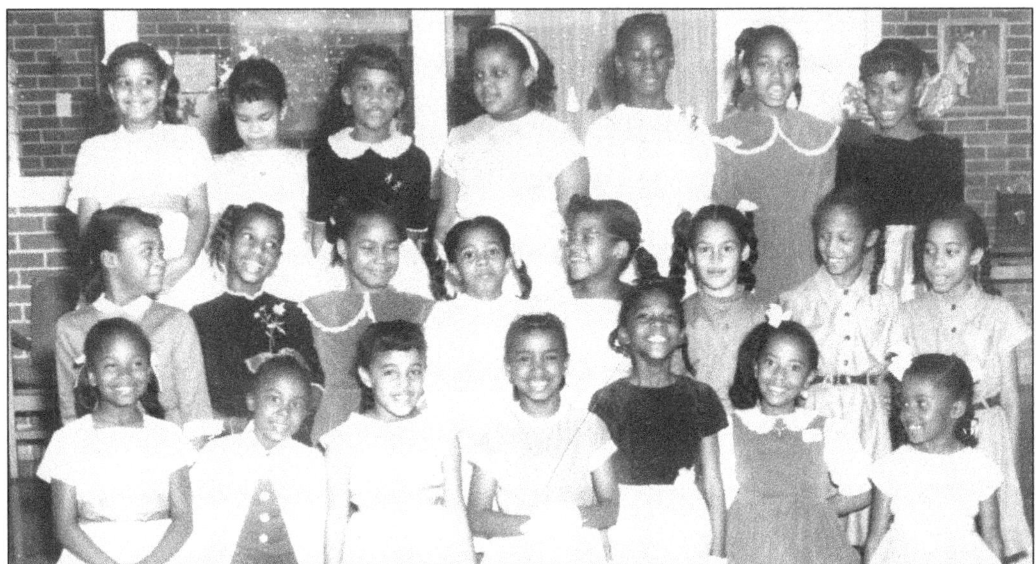

In the early 1960s, this Brownie Troop was active at Camphor Memorial United Methodist Church. Pictured are, from left to right, (first row) Debra Jefferson, Charnette Amacker, Pamela Dawson, Muriel Felder Haysbert, Robbye Lynn Thomas, Teri Carter, and Jannette Cox; (second row) Dianne Clark, Denise Baranco, Janice Jenkins, Gail Ann George, Beverly Robinson, Vallory Simms, Lydia Lawrence, and Olga Hayward; (third row) Vanessa Gray, Denise Davis, Karlene Crawford, Althea Yancy, Eunice Moore, Dianne Jenkins, and Lois Reese. (Courtesy of Muriel Felder Haysbert.)

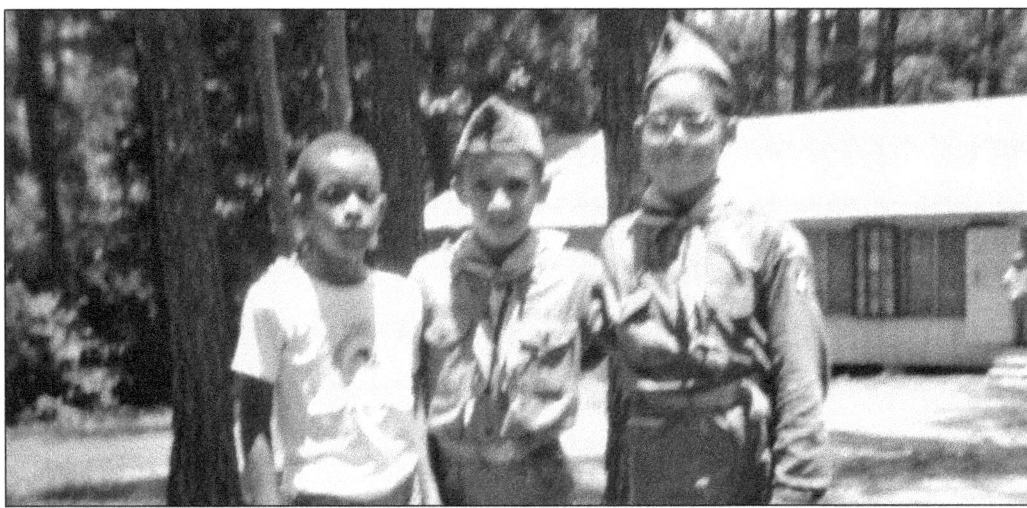

Boys Scout and Cub Scout troops in Scotlandville were based in sponsors' homes. One such sponsor was Scoutmaster Vanue Lacour, a member of the original law faculty at Southern. Scoutmaster Lacour, a resident of Southern Heights, took his troop members hiking, where they used the scouting handbook in their study of nature. Summer trips to Camp Carver, one of five black scouting camps in Louisiana, provided a week of sleeping in tents, cooking on campfires, and working to accumulate merit badges. Swimming lessons also were given in the shallow water of a rushing river, with roped boundaries and chaperones strategically placed to prevent the boys from accidentally washing downstream. Pictured from left to right are James Slaughter, James Cook Jr., and Raynaud Henton. (Courtesy of Dr. James Carl Cook Jr.)

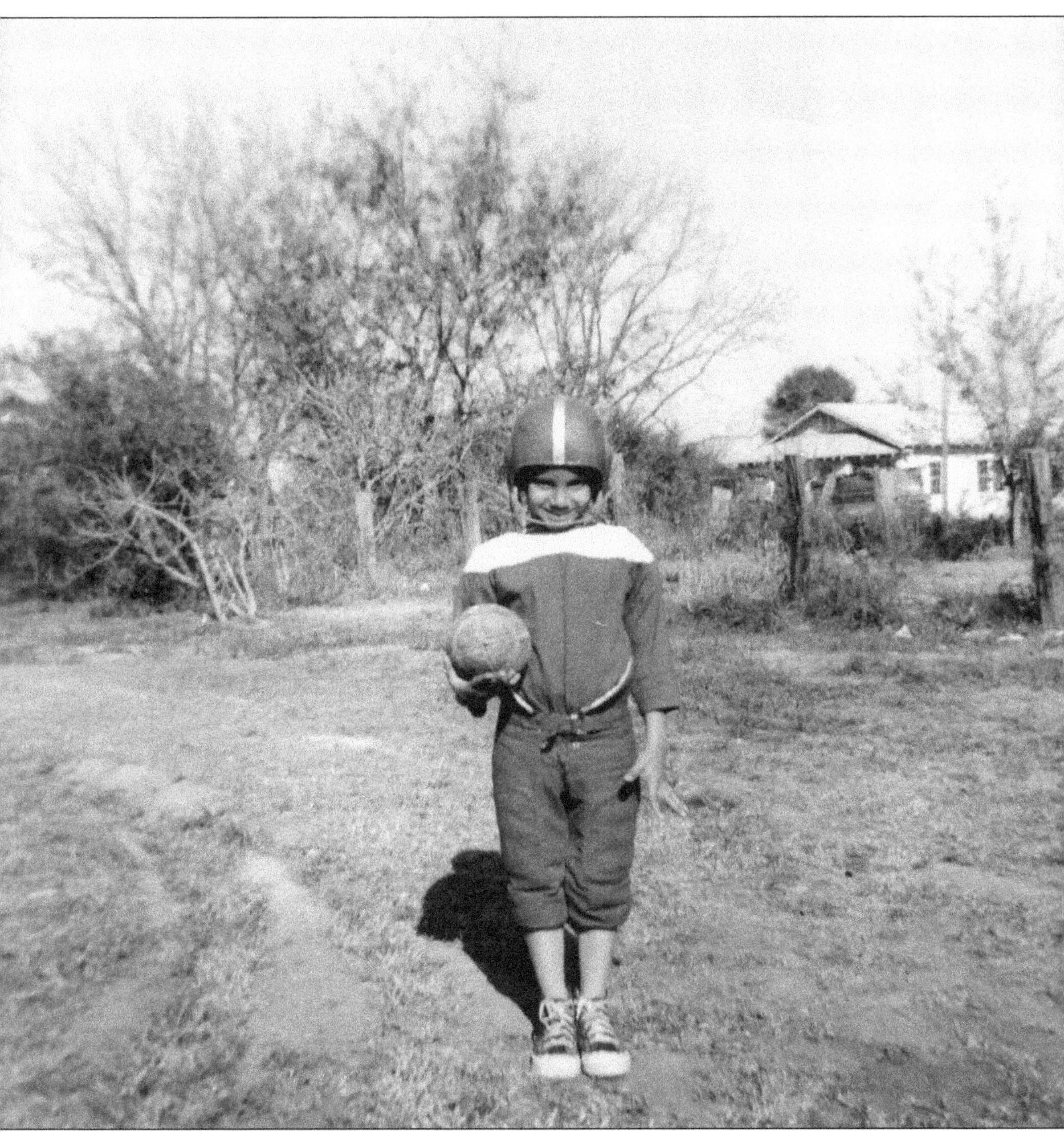

Sandlot baseball, basketball, and football occurred whenever and wherever teams could gather, including in the backyard of the Cook family home on Scenic Highway and Fairchild Street. Many players had their own uniform, pads, and helmets. Harold Cook enjoys his sports uniform and gear that came on Christmas delivered by that ultimate sponsor, Santa. He and his friends also loved track and field, holding impromptu relay races in the streets or climbing the fence of the Southern football stadium to use the track to try the hurdles and the high jump and pole vault pits. James Jr., currently a cardiologist in Oregon, was on the Little League Reds team sponsored by a Scotlandville merchant. University employee Benjamin Kraft was a coach of another team on which two of his sons played, one of whom is now Dr. Leon Kraft, a Baton Rouge cardiologist. (Courtesy of Dr. James Carl Cook Jr.)

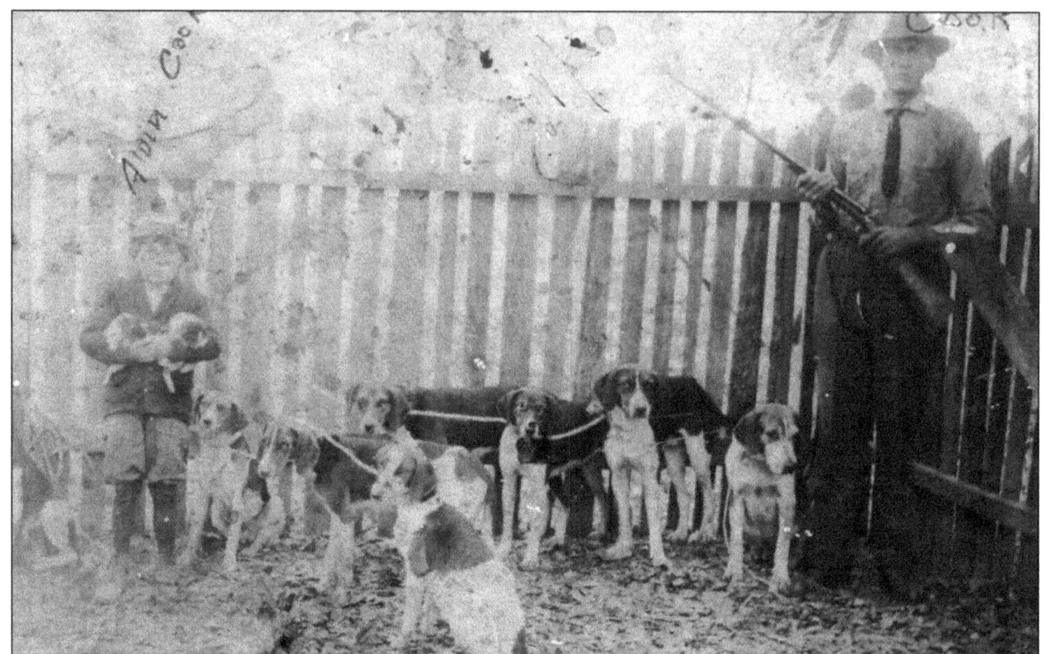

Hunting was a popular pastime for many men of Scotlandville as it was for many throughout Louisiana. Avid hunters Bertrand and nephew Alvin Cook are pictured with their hunting dogs and pups. These hounds have a great sense of smell and tracking instinct, which make them suitable for hunting rabbit, deer, and other small game native to Louisiana. (Courtesy of Dr. James C. Cook Jr.)

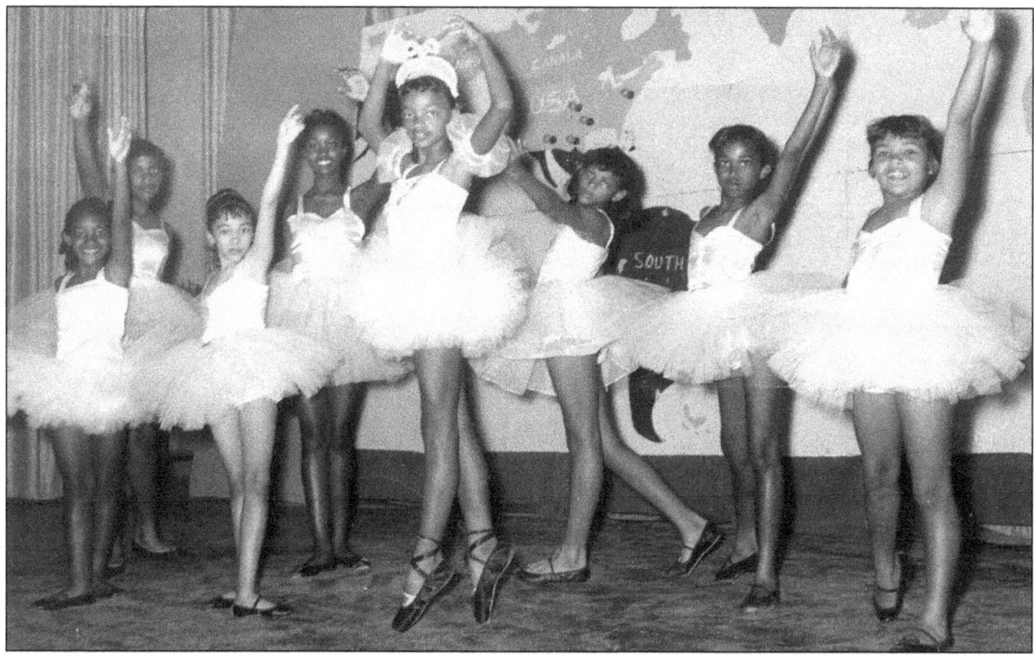

Providing an environment where artistic expression and talent thrives, educational dance programs, whether in public or private classes, were viewed as important for healthy emotional and intellectual development. Students of instructor Nell Rose Jordan (also coach of cheerleaders and girls' sports at Southern Lab) showcase their talents at a dance recital. (Courtesy of Doveal Essex.)

Six

Neighborhoods

Not Just Housing, But a Way of Life

The individual who was responsible for developing the area or village of Scotlandville, according to Southern University's president, Felton G. Clark, was a man by the name of A.R. Bacon, who "operated excursions from New Orleans to Scotlandville in an attempt to sell the property," Clark said.

"If you boarded the train in New Orleans with your destination Scotlandville, you were given a free ticket." His real estate venture involved buying a ticket for a drawing of two lots. One's name was written on the ticket and if drawn, he or she became a landowner. "Certainly, some persons came for this opportunity and more. The "more," Clark felt, was "a need for expression. . . . They came to get a cross section of abilities developed that would enable them to stand tall in the walk of life."

When they moved their families to Scotlandville, fathers and mothers were optimistic that they could secure jobs and their children could receive an education. So, many families came from East Baton Rouge Parish; from southern areas, such as Dutchtown and Burtville; and from the north of Scotland, from areas such as Baker and Zachary, Louisiana. They came and forged a partnership with the university, not by design, but by drift. University officials and the townspeople were risk-takers.

Clark called movements of persons to Scotland "Cycles of Migration." He stated: "The early cycle of migration was principally from the adjoining parishes of West Baton Rouge [towns of Port Allen and Brusly], and East and West Feliciana parishes. More specifically, they moved from Clinton, Fulsom, Norwood, Lindsay, St. Francisville, and Tunica."

In later years, migrants came from northern, eastern, and western points and from the adjacent states of Arkansas and Mississippi and even from the farther states of Alabama, Tennessee, Kansas, Illinois, and California. Similarly, white families moved into the community from places either within the parish or the adjoining ones.

By 1977, Scotlandville was the largest African American community in Louisiana. No doubt because of Southern University, the community was reported to have the distinction of having the highest number of individuals with doctorates per capita of any community in the state. It was fully incorporated into Baton Rouge in the mid-1980s.

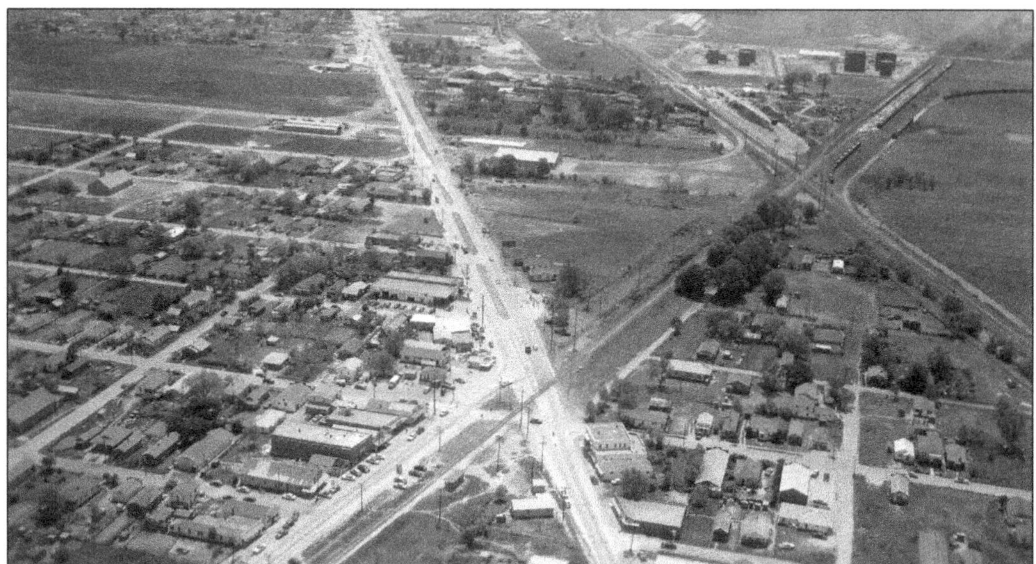

This aerial view of Scotlandville was taken in 1954. Sociologist Jerome J. Salomone in 1971 reported that Scotlandville divides into "four discernible human ecological areas" that include uniquely mixed-income housing. Area one, south of Harding Boulevard, included the first planned neighborhood for middle and upper middle-class residents; settled earlier, area two, between Harding and Rosenwald Road, was densely populated, with less planning; area three, north of Rosenwald and south of the industrial tank farms, was sparsely populated, converted from open farmland to residential; and area four consisted of old housing structures between Scenic Highway and the Louisiana and Arkansas railways. The mixed-income housing throughout was said to be encouraged by Dr. J.S. Clark to help all areas. (Courtesy of the Louisiana State Library.)

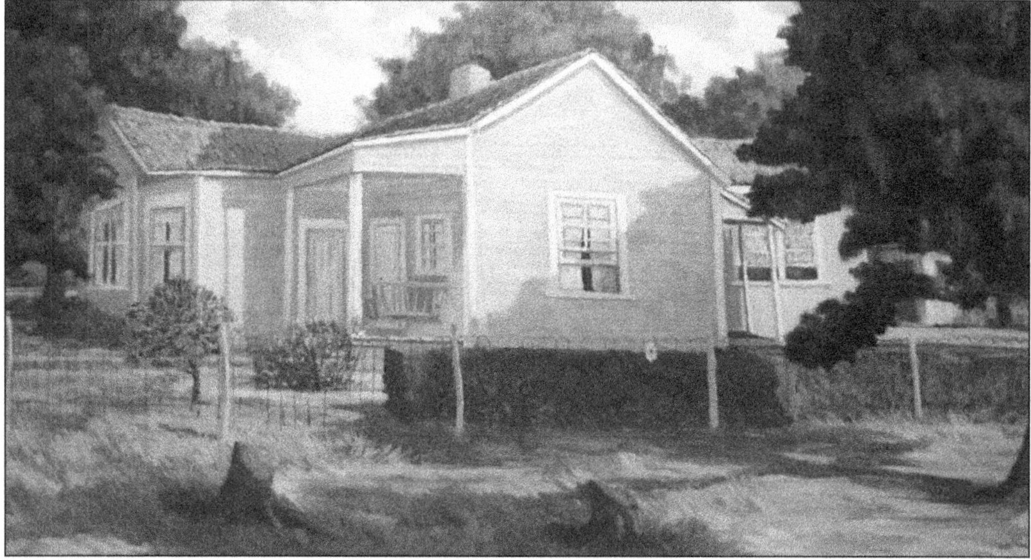

Salomone also states in his report that Scotlandville residents tended to be property owners. The William "Dreher" Kelly residence on Rosenwald Street is represented in this drawing. Portions of the family property would later provide the site for the Kelly Terrace Housing Development, one of 13 family developments owned and maintained by the East Baton Rouge Parish Housing Authority. (Courtesy of Nolan Kelly.)

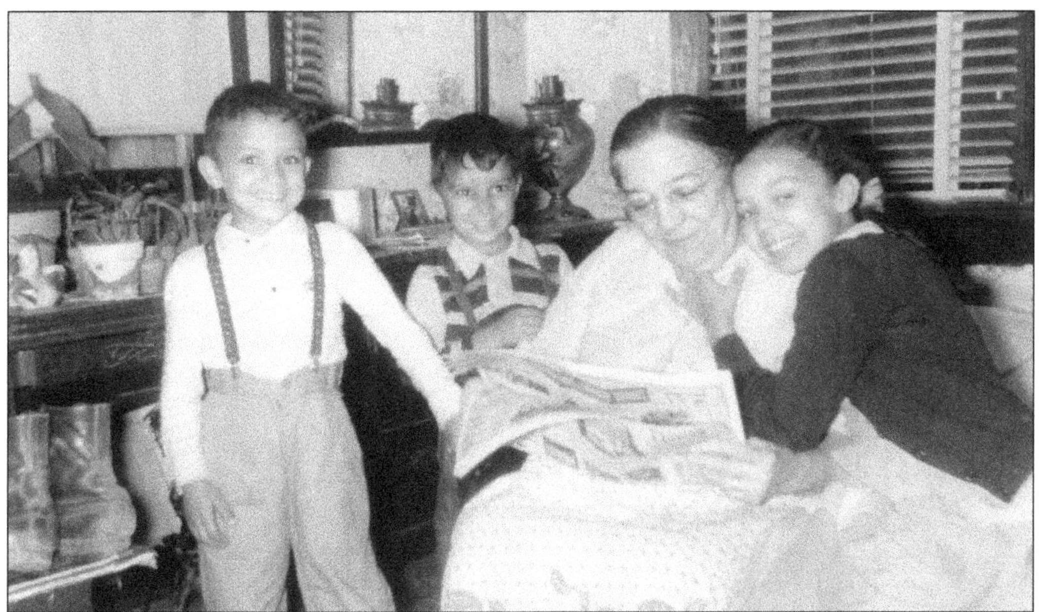

Ora Hunter Cook is pictured with her grandchildren Linda, at right, and Harold and James Carl Cook, in the bedroom of the Cook family home. The house was a wood structure on the corner of Scenic Highway and Fairchild Street. James Alexander Cook and his siblings and friends built the home during the Great Depression. James and Ora Cook reared five children in that home. After Alvin, Bessie, Harold, and Carl left home, the last remaining sibling, James Carl, took care of his parents and the property until their deaths. James and his wife, Ruby, are pictured below in their living room dressed for one of the regularly recurring balls held in Baton Rouge and New Orleans. Some notable entertainers who played for these events included Louis Armstrong, Duke Ellington, and Cab Calloway. The early remembrances of their oldest son, James Jr., are of eight people living in that house with four bedrooms and one bathroom. (Both, courtesy of Dr. James Carl Cook Jr.)

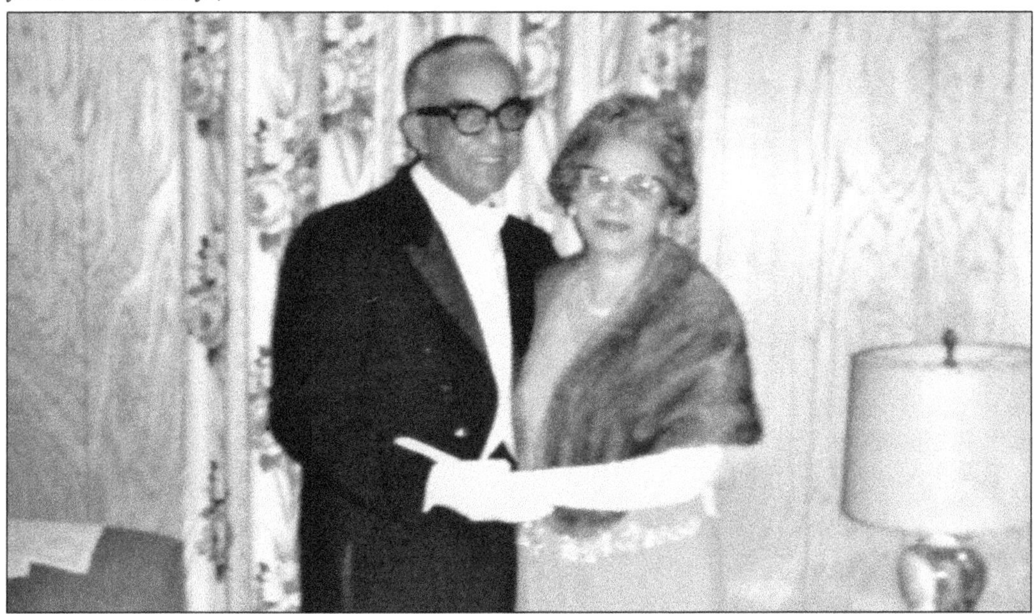

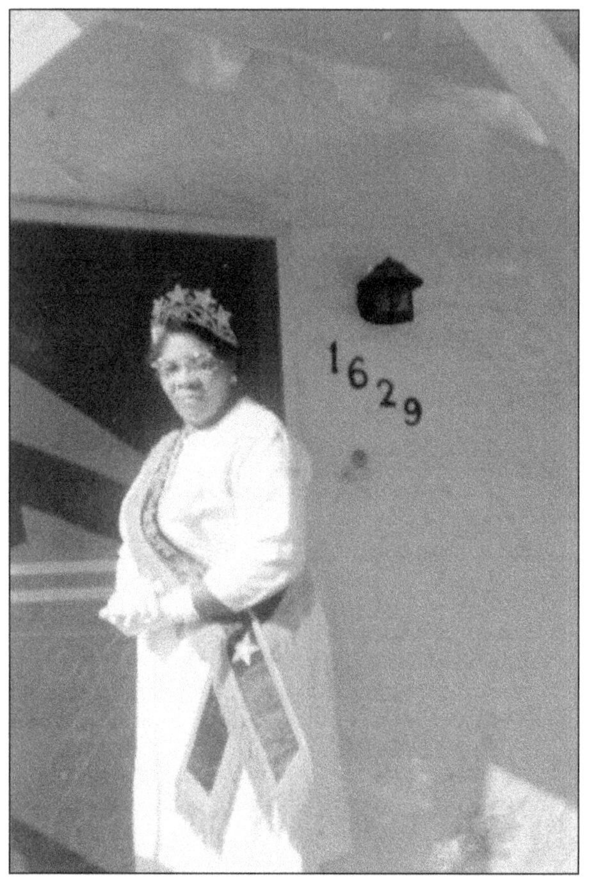

Wood-framed houses with occasional ones made of stucco, aluminum siding, and brick scattered among them were the typical Scotlandville housing in the early years. Ella Brazier, a member of Mount Pilgrim Baptist Church and the Order of the Eastern Star, is pictured at left at her home on Central Road. Brazier, a dormitory matron at Southern for more than 30 years, had five children who became Southern graduates. Knowing firsthand the need for student housing as the university's enrollment grew, she opened her doors to students, as did a number of faculty and staff members who lived near the campus. Covered doorways or porches for protection from inclement weather were another feature of many homes in the area. Below is one of the first brick homes in the Scotlandville area with a resident enjoying his front porch. (Left, courtesy of Eric Pugh; below, courtesy of Shirley Kelly Hammond.)

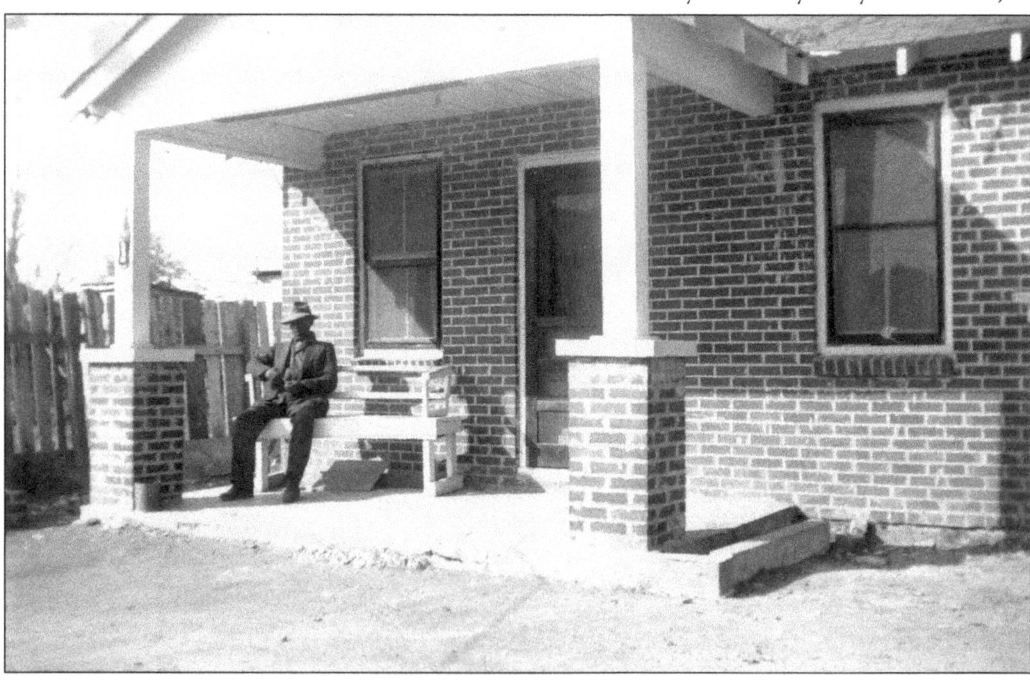

Louis Green moved his family to the old Harding Field when he accepted employment at the Juvenile Detention Center. His children, Marjorie Ann and Sandra Marie, liked to skate the wide streets of the World War II military airfield. (Courtesy of Marjorie A. Green.)

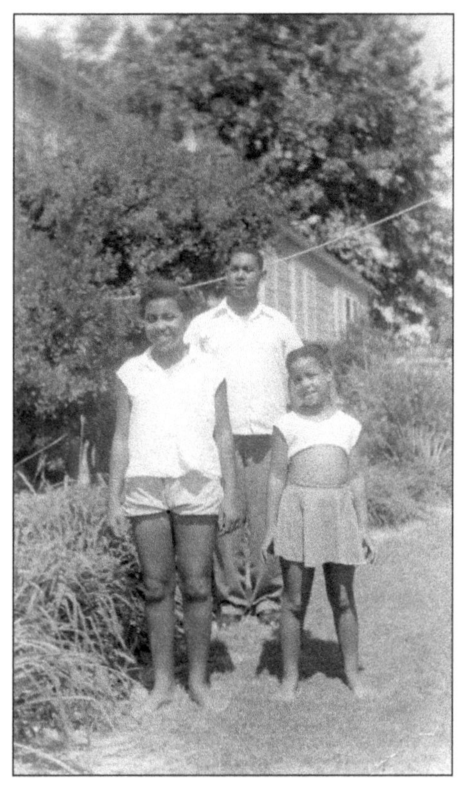

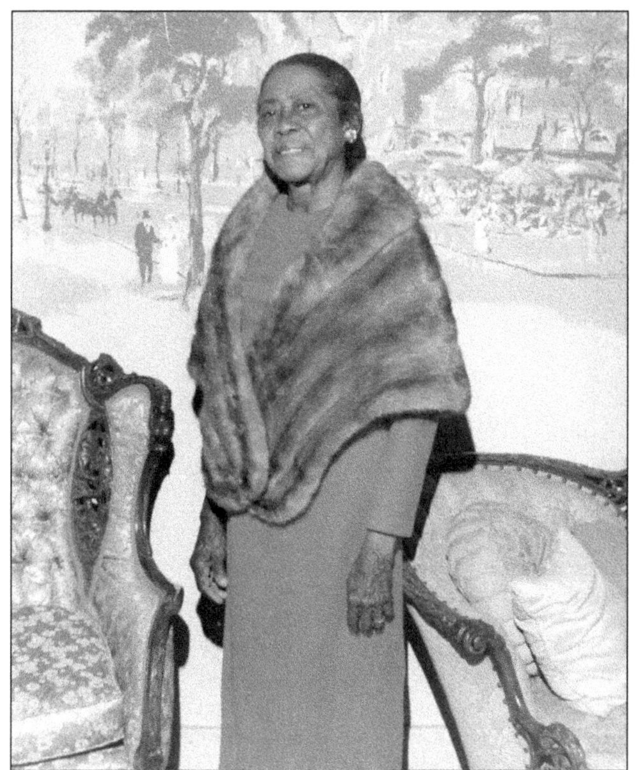

Amanda Kelly Mackie is pictured preparing to host a party in her home on Scenic Highway. She moved into the neighborhood after owning several residences throughout the Scotlandville area. Mackie displayed in her home the works of SU faculty artists, including the wall mural behind her. (Courtesy of Beverly A. Vincent.)

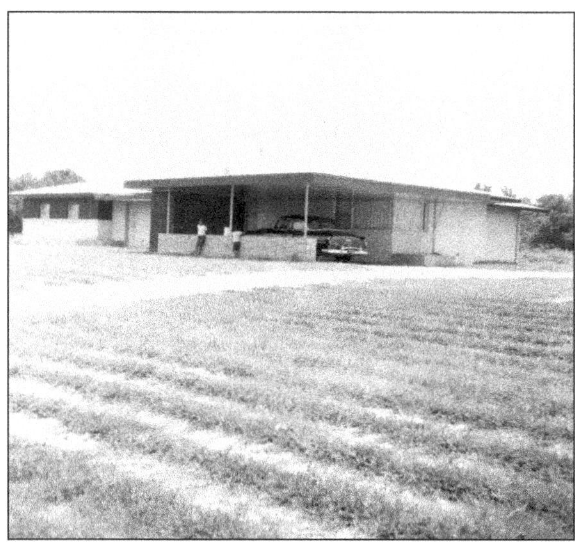

The community's second residential area, Southern Heights, was established in 1952. Developers including Horatio C. Thompson, Brady Kennedy, and Collis Temple Sr. purchased strips of land and subdivided them into lots that were sold to potential homeowners. Architects included architect Henry "Dickey" Thurman, SU dean of engineering; and James Hunt, supervisor and administrator. Contractors included Lewis Darensbourg, Calvin Thierry, and J.C. "Pappy" Patin. Pictured is a ranch-style brick home, featuring a large front yard able to accommodate a side-entry garage. (Courtesy of Phyllis White.)

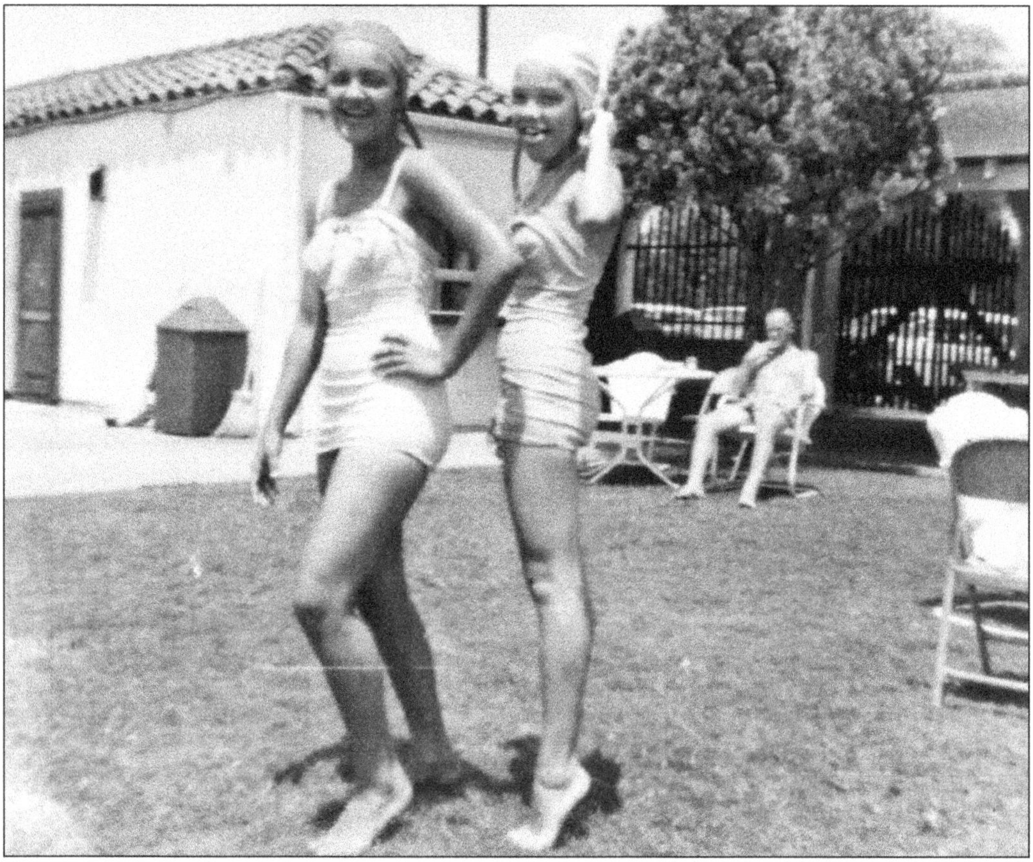

Prof. William H. Fletcher, seated in the background, a visual artist on the faculty at Southern, had the only private in-ground swimming pool in Southern Heights. Professor Fletcher also had a tennis court on his property behind the home. University colleagues and neighborhood friends regularly joined him there. Here, his daughter and her classmate, one of the daughters of James Cook Sr., enjoy themselves poolside. (Courtesy of Dr. James Carl Cook Jr.)

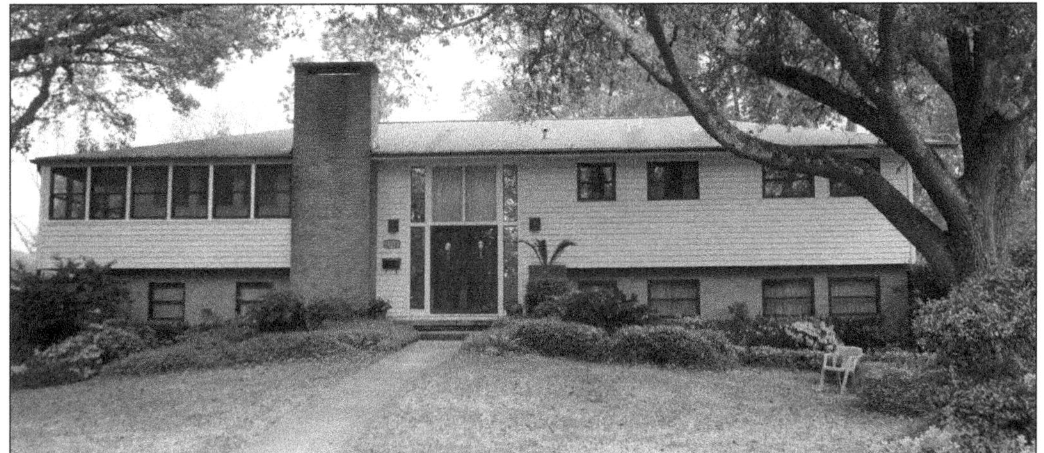

Retired educators Henry and Doveal Essex have lived in Southern Heights on Seventy-ninth Avenue for almost 60 years. According to Henry, they paid $14,500 for their initial Crawford home, a prefabricated house manufactured by the Crawford Corp. in 1954. Later, the couple built and purchased on the same street one of the first bi-level homes in the subdivision. (Courtesy of Steve Jarreau Photography.)

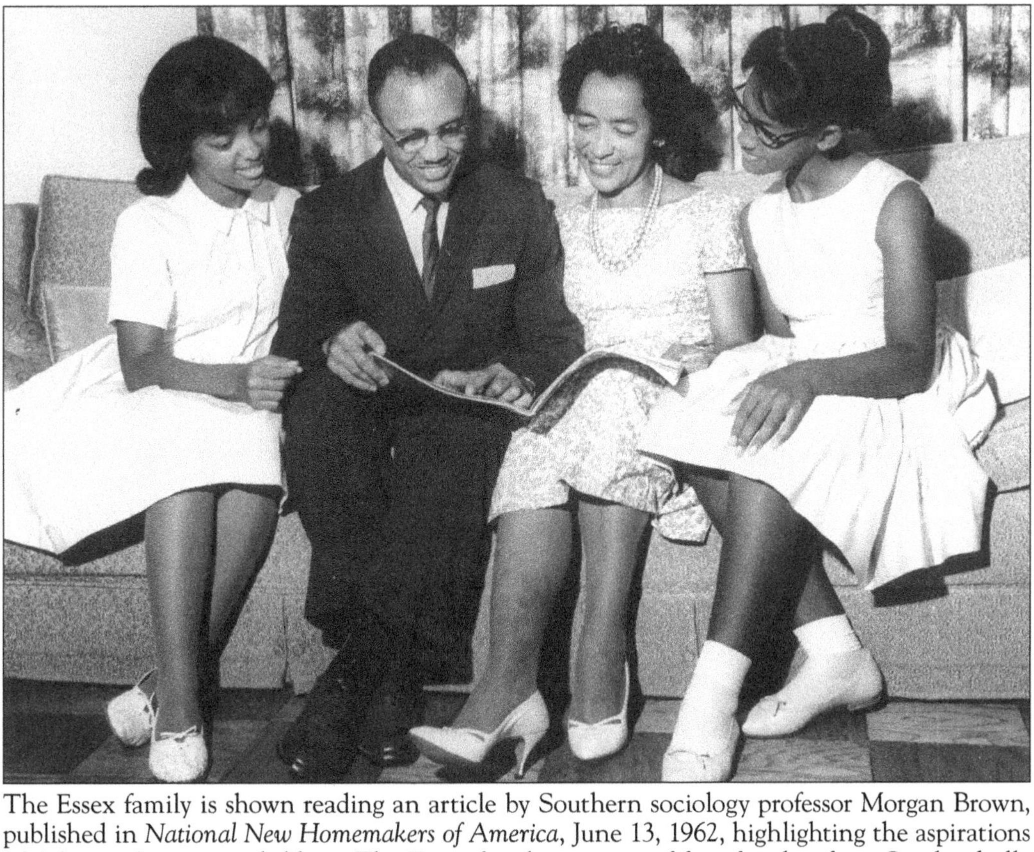

The Essex family is shown reading an article by Southern sociology professor Morgan Brown, published in *National New Homemakers of America*, June 13, 1962, highlighting the aspirations of African American children. The Essex family was one of four families from Scotlandville featured in the article. Pictured are, from left to right, Connie, Henry, Doveal, and Sylvia Essex. (Courtesy of Doveal Essex.)

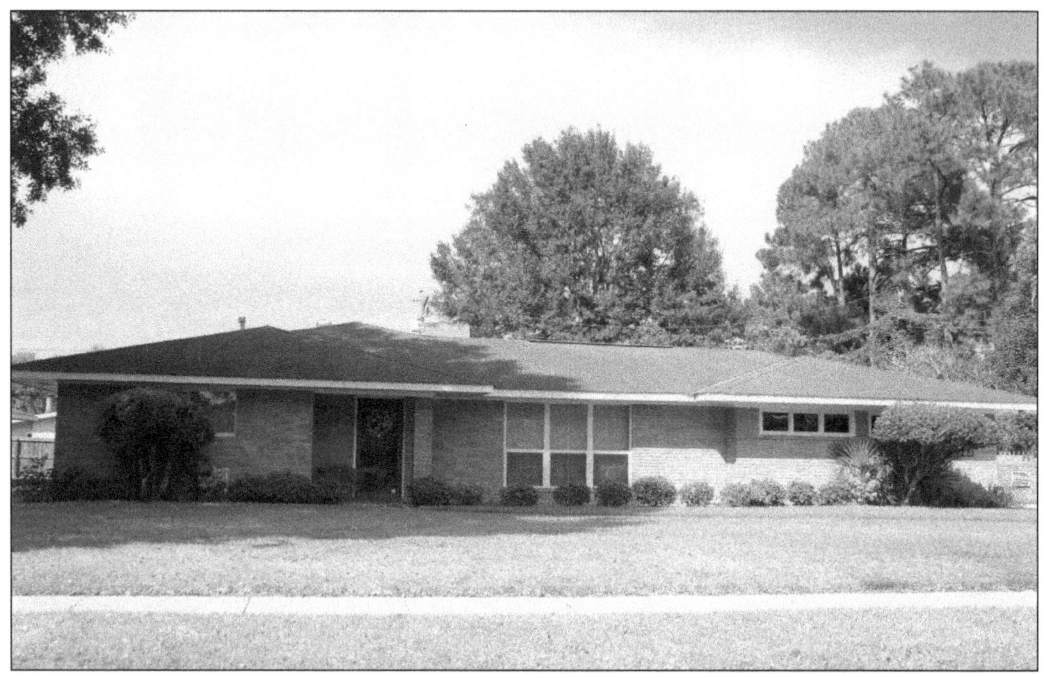

In 1963, Advance Inc. developed the first Scotlandville subdivision with sidewalks, Park Vista. The first filing attracted property owners Eddie Beauchamp, Louis Mobley, David Wheelock, George Rogers Clark, Eddie Johnson Sr., Hebert Collins, Calvin Thierry, and Charley Causey. Charter officers of the homeowners association, Park Vista Improvement Association, established in 1965, were Pres. McHenry Jackson; Vice Pres. Robert Andrews; recording secretary Percy Milligan; corresponding secretary Bertha Stevenson; treasurer Tolar White; and parliamentarian Press Robinson. (Courtesy of Aolar A. Wilson.)

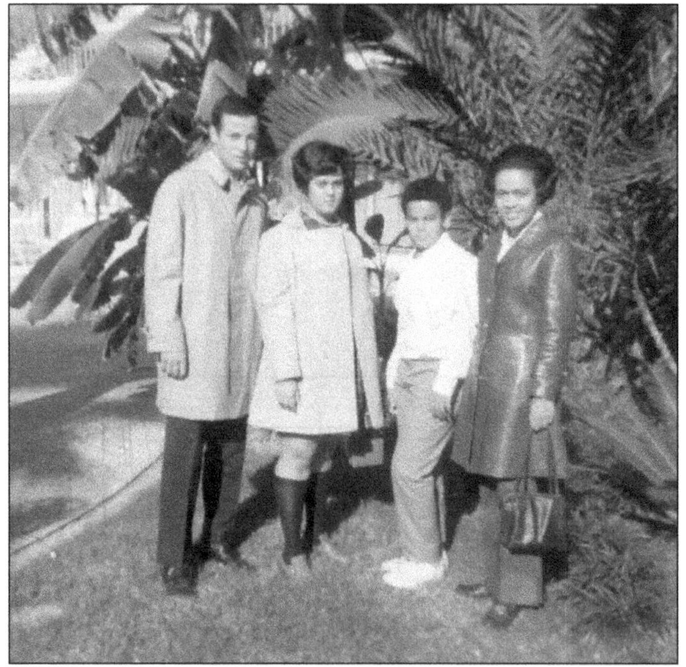

Otis D. Stewart, a US postal employee, and his wife, the former Bertha Robinson, one of the first teachers at North Scotlandville Elementary School, reared four children in their residence on the north side of Harding Boulevard. Pictured on the lawn of their home are the Stewart children, from left to right, Otis Jr., Alyce Maria, Michael Keith, and Brenda Diane. All chose careers in education and law, and three are Southern graduates, including Brenda S. Birkett, retired SU vice chancellor for academic affairs. (Courtesy of Bertha R. Stewart.)

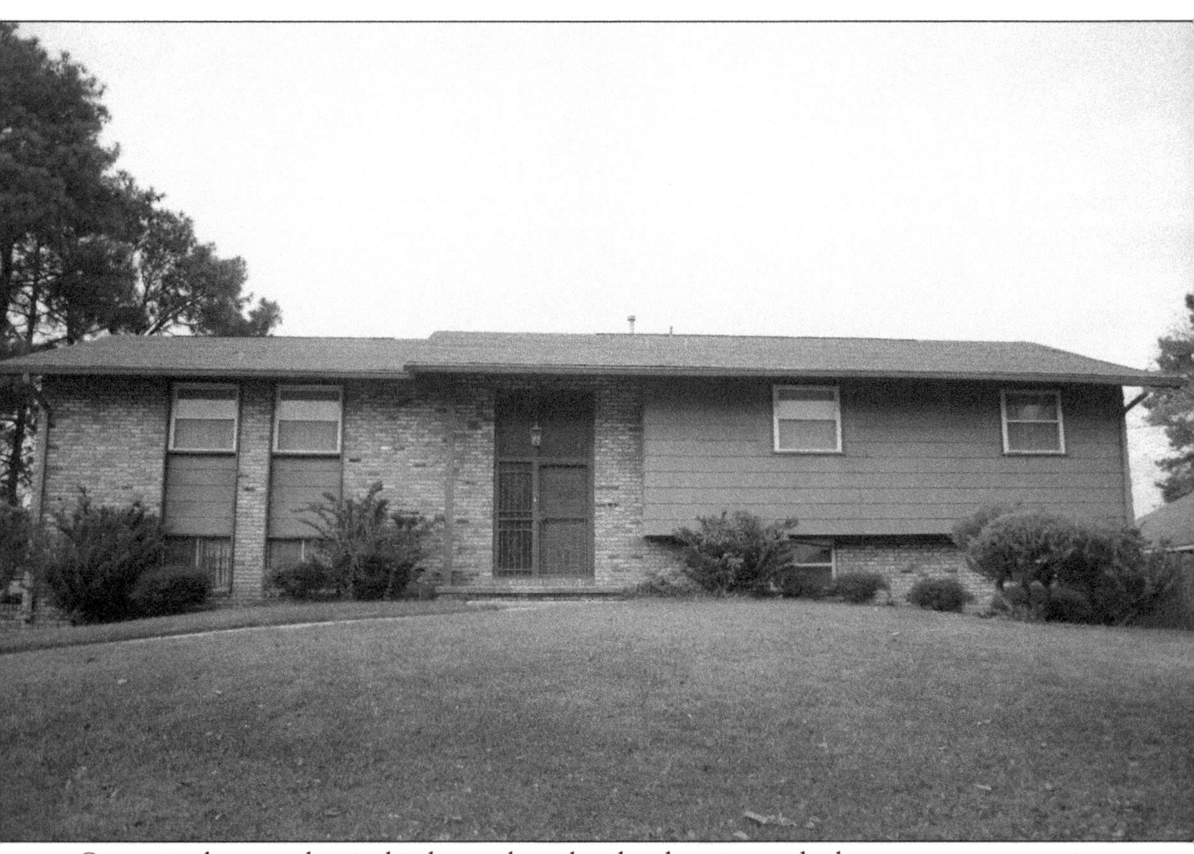

Careers in the petrochemical industry, the railroads, education, and other government agencies, along with self-employment, provided significant incomes for the time. Housing was available in a wide variety of price ranges and styles in subdivisions developed during the 1960s and 1970s. These residential housing developments included Pryce Place, off Elmgrove Garden Drive; Crestworth subdivision, west of Scenic Highway off Blount Road; and Golden Ridge, east of Highway 19 off Blount Road. Golden Ridge no longer exists, as the property owners were bought out with the expansion of Ryan Airport. This home in the Crestworth subdivision is the residence of Nathan Wilson, a 1963 graduate of the SULC who opened his law practice in Scotlandville. (Courtesy of Steve Jarreau Photography.)

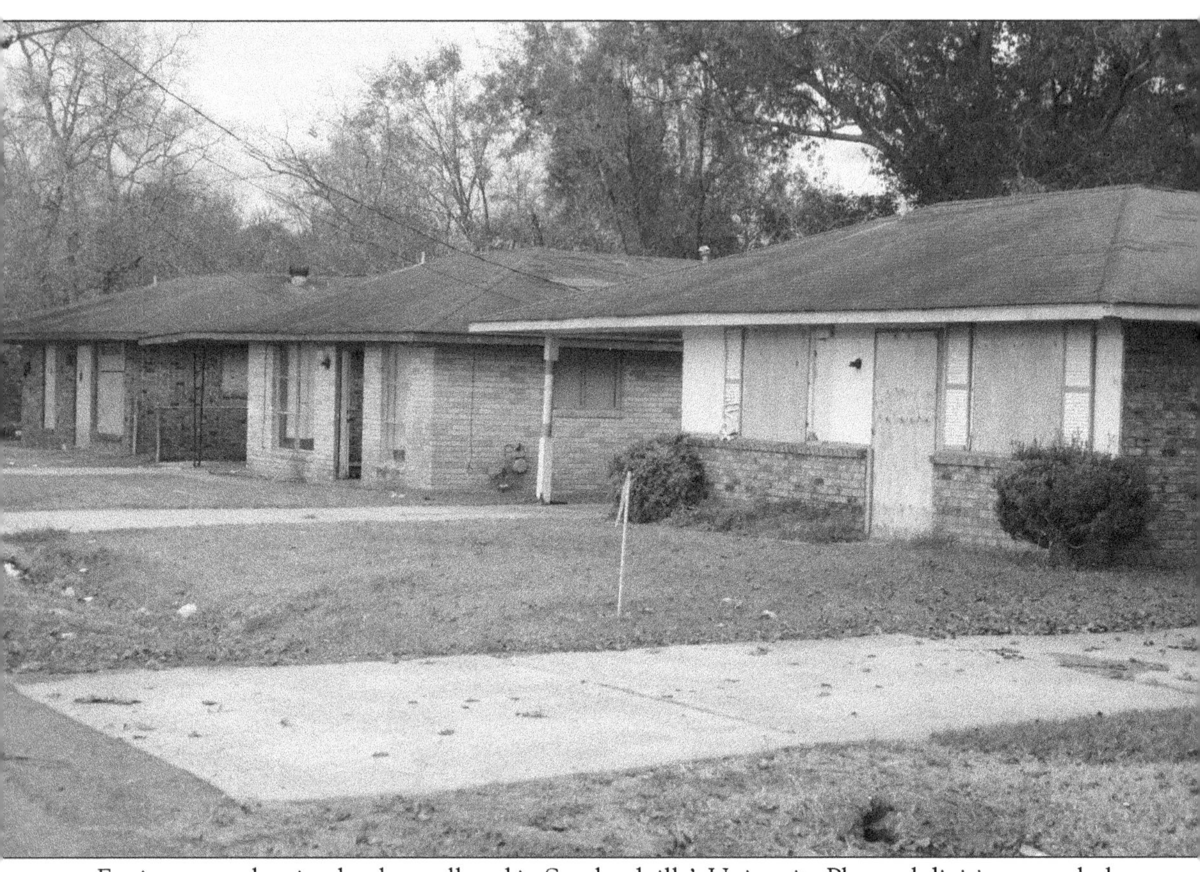

Environmental racism has been alleged in Scotlandville's University Place subdivision, popularly called "the Avenues," adversely affected by the expansion of nearby sewage treatment facilities. Environmental racism refers to institutional rules, regulations, policies, and government or corporate decisions that deliberately target communities of low income and residents of color for locally undesirable land uses. Lawsuits began in 1996. Only recently has the Metro Council governing board voted for a buyout of roughly 47 homes near the treatment plant. Many of the homes boarded up and awaiting demolition were once built and owned by university faculty, refinery workers, and other taxpayers. Residents who remain suffer from the obnoxious odor. Vacant lots remain vacant, as no one is buying or building in the area. (Courtesy of Steve Jarreau Photography.)

Seven

POLITICS

MAKING A WAY OUT OF NO WAY

In 1900, Scotland was a part of the Third Ward of East Baton Rouge Parish. This ward encompassed a large section of the parish, and Scotland is not specifically labeled on the 1900 US Census. According to author Ruby Ennis in *Generation's Recordings*, "as with African Americans throughout America during the era of Jim Crow, African Americans in Louisiana were treated as second class citizens. The farming families of Scotlandville, who were victimized by this system, would become part of a continuing activism, which was known as the civil rights movement, for positive changes in securing equal justice for all."

Following World War II, returning African American soldiers began to put into practice the "Double V" campaign, victory at home as well as abroad. Veterans like Acie J. Belton of Scotlandville, discharged from the military in 1946, immediately launched a voter registration drive. At the time, there were only 137 black registrants in East Baton Rouge Parish, mostly Republicans. Louisiana was an overwhelmingly Democratic state at the time, which meant that the black voters only had a voice in the presidential race every four years.

For black residents, long shut out of government, participation in back-room politics was their only means of seizing any political power, said Belton in a 1991 interview. Political power meant jobs, better education, and respect, much of what was missing in the black community when Belton became a political and civil rights activist.

Between 1946 and 1949, the number of registered black voters in the parish increased to more than 2,000, mostly from the Scotlandville area. The Second Ward Voters League, a black political organization long led by Belton that still endorses candidates, was born during that registration movement. From representatives and senators in the statehouse to mayor-president of the city and parish, from marching for environmental and social justice to sitting in for desegregation, Scotlandville residents' involvement in politics—from that time to the present—has been varied and strong.

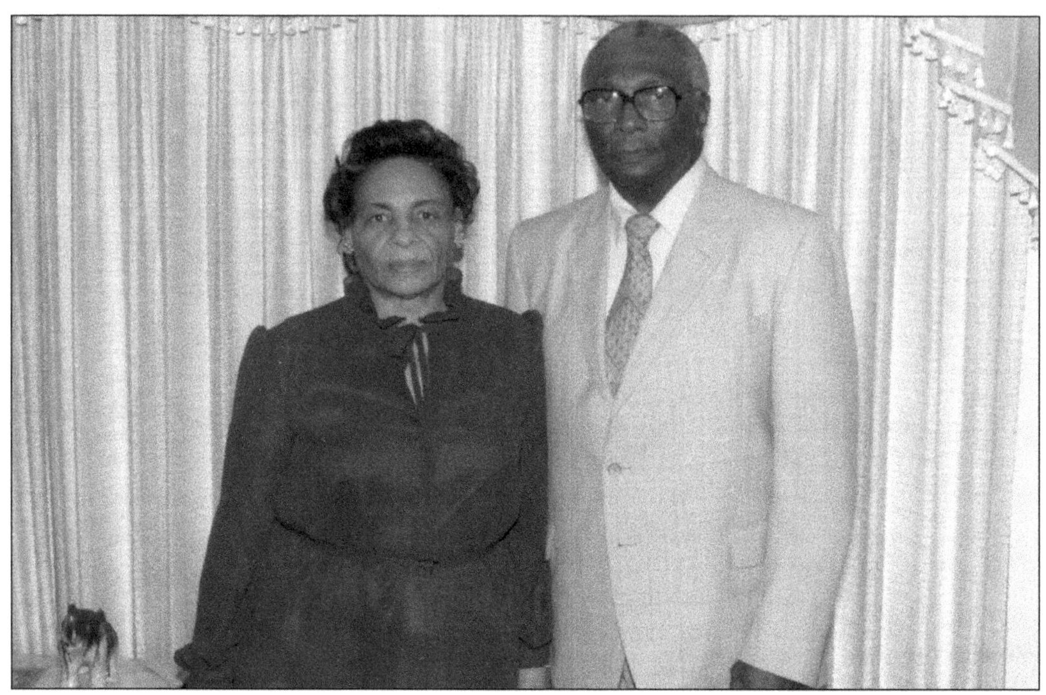

World War II veteran and Exxon refinery worker Acie Belton (1916–1995) is pictured with his wife, Sallie. In 1946, Belton became founding president of the Second Ward Voters League, which initiated a successful campaign to increase the number of registered black voters. Other league founders were Nicholas Harrison Sr., Raymond P. Scott, O.M. Amacher, A.A. Lenoir, T.J. Jordan, Arthur Franklin, Henry Franklin, G.B. Robinson, Bonnie V. Moore, Simon Lewis, and Vaughn Parris. (Courtesy of Dr. Wesley J. Belton.)

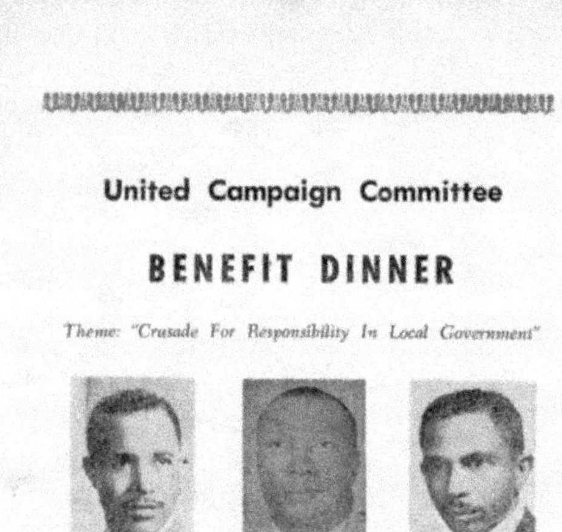

United Campaign Committee

BENEFIT DINNER

Theme: "Crusade For Responsibility In Local Government"

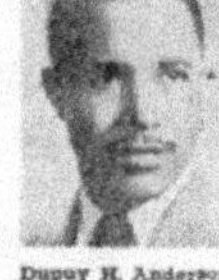

Dupuy H. Anderson
Candidate For
School Board
Ward I

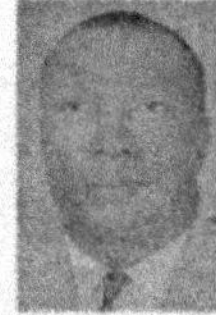

Acie J. Belton
Candidate For
School Board
Ward II

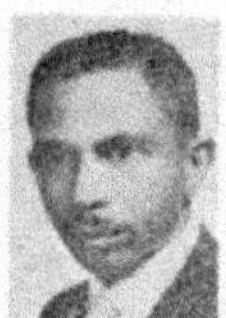

Johnnie A. Jones
Candidate For
District Judge

SCOTLANDVILLE SENIOR HIGH SCHOOL DINING ROOM

SATURDAY, JULY 14, 1962

Eight o'clock p.m.

This flyer announces a fundraising event for black Democratic candidates Dr. Dupuy Anderson, Acie Belton, and Johnny Jones. Anderson was a dentist, whose daughter Freya would in 1964 be among the first African American students to successfully sue LSU for admission as undergraduates. Jones, a member of the 1953 SU law class, practiced civil rights law and was involved with many legal cases to advance equal rights for all. He was later elected to the Louisiana legislature. (Courtesy of Dr. Wesley J. Belton.)

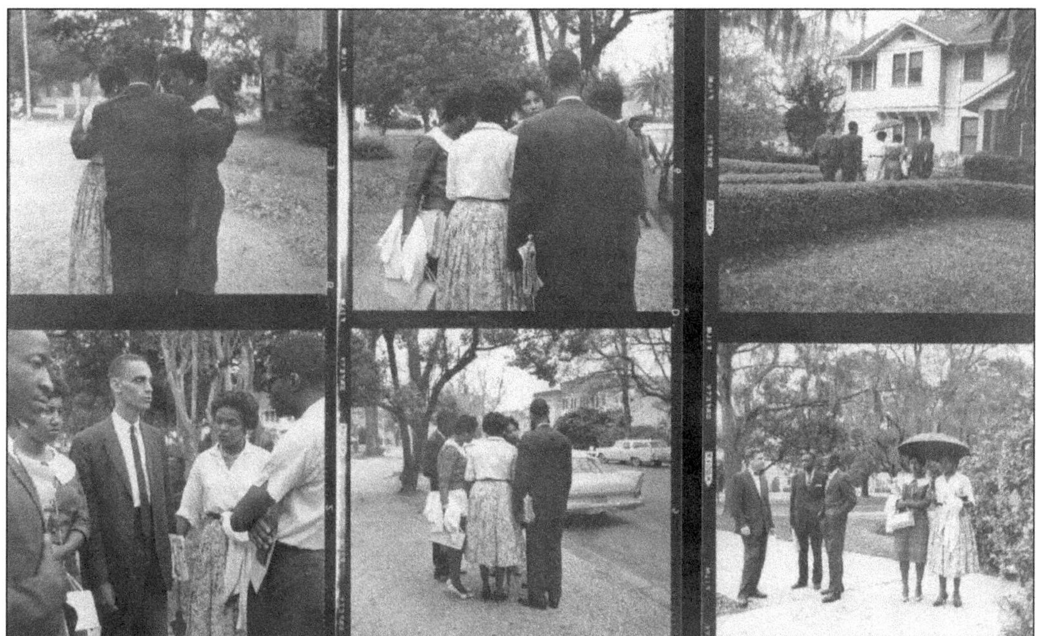

In March 1960, sixteen SU students conducted sit-ins at Kress Department Store, Sitman's Drugstore, and the Greyhound Bus Station in Baton Rouge protesting racial segregation laws. The students were promptly arrested, charged with disturbing the peace, indefinitely suspended from Southern, and convicted in state district court. Their convictions were overturned in the first sit-in case heard by the US Supreme Court. Historians noted that sit-in protesters, including Vernon Jordan and John Garner of Scotlandville, helped crystallize great moral force and gave the civil rights movement renewed vitality. Southern law graduate Johnnie Jones was one of the attorneys for the students. These students could be whom Pres. John F. Kennedy was speaking of in his June 1963 national address: "Those who do nothing are inviting shame as well as violence. Those who act boldly are recognizing right as well as reality." (Above, courtesy of Dr. Janette Hoston Harris; below, courtesy of The Archives Department/John B. Cade Library/Southern University and A&M College.)

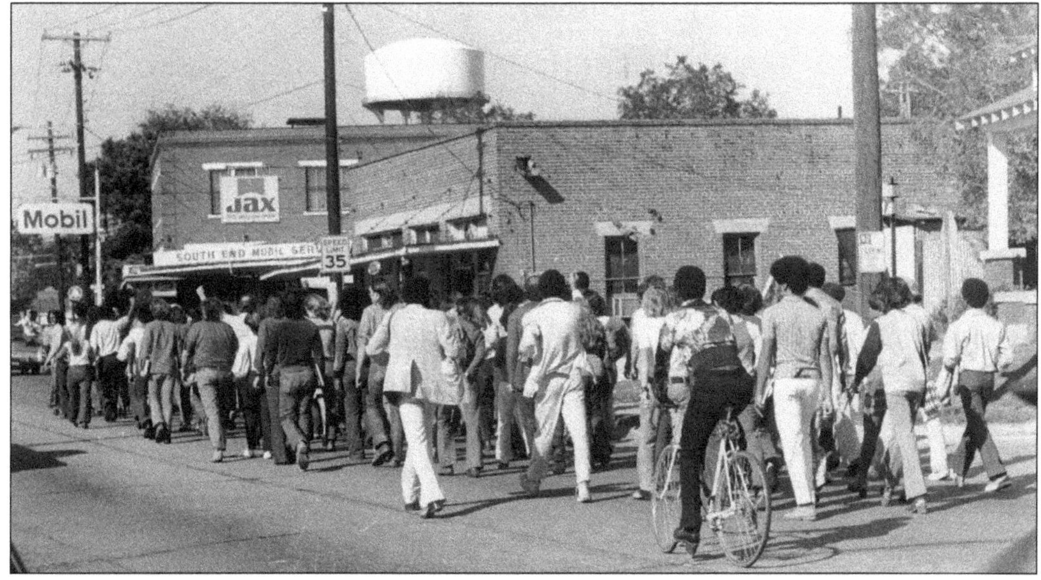

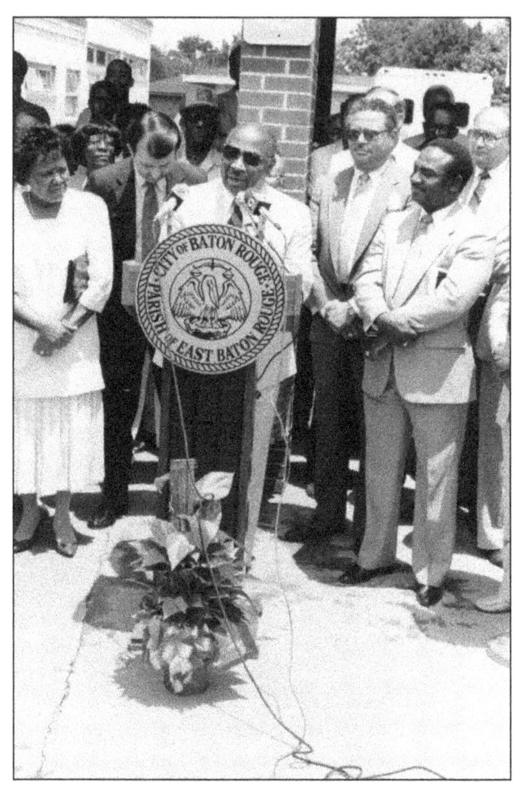

New fire chief Thomas Woods (1935–2011) gives his acceptance speech at Scotlandville Fire Station, where he began his career in 1956, while attending Southern. Pictured are, from left to right, his wife, Ola Jeanlouis Woods; Mayor-President Pat Screen; Woods; and Louisiana legislators Joseph Delpit and Richard Turnley. In addition to becoming Baton Rouge's fire chief in 1986, the US Army veteran also served as first fire chief for the City of Baker, as a member of the Baton Rouge Metro Council, the first African American East Baton Rouge Parish and City of Baton Rouge mayor-president pro-tempore, vice chairman of the Baton Rouge Metropolitan Airport Commission, chairman of Capital Improvement Committee, and president of the Black Caucus of the Louisiana Police Jury Association. He is pictured below standing before the portraits of Baton Rouge fire chiefs before him. (Both, courtesy of Ola J. Woods.)

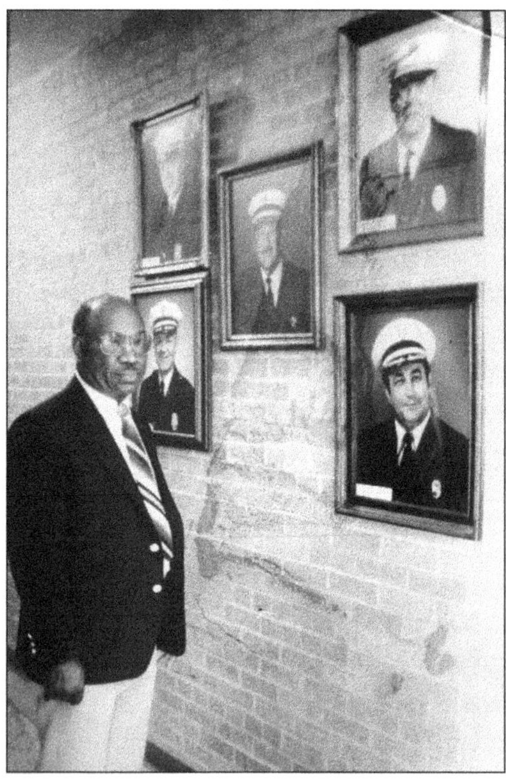

Press L. Robinson retired in 2005 as a Southern University administrator and professor of chemistry after 41 years of service. Robinson's tenure included leadership in academic and student affairs at the system level and on the campuses of Baton Rouge, New Orleans, and Shreveport. The first African American elected to the East Baton Rouge Parish School Board in modern times, he served 22 years, including one term as vice president and three terms as president. Robinson is currently president of Duplichain University. (Courtesy of Press L. Robinson.)

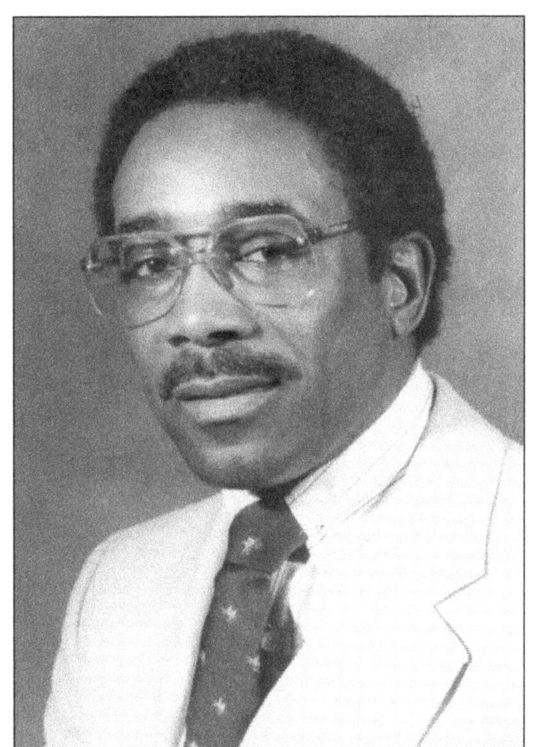

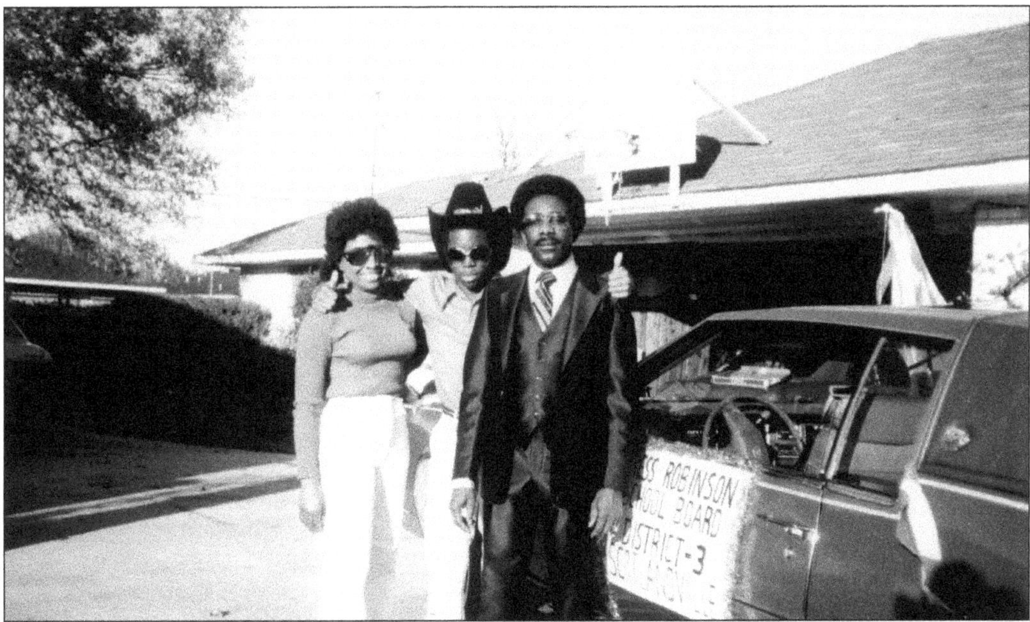

Press L. Robinson, at right, with his wife, Ruth W. Robinson, and son Press L. Robinson Jr., prepare for participation in the Southern University homecoming parade in the Scotlandville area. Homecoming and holiday parades provided opportunities for political candidates to gain greater visibility in the community as well as greet constituents. These festive events brought together all segments of the community for special moments of fellowship, and enhanced vital relationships. (Courtesy of Press L. Robinson.)

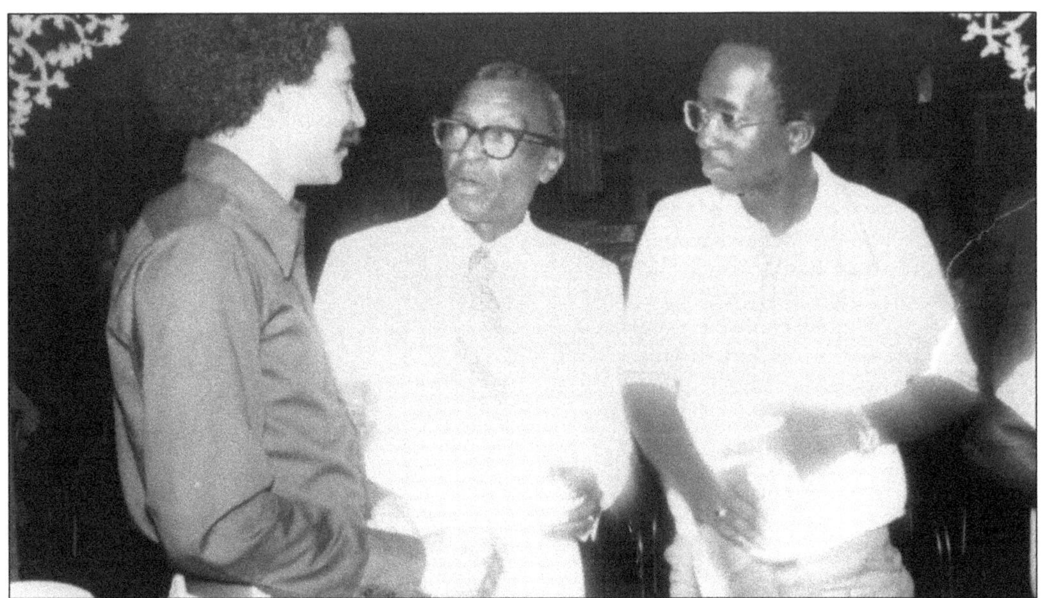

Jewel J. Newman (1921–2014) was elected to represent the Scotlandville community as a city councilman from 1972 to 1984 and as a state legislator from 1984 to 1988. Among his many contributions to public service, he started Scotlandville's first Little League baseball team, assisted in establishing the Bishop Ott shelters and a thrift store for the needy, and brought the predecessor of the DARE program to parish schools. He was a major player in the incorporation of Scotlandville into Baton Rouge. The Jewel J. Newman Community Center on Central Road was named in his honor. He was the father of six children. At the time of his death, he had been married to the former Sallie Gillespie for more than 50 years. Newman is pictured above at center with university administrators Norman St. Amant (left) and Nathaniel Harrison (right), and below addressing the Louisiana legislature. (Both, courtesy of Judge Trudy White.)

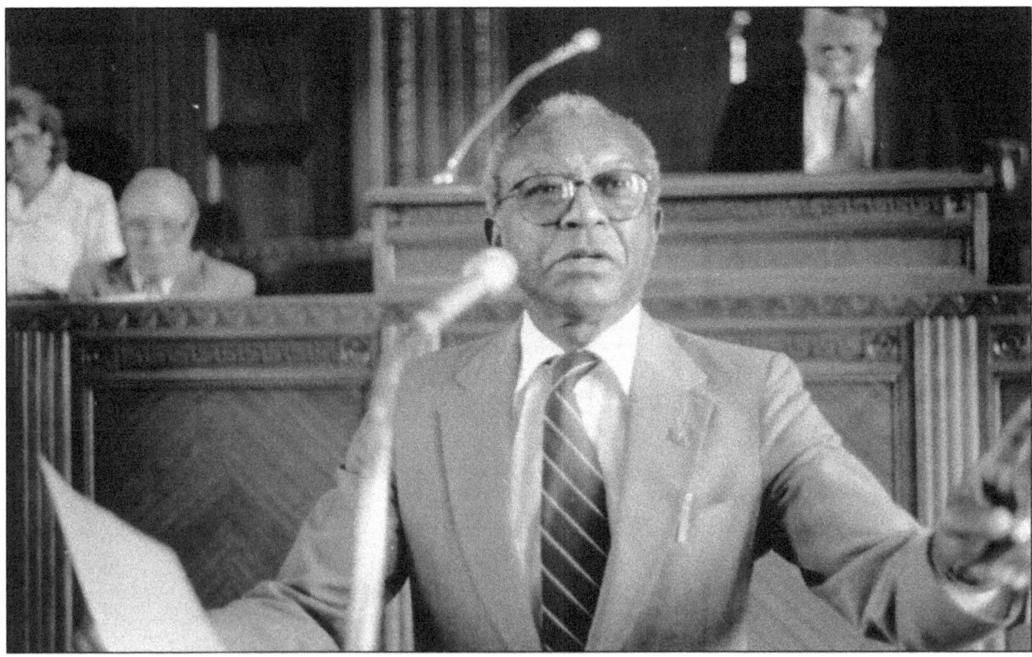

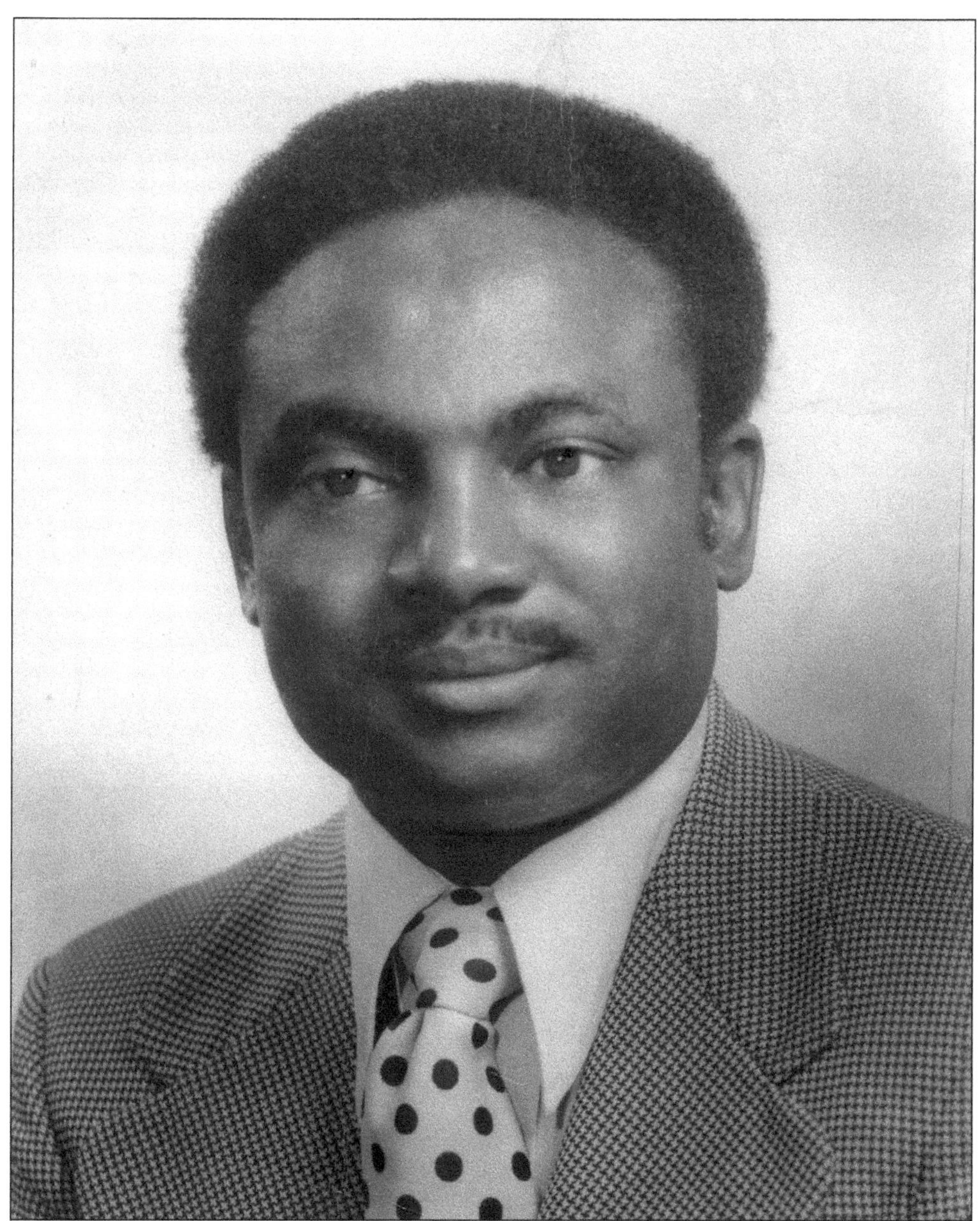

The year 1972 was a seminal year for elected officials from Scotlandville. With the election of its first African American city councilman also came the election of one of the first black legislators from the area since Reconstruction. Richard Turnley Jr. (1933–2013) was elected to the state's House of Representatives in 1972 and served until 1984, when he was elected to District 14 of the Louisiana Senate. He was a founder of the Louisiana Legislative Black Caucus in 1977. During his tenure, the 1971 graduate of Southern University and 1973 graduate of the Southern University Law Center championed equal rights of African Americans and America's senior citizens. He fought aggressively for the passage of a Louisiana law that discouraged discriminatory housing practices in the state and started a food cooperative in the Scotlandville area. The longtime STPFCU chief executive officer Turnley and his wife, the former Joyce Huntsberry, had three children, Tamara, Sharon, and Richard III. (Courtesy of STPFCU.)

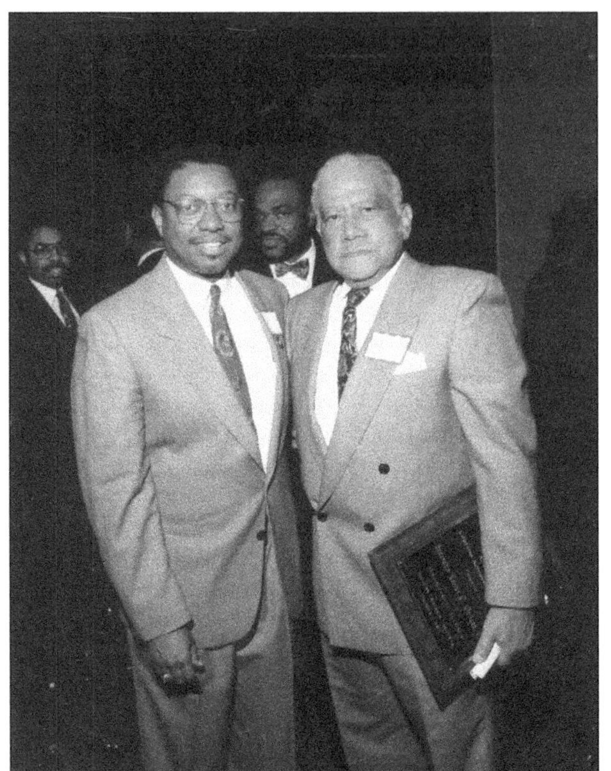

The Honorable Melvin "Kip" Holden began his political career as a city councilman in 1985, representing the Scotlandville area, and was later elected state representative (1988–2002) and state senator (2002–2005). Serving his third term as the first African American mayor-president of Baton Rouge and East Baton Rouge Parish, he is credited with revitalizing downtown Baton Rouge with increased hotel room capacity, attracting an IBM headquarters and major entertainment and sporting events, and creating the Baton Rouge Film Commission. Holden and fellow SULC alumnus Louisiana Supreme Court Justice Revius O. Ortique Jr. continue to inspire aspiring elected officials. (Courtesy of SULC.)

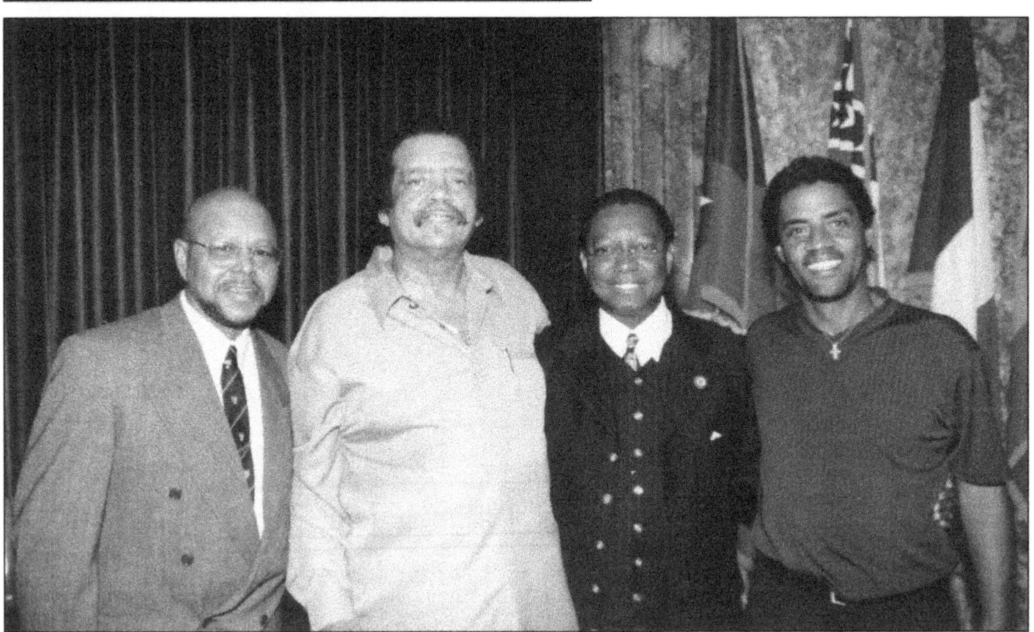

Through his careers as radio and television reporter and public relations professional, as well as his career in politics, Holden—still a Scotlandville resident—is a cultural ambassador of all things East Baton Rouge Parish. He is pictured here second from right with blues greats Raful Neal (second from left, 1936–2004) and Kenny Neal (far right). (Courtesy of Mayor-President Melvin "Kip" Holden.)

Avon R. Honey (left, 1947–2010), son of the late Edward and Matilda Flowers Honey, was a member of the Louisiana House of Representatives representing the 63rd District after a successful campaign in a special election in 2002 to fill the seat vacated by Melvin "Kip" Holden, who was elected to the state senate. The 1965 Scotlandville High graduate earned a bachelor's in education in 1973 and a master's in guidance and counseling in 1983, both from Southern University. Executive director of the TRIO programs at Southern, Honey was married to the former Linda Gray and was the father of two. As legislator, he was chairman of the House Committee on Labor and Industrial Revelations, Ways and Means, and the Joint Committee on Capital Outlay. Pictured below are, from left to right, Rev. Ken Ward, Louisiana House chaplain; Honey; Rev. Darlene Moore, pastor of Camphor United Methodist Church in Scotlandville; and unidentified. (Both, courtesy of Louisiana House of Representatives Office of Communications.)

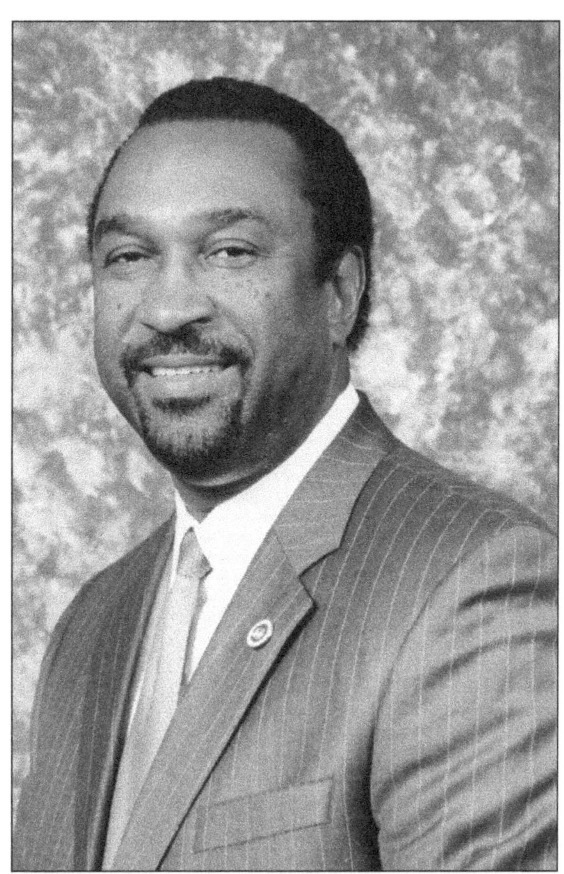

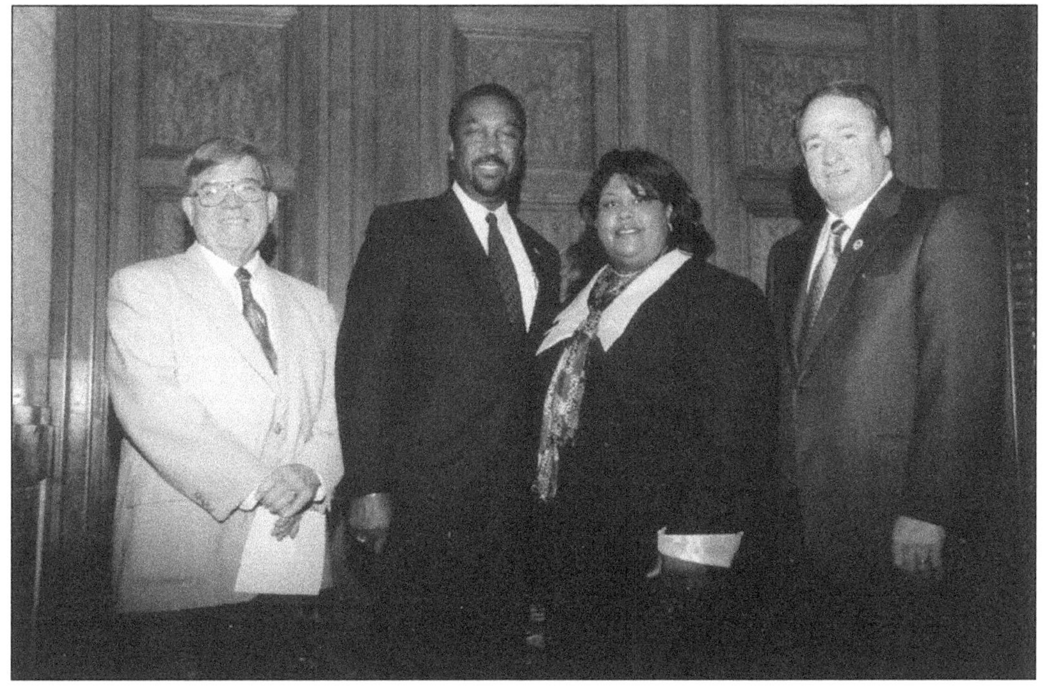

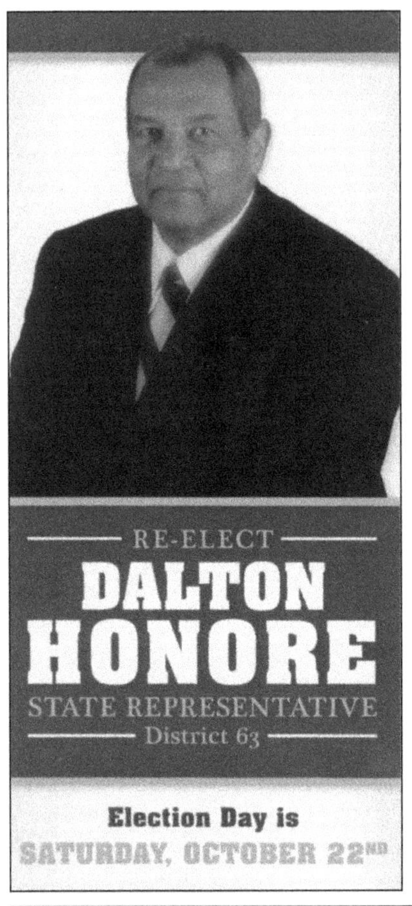

In May 2010, Dalton A. Honoré was elected to serve as Louisiana state representative, completing the term of deceased representative Avon Honey. Pictured below in 1965 with community activist Jewel Newman, the Southern University and LSU Basic Law Enforcement Academy graduate was appointed the first African American deputy sheriff in East Baton Rouge Parish. Assigned to the Scotlandville Substation, he rose to the rank of captain and substation commander. After 12 years, he left the Sheriff's Office to start a private business. He also has been a legal investigator with the Parish Attorney's Office. Honoré and his wife, JoEthel Honoré, reared three children. His community involvement includes membership and volunteer work with the American Legion Post No. 502 and Baton Rouge Alumni Chapter of Kappa Alpha Psi Fraternity. He is also an active member of Immaculate Conception Catholic Church, the Southern University Century Club, Scotlandville High School Alumni Association, the Southern University 6th Man Club, and Southern University Foundation Board of Directors. (Left, courtesy of Charles Vincent; below, courtesy of Judge Trudy M. White.)

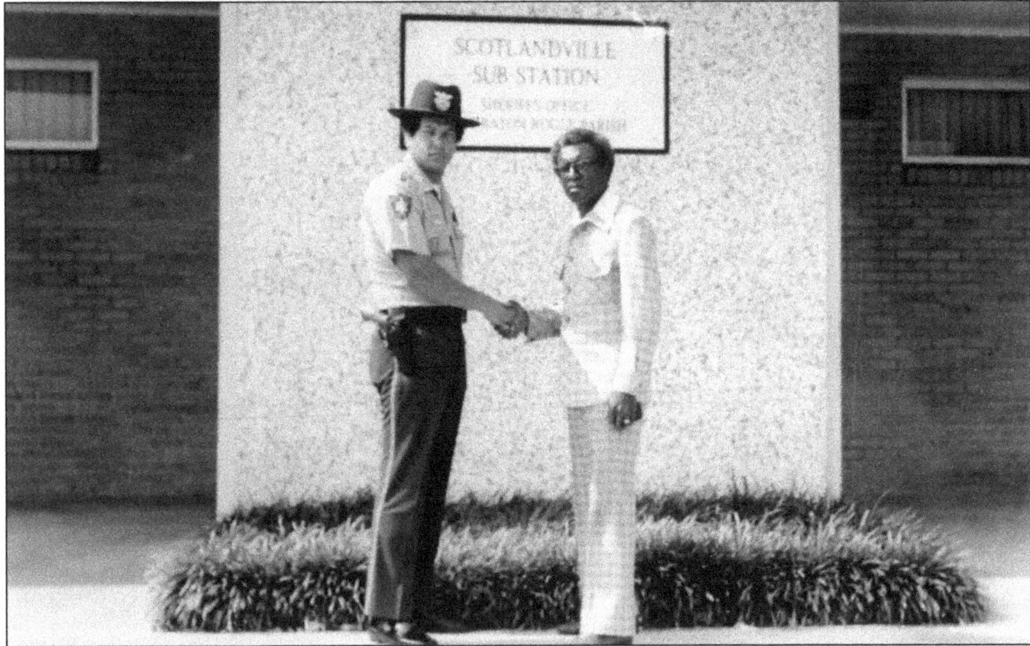

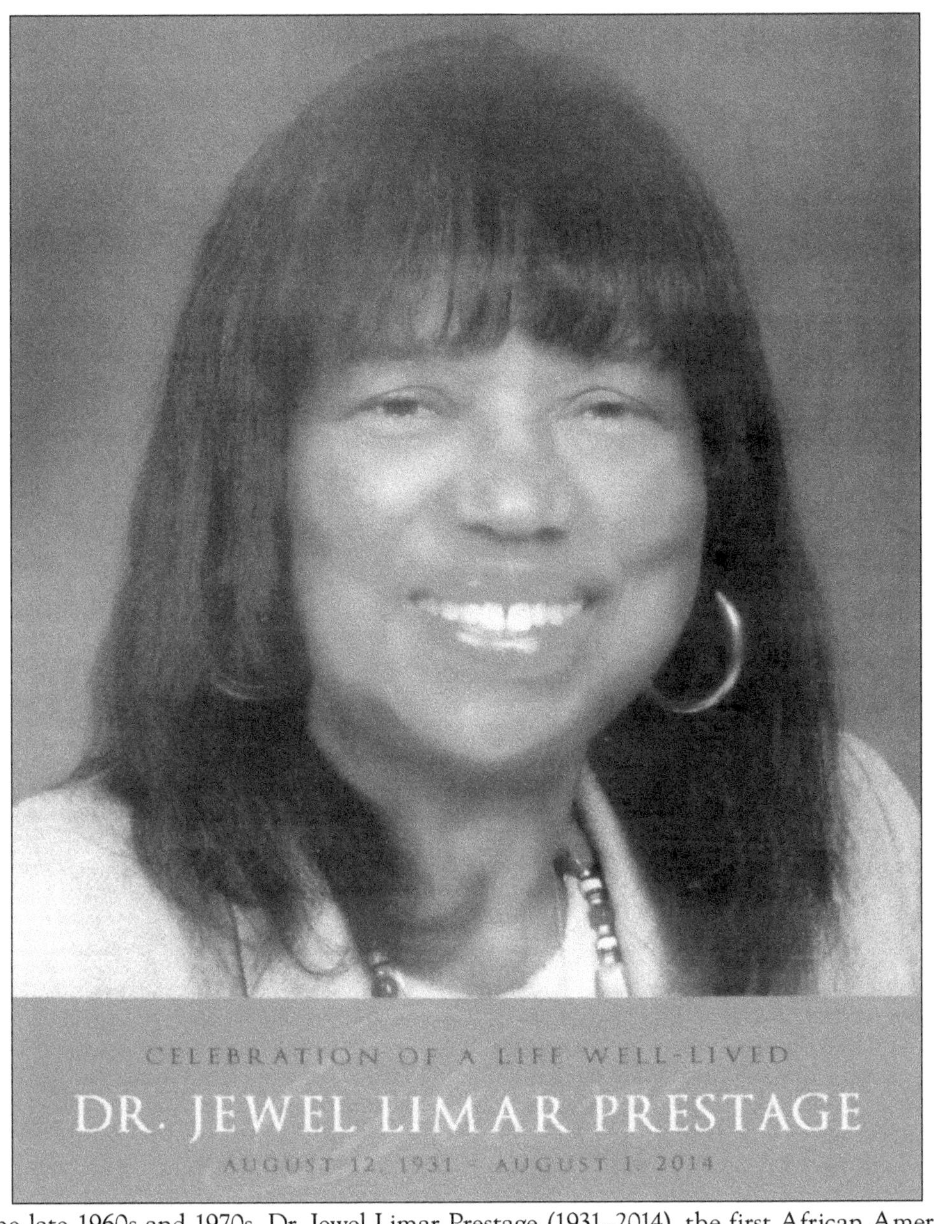

In the late 1960s and 1970s, Dr. Jewel Limar Prestage (1931–2014), the first African American woman to earn a doctorate in political science at an American university, prepared many Southern politicians for new public service opportunities that became available with the passage of the Voting Rights Act of 1965. Prestage served as chair of Southern's Department of Political Science for 18 years. The 1952 Southern graduate earned a master's degree in 1952 and a doctorate in 1954 from the University of Iowa, at the age of 22. After retiring as dean of her alma mater's School of Public Policy and Urban Affairs in 1989, she joined the political science faculty at Prairie View A&M University in Texas. She retired in 2002 as dean of its Benjamin Bannaker Honors College. Affiliated with many of the nation's major political science organizations, Prestage was founder of the National Conference of Black Political Scientists. Her husband, Dr. James J. Prestage, was chancellor of Southern's Baton Rouge campus from 1982 to 1985. The couple, both longtime residents of Scotlandville, had five children. (Courtesy of Pastor Clee Lowe.)

Bibliography

Cade, John B. *The Man Christened Josiah Clark*. New York, NY: The American Press, 1966.

Cotton, Melesha. "My Backyard is a Swamp: A Call for Action to Impact our Community." Baton Rouge, LA: unpublished, April 2012.

Danesh, Yousef. "The Unsuccessful Struggles of a Black Community to Incorporate: A Case Study." *Journal of Black Studies*. November 1999: 184–203.

deJong, Greta. *A Different Day: African American Struggles for Justice in Rural Louisiana, 1900–1970*. Chapel Hill, NC: The University of North Carolina Press, 2002.

Emanuel, Rachel L., and A.P. Tureaud. *A More Noble Cause: A.P. Tureaud and the Struggle for Civil Rights in Louisiana*. Baton Rouge, LA: LSU Press, 2011.

———. *Taking A Seat for Justice: The 1960 Baton Rouge Sit-ins*. Baton Rouge, LA: Louisiana Endowment for the Humanities, 1996.

Ennis, Ruby Robinson. *Generations Recording: Genealogical Findings and Memories of the Gaines and Robinson Families*. Bloomington, IN: AuthorHouse, 2011.

Fairclough, Adam. *Race and Democracy: The Civil Rights Struggle in Louisiana, 1915–1972*. Athens, GA: University of Georgia Press, 1999.

Kalmback, Fred. "Acie Belton Looks Back On Activism: Civil Rights Figure Recalls Old Politics." *Baton Rouge Advocate*, February 16, 1991.

Salomone, Jerome J. *Before the Highway: Scotlandville, Louisiana A Black Community in the Path of an Interstate Highway*. New Orleans, LA: LSU Urban Studies Institute, 1971.

Simms, Ruby Jean. "Boley, A.A.; Butler, Melvin; Clark, Octavia; Douglas, Emmitt; Jordan, Anna T.; Mackey-Kelly, Amanda; Jordan, T.J.; Kelly, Mayberry, E.N.; Meadows, M.C.; and Sewell, Vanderbilt." *The Dictionary of Louisiana Biography*. Lafayette, LA: The University of Southwestern Press, 1989.

———, and Peter Breaux. "Southern University and Scotlandville, Louisiana: A Partnership via Drift or Design, 1914–2011?" *The Scotlandville Comprehensive Development Plan*. Baton Rouge, LA: Southern University School of Architecture, 2011.

———, and Pearl L. Hall. "Southern University Moves to Scotlandville." *The Southernite* (Part I, May 1979) and (Part II, Summer, 1979): 2–2.

Steptoe, R., and R. Green and W. Paynes. *Scotlandville before the Highway: An Analysis of the Land Use, Population Density and Minority Businesses before the Scotlandville Bypass, Vol. 61 No 1*. Baton Rouge, LA: Economic Research and Transportation Center, Southern University, 1974.

Vincent, Charles. *Black Legislators in Louisiana During Reconstruction*. Baton Rouge, LA: Louisiana State University Press, 1976; reprinted by Southern Illinois University Press, 2011.

———. *A Centennial History of Southern University and A&M College, 1880–1980*. Baton Rouge, LA: Moran Press, 1981.

———. "Southern University and World War I: Aspects of the University and its Leadership Participation." *Journal of Social and Behavioral Science*. Fall 1979: 118–122.

INDEX

www.ingramcontent.com/pod-product-compliance
Lightning Source LLC
LaVergne TN
LVHW060626110826
845147LV00015B/947

9781467113144